WHY CANADIAN UNITY MATTER
WHY AMERICANS CARE

Democratic Pluralism at Risk

Why is Canadian unity important to democratic pluralism worldwide?

Democratic pluralism is a system which enables different cultural and language communities to find representation under a single set of democratic institutions, however configured. Although the liberal political tradition has tended to avoid cultural matters in attempting to eliminate longstanding inequalities, it has created in democratic pluralism a dialectic of culture and politics that addresses the theoretical and practical problems related to social diversity. Canadian democracy is widely regarded as a monument to the success of democratic pluralism in its capacity to provide dignity, freedom, opportunity, and prosperity to its citizens throughout the polity. In this book Charles Doran argues that the secession of Quebec would put these achievements at risk, raising the possibility that cultural-linguistic norms, not a mature liberal democracy, will fashion the kind of state that future generations will inherit.

Drawing on a variety of perspectives, Doran examines why Canadian unity is important not only to the United States but also to other liberal democracies around the world. In addition, he looks at the wider context of Quebec nationalism and the nature of the historical era that has shaped and conditioned the secessionist impulse.

CHARLES F. DORAN is the Andrew W. Mellon Professor of International Relations, Nitze School of Advanced International Studies (SAIS), Johns Hopkins University, Washington, DC.

Why Canadian Unity Matters and Why Americans Care

Democratic Pluralism at Risk

CHARLES F. DORAN

UNIVERSITY OF TORONTO PRESS
Toronto Buffalo London

© University of Toronto Press Incorporated 2001
Toronto Buffalo London
Printed in Canada

ISBN 0-8020-4873-0 (cloth)
ISBN 0-8020-8391-9 (paper)

Printed on acid-free paper

National Library of Canada Cataloguing in Publication Data

Doran, Charles F.
  Why Canadian unity matters and why Americans care : democratic
  pluralism at risk

  Includes bibliographical references and index.
  ISBN 0-8020-4873-0 (bound)   ISBN 0-8020-8391-9 (pbk.)

  1. Quebec (Province) – History – Autonomy and independence
  movements.   2. Secession – Quebec (Province).   3. Pluralism (Social
  sciences) – Canada.   4. Canada – Foreign public opinion, American.
  5. Public opinion – United States.   I. Title.

  FC2926.9.S4D67 2001   971.4'04   C2001-930741-1   F1053.2.D67 2001

The University of Toronto Press acknowledges the financial assistance to its
publishing program of the Canada Council for the Arts and the Ontario
Arts Council.

University of Toronto Press acknowledges the financial support for its publishing activities of the Government of Canada through the Book Publishing
Industry Development Program (BPIDP).

Contents

Preface

Liberal democracy has never been more sophisticated in terms of procedure or process. Elections, institutions of government, referenda,
opinion polls, and communications to and from voters have been perfected beyond what Locke or Rousseau might have imagined. But from
the United Kingdom to Indonesia, the reinforcing principles of civil
society everywhere appear to be under siege. Multiethnic cultural and
social interaction, minority participation, equal opportunity for jobs
and advancement, communal cooperation, and tolerance all seem to be
up for reconsideration.

A paradox emerges. Formalities of democracy are cosmopolitan and
highly successful, but the underlying vitality and cohesion of society
are in jeopardy. The larger national identity is under siege from a resurgence of cultural consciousness and a deepening of solidarity at the
communal level. Liberal democracy, rightfully celebrating its protection of individual and minority rights, must suddenly accommodate
long-standing or new group concerns, understandable and legitimate,
about preservation of culture, language, and tradition for diverse communities within the society. In democracies and non-democracies alike,
the disparate interests within society are pulling the nation apart,
claiming the right of self-determination and actively seeking autonomy or secession.

Is modern liberal democracy able to handle the stress of societal
diversity? Modern liberal democracy must confront anew the ancient
political dilemma of creating harmony within diversity, for if a society
is completely homogeneous in every attribute of its social and cultural
consciousness, then no mediating political influence would be necessary to preserve harmony. Older, rural, clerical societies possessed

some of these characteristics. But modern society, of the twenty-first century, is not like this, and the ability to manage political and cultural diversity is regarded as an attribute of mature liberal democratic institutions. Given the stress between modern multicultural society and those institutions of government, however, can even the mature liberal democracy preserve harmony amid diversity without cracking or fragmenting? Liberal democracy as never before is on trial.

The purpose of this book is to examine the U.S. attitude towards possible secession on its border as we contemplate the twenty-first century. Americans care about Quebec secession, it is argued, because secession puts at risk the principle of democratic pluralism and, thereby, liberal democracy itself. Canadian unity, according to this thesis, is a test case for liberal democracy worldwide. Americans are in no sense alone in caring.

In attempting to find the impulse for separation, the book first assesses three complex, interactive social-psychological processes that drive contemporary divisive nationalism. The objective throughout is to cut through the mystery and folklore regarding possible Quebec secession from Canada, to understand not only the uniqueness of Quebec nationalism but also its commonalities with broader movements in the contemporary system. Likewise, this book seeks to encompass a variety of perspectives. It weighs the political impact of secession on Quebec, Canada as a whole, and the United States and it examines conflicting theoretical arguments about the economic costs of secession. It places the issues surrounding secession in the larger milieu of North American economic integration. At its heart is the attempt to think about Quebec secession in the context of North America and the world in the twenty-first century. The analyst inevitably must confront the implications of secession for democratic pluralism and modern liberal democracy.

Liberal democracy is defined for purposes here as a state that displays adequate representation, tolerance towards minorities, equal opportunity for each individual to develop to his or her fullest potential through cooperation between community and government, equality before the law, and freedom of expression. Modern liberal democracy has evolved through long struggle to eliminate tremendous prejudice, errors, and wrongs such as slavery and ethnic discrimination, and out of this struggle it has created a condition of democratic pluralism between different ethnic, cultural, and linguistic communities. Traditional liberal arguments at best ignored culture, and hence their weaknesses and inconsistencies and prejudices had to be exposed and rejected. In practice, however, the liberal tradition has created in democratic pluralism a dialectic of culture and liberal politics that resolves the theoretical conundrums so dear to both.

From the perspective of democratic pluralism, the undoing of modern liberal democracy is the proclamation, increasingly heard, that a single 'nation' *must* or *should* underlie the polity, and that the citizens of the polity *must* or *should* assimilate towards a single language and a single culture. That some liberal democracies have been and will continue to be based primarily on a single 'nation' in which a single dominant language is spoken is not at issue. But that liberal democracies *must* or *should* be so constituted is the fallacious claim thought to justify the fragmentation of modern liberal democracies along cultural-linguistic lines.

Canada is a liberal democracy composed of a large French-speaking population most of which lives in Quebec; a larger English-speaking population, most of which lives outside Quebec; and an Aboriginal population of diverse origins, most of which is scattered across the far North. Each large, diverse community is nonetheless able to share a common set of confederal political institutions. Just as assimilation is not required in Canada as a whole, so assimilation is not required in Quebec or in areas of primary Aboriginal residency. While French is (and will always be) the predominant but not exclusive language in Quebec, so English is (and will always be) the predominant but not exclusive language in other parts of Canada. At a minimum, Quebecers and English-speaking Canadians are able to obtain public services and read government documents and laws in their preferred language. To an outsider, this concept of bilingualism defines Canada more effectively and positively than virtually any other single idea. These are the facts of Canada, but also the social underpinnings of its political institutions.

This book argues that the very uniqueness of Canada makes Canadian unity matter very greatly for liberal democracy worldwide. The attempt to base liberal democracy on the outmoded concept of 'nation' is the outstanding political error of our time. Canada and most other large advanced industrial democracies will be composed of territorial groupings in which the predominant ethno-linguistic or cultural-linguistic community differs from some of these other groupings. This will increasingly become the political norm for liberal democracy. The index of the success of liberal democracy as a form of government will be its ability to make democratic pluralism work inside populous, complex states. Divisive nationalism is its greatest threat.

Divisive nationalism in the twenty-first century has much in common with *dependencia*, a quintessential twentieth-century idea. Both cast the smaller political entity as on the 'periphery,' subordinate and comparatively powerless. Both characterize the smaller entity as subject to manipulation, collusion, and exploitation that contributes to economic stagnation. Yet the modern Western state, including its separatist component, is rich, powerful, and politically mature, with sophisticated political institutions and a long history of internal cohesion. Despite all of this political and economic achievement, divisive nationalism attempts to build states by breaking them, a comparatively new phenomenon among the rich, highly institutionalized countries that were thought to have evolved beyond such liabilities. Transformation of the system may contribute to the forces of divisive nationalism today, especially inside empires such as the Soviet Union. In contrast to empires, states are cohesive; most states are likely to survive. A problem for Canada is that as a state it is the outgrowth of an earlier 'Empire on the St Lawrence.' If the state that has grown out of that past now fractures, however, the impact on democratic pluralism is likely to be serious, lasting, and global.

What about the possible economic impacts of secession? Will the economies of fractured states prosper as much as they had prior to the breakup? Recently, because of the effect of global trade liberalization, some economists have begun to argue, counter to neoclassical thought regarding regional economic integration, that small market size does not restrict either the level or rate of growth of per capita income. If rate of growth does not increase with market size, entry into larger regional economic trade areas would hold no benefit for small state economies. More than this, small communities could secede from larger states without exacting any economic penalties to themselves whatsoever. Absence of a growth–size relationship would be a great boon to the secessionist argument.

Strangely, however, secessionists also claim as correct that very neoclassical promise of enhanced economic growth for small state economies within a regional trade area such as NAFTA and the EU. And they claim the right of the secessionist entity to enter into full membership in the regional trade area. How can both the presence and the absence of a relationship between size and growth be correct? This book reconciles the neoclassical and contemporary arguments, asserting the presence of a size threshold and of differing levels of integration within the world trading system. It concludes that the secessionist state's economy is likely to experience a reduced rate of growth in per capita income when it withdraws from the larger state economy.

Yet another paradox emerges. In divisive nationalism today, the separatist community wants autonomy from the state with which it is affiliated but says that it will allow transfers of sovereignty to a regional trade area or union. Such paradoxes are manifestations of a deeper societal problem, and they expose contradictions and potential dangers within the secessionist panacea. Also problematic, especially but not only in weak democratic states, is the impact of divisive nationalism upon civility, including, for example, challenges to citizenship or discouragement of intermarriage. Civility requires toleration, which requires acceptance of constraints and limits on one's own political or cultural preferences. North America, long a haven for the 'Romeo and Juliet' in search of freedom from ancient societal intolerance, is today a celebration of multiethnic and multicultural individuality that respects all societal groups, new and old. Democratic pluralism, as it has been evolving in North America and other modern liberal democracies, provides the base for a workable solution to the many concerns and needs of cultural communities. It warns, moreover, of the contradictions and dangers lurking within a conception of state that is based on elevating one culture above others.

Canadian unity is thus a barometer of the modern democratic nation-state's ability to prevail over divisive nationalism and cultural and ethnic diversity. During state-creation, the clarion call was 'unity amid diversity.' Democratic pluralism evolved with the maturation of the nation-state. Although the state might withstand an assault by divisive nationalism, democratic pluralism might suffer tragically. As the current of divisive nationalism surges around the globe, to what extent can a state contain its flow? Will a prominent example of secession decidedly increase that flow?

Although the debate over Canadian unity is a debate about many things upon which this book touches – compatibility of values, whether liberal institutions are strong enough to meet the needs of all citizens, recognition of cultural identity and distinctness, political autonomy, the shifting locus of political centralization on different issues, anxiety over linguistic survival versus fear of political partition, the frustrations of constitution-building – ultimately this book is about the risk that secession poses to democratic pluralism not only in the

Quebec and Canadian fragments but throughout the world. Many Quebecers still seek a federal solution, pursuing political autonomy for Quebec inside Confederation (a type of civic nationalism), and its non-francophone minority has consistently opposed separation. Secession means failure of the Canadian federal experiment with unity across the culture-language divide. This failure thus does not bode well for the ability of other democracies to establish political harmony among their own regional communities, some of which share exactly the kind of doubts, fears, and aspirations as those of Quebec secessionists.

The problem of harmony amid diversity will not go away through breakup. The problem of cultural and linguistic difference will continue to beg for resolution. Inside Quebec, perhaps increasingly disparate cultural minorities, although French-speaking, will escalate demands on an autonomous Quebec. Likewise, the Cree, justifiably concerned for their own cultural survival, and whose lands encompass almost half of Quebec, will have precedent to further their own claims to self-government or even secession. Outside Quebec, critical relations with a politically more distant English Canada and a more directly involved United States will rise in importance and be conducted along lines that feature linguistic difference.

Secession not only means that federal political institutions fail. It also means that cultural-linguistic preference rules societal organization and institutional development. Secession means that ultimately individual interaction will also be shaped by awareness that cultural-linguistic norms, not the norms of democratic pluralism, will fashion the kind of democracy, albeit otherwise liberal, that future generations will inherit.

Hence, regardless of where it turns, the modern nation-state faces the turmoil of cultural and ethnic diversity, either internal to the state or in relation to its neighbours. Such diversity lies at the core of the multiethnic society in the new millennium. Multiethnicity is a social phenomenon, largely independent of the architecture of the nation-state itself. Yet it is the architecture of the nation-state that is expected to preserve the harmony of both social and political relations today. And, as is emphasized throughout this book, although most modern nation-states are not culturally or ethnically monolithic, most separatist communities *are* culturally, ethnically, or linguistically identifiable in territorial terms. The issue thus cannot be separated from its implications for democratic pluralism and toleration in a mature liberal democracy.

Where liberal democracy is weak, where the task of economic development distracts governments, and where violence is pervasive, there democratic pluralism is likely to be weak and that weakness most likely a spur to secession. But in politically stable advanced industrial states, with long-standing democratic government, which have so long nourished democratic pluralism, secession would seem to proclaim failure of the best hope of mature liberal democracy. Ultimately, cooperation itself comes into doubt. If diverse peoples cannot cooperate inside the state, what likelihood is there that they will cooperate as independent actors? If different cultural communities cannot solve their problems inside the democratic polity, how can they be expected to cooperate as independent actors within a larger region?

Many scenarios regarding future association between the federal government of Canada, Quebec, and the other provinces are possible. Not all of these impact upon the United States in the same way. Whatever Ottawa, Quebec, and the other provinces decide, all of the governmental institutions of North America must take steps to ensure that democratic pluralism continues to deepen its roots. In a metaphor dating from its first colonization, North America has always regarded itself as a 'beacon' for others to follow. Canada and the United States must be able to show that democratic pluralism works at home if others abroad are to emulate the values and institutions of these two countries. Success in North America will help preserve democratic pluralism worldwide.

Mingling these themes, the book tries to draw conclusions that could help North America prevent a misstep in an era when integration, not fragmentation, is the key to interdependence, prosperity, and global influence.

WHY CANADIAN UNITY MATTERS AND WHY AMERICANS CARE

Democratic Pluralism at Risk

CHAPTER ONE

Challenges to Democratic Pluralism

To most North Americans, the name of Brussels is identified with the European Union. Yet Brussels, a largely French-speaking urban centre, is located in the heart of Dutch-speaking Flanders, the breakaway province of Belgium. Few North Americans would equate the European Union with the breakup of Belgium. Fewer still perhaps realize that because French-speaking Brussels is in the centre of Dutch-speaking Flanders, Brussels is the geographic insurance policy *against* Belgian fragmentation. Yet this juxtaposition between regional evolution and devolution along ethno-linguistic lines establishes the blueprint for cultural and territorial turbulence inside the state during the twenty-first century.

According to a study published in 1990, perhaps 8,000 movements worldwide, at the substate level, attempt to feature cultural distinctiveness.[1] Many of these movements involve groups that are ethnically and linguistically different from the dominant culture. Quite a few are folkloric rather than generative and self-perpetuating. Approximately 100 have engaged in serious political or intercommunal conflict at some time in the past half century.[2] Most are resolutely peaceful. Of these, only a small fraction have become politicized and could be said to aspire to national independence.

In contrast to the earlier nationalisms that were essentially unifying in nature, 'the characteristic nationalist movements of the late twentieth century,' according to E.J. Hobsbawm, 'are essentially negative, or rather divisive.'[3] The new type of nationalism, catalysed but not caused by the latest systems transformation after the Cold War, is expressed as secession. The shattering of Yugoslavia, the bloody attempted departure of Chechnya, the terrorism and repression regarding Kurdish Iraq and Turkey, the ideological civil war in Azerbaijan, and the 'velvet divorce' of the Czech Republic and Slovakia reflect ongoing or completed efforts at secessions. The rumblings in Scotland, Wales, Northern Ireland, Brittany, Flemish Belgium (Flanders), the Basque country, Catalan, Northern Italy, and Quebec, as well as a number of other places globally, also suggest or proclaim secessionist inclination, although often expressed in the language of autonomy.

One of the characteristics that makes this divisive nationalism so unique is that it takes place inside the so-called politically mature nation-state. One striking difference marks secession in the mature polity versus secession in the developing polity: the degree of political stability. All the conditions for secession in the developing polity – executive instability, violence, and low political participation – are absent in the mature polity (in most cases), and still secession threatens.[4] Proponents of secession express worry that their culture is at risk of extinction, or that they are disadvantaged economically, socially, or politically. Yet, if these threats are present in the mature liberal democracies, they can be eliminated through its democratic institutions and processes.

The modern crisis of democracy and the nation-state, however, lies elsewhere. The crisis is less about governmental institutions and procedures and more about the cleavage between society and the state. Certainly, 'strong democracy' involves participation of people in some aspects of self-government at least some of the time.[5] Perhaps one problem is a sense of distance from the federal government and a lack of participation in federal politics. A study of Italian regional government, for instance, shows a significant correlation between institutional performance and citizen satisfaction.[6] Other analyses claim that a livelier sense of moral deliberation in democracy will enhance citizen satisfaction.[7] Each of these tactics undoubtedly has merit in the quest to get beyond mere procedure and to heal the cleavage between society and the state.

The problem may lie still deeper, requiring much greater attention, insight, and skill if it is not to fracture the state completely. The problem may be that in some instances communal identity is becoming stronger than identity with country. At a time when globalism, supranationalism, and regional blocs seem to have triumphed, regional identification buttressed by cultural and linguistic similarity within that region is more compelling than federal identity. The state has lost touch with large sectors of society. Large communal groups have rejected sometimes century-long association with the federal state, or the long-standing failure to establish those ties to the federal state has suddenly become evident. But the issues at stake do not just involve the 'sense of belonging' or the strain between state institutions and the voice of communal dissent within society.

The deeper issue and one of far greater consequence is that the desire (and legitimate right) to protect and promote one's own culture, language or ethnicity has become an effort to create a homogeneous state by breaking away from a larger, more diverse cultural entity. The deeper issue is a population's rejection of the capacity or willingness to communicate and to cooperate politically within a single democracy, that is, within a single federal state, vis-à-vis another population of differing culture, language, or ethnicity. In *Polyethnicity and National Unity in World History,* William H. McNeill warns that the very preferences of liberal democracy have created dangerous blinders: 'Our preferences may well continue to support the pretense of ethnic unity within sovereign nation states for some time to come. But the reality is otherwise.'[8] Is democratic pluralism in North America a mere pretense?

Democratic Pluralism: What It Is and Why It Is Necessary

Democratic pluralism is defined as a condition of society in which diverse ethnic, racial, religious, or social groupings 'maintain their autonomous participation in their traditional culture within the confines of a single civilization' or state.[9] Democratic pluralism seeks to harmonize and to integrate politically. Although assimilation may be a goal in some states at some time (whereas other polities may reject it as counter to the ethos of the society) democratic pluralism is a political and legal guarantee that assimilation is *not* required. In democratic pluralism, regionally specific cultural-linguistic communities retain their 'traditional culture' while participating fully in the processes and institutions of the state. Above all, democratic pluralism ensures cohesiveness and political accord within the state. In a mature democracy, democratic pluralism is completely liberal.

Democratic pluralism is denied when culture, language, or ethnicity is held to be a higher value or norm than other characteristics of human nature and social interaction, a value that becomes justification for secession. In the mature liberal democracies, self-segregation according to culture or language is not necessarily a result of immediate oppression or exploitation or even the prospect of greater economic opportunity.

More pointedly, the drive for separation in a mature liberal democracy is not based on a revolt against tyranny. Tyranny is used here as defined by James Fishkin, building upon the term used by James Madison in his *Federalist Papers* No. 10 (his treatise on liberal democracy), and by Robert Dahl in assessing modern liberal democracies.[10] If tyranny occurs when there is 'an avoidable severe deprivation ... of a person or group's most basic rights or fundamental interests,' then surely tyranny is not at the basis of separation within the modern democratic polity.[11] In a society guaranteeing the legitimate rights and interests of individuals and groups, there is no tyranny against which to revolt. The non-francophone minority in Quebec cannot legitimately claim that tyranny of the majority exists against themselves, nor can Quebec claim a tyranny of the majority within Canada against Quebec.

Even in a liberal democracy where the human rights of individuals and groups are not threatened, separation occurs for the singular purpose, however motivated, of not wanting to associate politically in a single democracy with citizens of differing ethno-linguistic affiliation. The philosophy of separation professes the 'incompatibility' of diverse cultural values and preferences (see chapter 3).

According to Michael Walzer's *On Toleration*, the mere presence of diversity can lead to an obsessive focus on one's own culture: 'Where pluralism is a social fact, as it commonly is, some of the groups will compete with others by seeking converts or supporters among uncommitted or loosely committed individuals. But their primary aim is to sustain a way of life among their own members, to reproduce their culture or faith in successive generations. They are in the first instance inwardly focussed.'[12] The result is the desire or the felt need to 'govern oneself,' which, in the context of the modern fragmentation of the nation-state, means wanting to associate politically with neighbours who speak the same language and share the same cultural orientation and not wanting to form or maintain a political union with those who are culturally different.

There is nothing wrong yet much of value with being inwardly focused. The only problem for a pluralist democracy is where 'territorially concentrated minorities' decide on inwardly focused grounds to separate politically from those who are culturally different. Once separated as a small, politically autonomous nation-state, an excessive concentration upon inward focus can get in the way of interdependence and can even become the source of conflict. Thus in a pluralist democracy, as in international society, inward focus must be balanced by a sense of outward focus.

The end of this chapter returns to the relationship between the individual and the collective in the evolution of liberal thought in modern democracy. Perhaps only in the most recent phase of its evolution has liberal thought begun to fully take cultural pluralism into account at both the individual and the collective levels. In the twenty-first century, the final battle of liberal democracy that the individual must face may be the battle for cultural pluralism, for the mature form of political association characterized by democratic pluralism.

Unfortunately, in the vernacular of American politics, the term 'pluralism' has multiple meanings. Hence, democratic pluralism is sometimes confused falsely with the debate over absolute and relative values, or over prayer in the public schools, or with declining emphasis on the classics in education.[13] Understanding of pluralism, in particular of 'democratic pluralism,' is also clouded by equally contentious debates over the term 'multiculturalism.' Conceptually, multiculturalism in Canada and multiculturalism in the United States mean very different things. In Canada, multiculturalism fits nicely into the conceptual framework of democratic pluralism. But, as James Kurth argues, multiculturalism in the United States has become an ideology, not coterminus with other cultural perspectives, but as a set of values to replace those of Western civilization.[14]

Such a strategy is the antithesis of that of democratic pluralism, which requires toleration, reciprocity, and sharing. Democratic pluralism amends communitarianism. Encapsulating one of the lessons that Cary Nederman found within medieval political theory regarding the 'necessary foundations of a self-sustaining [civic] community,' democratic pluralism recognizes that 'the community (and therefore its good) is not a simple unity but a multiplicity ordered toward a single end,' and hence each segment of the community is open to 'the realization of one's interdependence in relation to the other segments of the community.'[15]

David Landes chronicles the complexity and diversity of circumstances, both rare and fortuitous, which were necessary for scientific innovation, entrepreneurship, and economic growth throughout recorded history. The ideology of alleged exploitation notwithstanding, serious education must not ignore the geographic inequalities and temporal contingencies which make possible a broad-based understanding of cultural, economic, and social causation in history.[16] David Bercuson, Barry Cooper, and Jack Granatstein have also focused on the damage that the history of 'limited identities' can do to learning 'history writ large.'[17]

Democratic pluralism, even as it acknowledges and welcomes many different languages and religions and traditions among its citizens, does not necessitate denial of the Judaeo-Christian intellectual ethos in the United States, the inheritance of British parliamentary institutions in Canada, or the justifiable preponderance of the French language in Quebec. Moreover, democratic pluralism, even as it admits the divergent interpretations of the 'common good' that exist in a diverse society, encourages a 'cooperative consensus' through the active participation of all citizens in the democratic process.[18] The issue today, as Anthony Smith warned in 1992 regarding the debate over 'European identity,' is the existence of multiple (competing) loyalties that could generate conflict or at least undermine existing levels of cooperation and consensus building at the political level.[19] An index of the presence of multiple loyalties in Canada is that 66 per cent of Quebecers identify themselves as hyphenated Canadians.[20]

How Democratic Pluralism Amends Communitarianism

Democratic pluralism thus is defined as the allowance and encouragement of individual communal groups to develop their own culture and value preference inside the larger democratic polity. This definition, however, can easily be misunderstood. One such potential misunderstanding is reflected in the debate between communitarians and liberals. Communitarians argue that the 'good' must accompany definition of the 'right.' By this they mean that moral values involved in a sense of what is good for society must be involved in a definition of justice or of rights. In that view, there are no rights that are universal, 'self-evident,' or that stand above all communal difference. For example, insufficient is the statement that religious freedom is a right because it is the result of 'free and voluntary choice.' According to the communitarian, the content of the religion is relevant to whether the right exists.

The definition of democratic pluralism offered above might be interpreted as an affirmation of this communitarian position on the right of religion based on its content, since the definition openly encourages communal groups to 'develop their own culture and value preference' inside the democratic polity. But such an interpretation would miss the mark. If indeed the communitarian argument is pursued to its necessary conclusion, it would undermine democracy in the very way that secession ultimately would do so. Consider the societal assumptions.

If the assumption is that society is totally homogeneous, then the communitarian position is workable. The values of the society (the good) can determine or at least help shape the rules of justice (the right). But if the assumption is that society is like most modern democratic societies, a place in which very substantial heterogeneity exists, namely, in the sense that the polity is composed of a number of distinct ethno-linguistic groups with different understandings of 'the good,' then problems arise for the communitarian position. Because the society cannot decide on a single definition of the good, the society cannot decide upon the nature of primary rights and duties. Because the society cannot decide on primary rights and duties, the polity ceases to function as a unified state. That is where the unfortunate logic of communitarianism leads in a heterogeneous society.

That is also why democratic pluralism requires a fairly abstract and a fairly general definition of rights and duties in which there is some chance that each of the communal groups and most individuals in those groups can find agreement. Consider the famous statement attributed to Voltaire, 'I disapprove of what you say [that is, regarding 'the good'], but I defend to the death your right to say it.' What, then, does democratic pluralism allow if not rights defined as the communitarians have recommended in terms of the good?

The answer is that democratic pluralism allows a wide range of delineation of preferences and behaviours that are regarded as fundamental to the preservation of the language and culture of the local community. The most basic rights and duties apply equally to all members of the polity, for these must be defined in conjunction with other communal groups and with other members of the polity as a whole through the democratic process. Such rights, shared by all, may indeed be regarded by all as inalienable. Such a degree of hard-fought and yet fragile tolerance backed by effective government enforcement occurs in only a few societies in the world. Only in a handful of advanced industrial democracies is the manifestation of such tolerance so deep and widespread that it can virtually be taken for granted. The polities of North America find themselves on the forefront of nations so fortunate as to be among the exemplars of this type of democratic pluralism.

Hence democratic pluralism provides two things: (1) It establishes through a constitution or sense of comity a framework of generally agreed upon principle, institutions, and law that emerges out of individual and group preference, but also surmounts that preference, such that all groups can and must accept the framework and operate within it. (2) It creates a set of procedures for decision making that will allow government to function, despite issues that divide the various communities and interest groups of which the larger polity is composed. Some of these issues can perhaps never be fully resolved, but they can be effectively mediated by means of the process of law making, adjudication, and administration.

Much as liberals have argued that such democracy is based on the rights of the individual, communitarians have argued that these rights do not 'bracket' moral judgment or values. Rather, the communities of which the individuals are a member often shape the ethical preferences of the individual. Individual preferences are then reflected in the decision outcomes that emerge from the overall democratic process. Sometimes the individual preferences are indeed determined by the group. In any case, these are the preferences that are used for the purpose of governance.

Thus democratic pluralism is the result of both 'pluralism' and 'democracy.' Both terms are essential to an understanding of the unified concept. Pluralism protects the culture and identity of the respective communities. Because the culture and the identity of the community are secure, the community is able to participate in the activities of the larger polity. But since the preferences of the respective communities often differ, the democratic process is essential to mediate those differences when making common policy. Communities and interest groups are more than mere aggregations of individuals. Yet, in the end, democracy is based on the preference of individuals who vote in elections even though the way they vote may be shaped by parents or by the attitudes of groups of which they are a member. In addition, the communal groups and interest groups have ways of affecting policy between elections that go directly to decision makers. Ultimately the nature of governments is determined by elections, and these elections are decided by the vote of the individual citizen.

An aspect of group action that makes governance inside the democratic polity rather more difficult is that many groups do not truly conduct themselves according to democratic norms. This fact tends to make them more assertive, more rigid, and less given to compromise with other communal or interest groups or with the government of the polity as a whole. For example, labour unions often 'vote' unanimously for their leadership, thus raising doubts about how democratic the underlying procedure was. Corporations often are run by the managers in the name of the shareholders but scarcely through the direct preferences of those shareholders. Religious groups rarely are models of democratic procedure, and some, like the Roman Catholic Church, publicly renounce democracy as a method of decision. It is therefore not surprising that democratic government is often challenged by communities, groups, and institutions that tend to see democratic government as something to be manipulated rather than accommodated on the basis of corresponding principle.

The wise government is the government that devolves as many decisions as possible to the local level in which communities can best express their collective wills. As within a federal system, on matters that cannot be decided at the local level, communities must yield to compromise with other communities and interest groups on policy that reflects an amalgam of their respective views. On matters of crucial significance to a communal group, however, that significance, because of the intensity of its expression if not the size of its numbers, is likely to prevail. On matters of more marginal significance, the communal group, like the individual, must be prepared to compromise. Hence democratic pluralism allows the communal group to protect its own core values while accommodating the larger polity through means of the democratic process. In the end, in democratic pluralism, no decisive conflict exists between democratic liberals and communitarians, or, for that matter, between either of these groups and conservatives. All can live within the framework of the single polity that observes the principles of democratic pluralism.

Varieties of Democratic Pluralism in North America

Democratic pluralism is nicely adapted to the peculiarities of Canadian society. While probably not a true 'vertical mosaic,' as Porter memorably described it, in Canada specific cultural-linguistic groupings have, in comparison to similar groups in other democracies, considerable political autonomy and support for that autonomy from the state. Moreover, Canada's mythology reinforces public policy in convincing Canadian citizens that they need not give up their prior cultural heritage to become Canadian. When children have the opportunity to attend school in French, for example, the community can preserve its language. The consequence is that, despite Greg Marchildon's apt metaphor about sugar dissolving in coffee, cultural communities in Canada probably do not melt into the rest of the society as readily as cultural communities in other countries.[21] Instead, they remain visible and quite distinct throughout the Canadian social and political landscape. Without that governmental support for educational opportunity, however, 'the sugar will dissolve in the coffee.'

Under these circumstances of prolonged and highly accentuated cultural autonomy, Canadian communities reflect the assumptions of the democratic pluralist model. They continue to express traditional patterns of speech in the home and in the workplace long after similar groupings in other countries would have assimilated into the larger milieu. Students in Toronto, for example, are able to attend schools in which the instruction is in one of sixty or more languages calibrated to the cultural identity of the local community. While the first language of the student normally becomes French or English, the second language, often used at home, is frequently that of the community's cultural inheritance. Similarly, the Ukrainian community in Saskatchewan is well-known for having acted as a repository for Ukrainian custom, music, folklore, religious art, and tradition during the long communist interregnum in Ukraine, when many of these cultural attributes were being spurned or repressed. Democratic pluralism in Canada allows cultural diversity to flourish inside the larger democratic framework of society. While for some this toleration and encouragement of cultural and linguistic diversity is insufficient, by the standards of most advanced industrial polities Canada offers a rare degree of pluralism. Despite controversy over Quebec's language laws, this statement is as true for Quebec in general as for any other part of Canada.

In the United States, democratic pluralism, although as real as in Canada, possesses slightly different nuance. While probably not a true 'melting pot' in the metaphorical sense, U.S. society displays a strong capacity for assimilation. For example, the Irish, Italians, Jews, and Puerto Ricans have all broken out of their original ghettos to merge with the larger population as later waves of immigrants from different areas of the world arrive and occupy parts of cities that were previously inhabited and characterized by some of these groups. And yet, after many generations, South Boston is still regarded as 'Irish.' So what does 'assimilation' really mean? It could mean any of the following:

- Retention of all linguistic, cultural, and religious characteristics but movement out of the original ghetto area
- Retention of all characteristics but learning of English as a second language
- Retention of all characteristics but use of English as the primary language

- Retention of cultural and religious affinity but little use of the original language
- Retention of cultural affinity but little else
- Intermarriage but with some symbolic association regarding the original characteristics

In even the last case, where assimilation is seemingly complete, important political consequences could be retained vis-à-vis the original cultural-linguistic association, for example in voting patterns or employment. But regardless of the nature of the retention of original cultural-linguistic characteristics, an individual or a community at any of these levels of association with the larger polity could be encompassed within the concept of democratic pluralism. Nothing at any of these levels of association is incompatible with participation in society according to the principles of democratic pluralism, although these principles may be most meaningful for well-defined cultural-linguistic communities located within a specific territorial space.

What is perhaps remarkable about the U.S. variant of democratic pluralism is that it includes communities at every level of cultural-linguistic association mentioned above in every part of the country. The Amish, for example, although a tiny population, have managed to retain their distinctive culture and religion for many generations in part because democratic pluralism allows them to do so. Groups such as the various Scandinavian peoples have, on the other hand, by choice assimilated almost completely. Others like the African Americans have done so primarily in terms of occupation or place of residence. Some like the Koreans and Chinese have, aided by a great push to obtain as much education as possible, joined the majority population in record time.

The other principle attribute of the U.S. experience with democratic pluralism is the commitment to the use of English in the workplace. That is why the Quebec insistence on use of French in the Quebec workplace does not seem strange to American ears. While many of the Hispanic groups such as the Cubans and Mexicans retain Spanish as a preferred language for virtually all discourse, no one in the United States doubts the advantages associated with knowing English for purposes of business and economic advancement.

Thus democratic pluralism means slightly different things in each country. Because ethno-linguistic communities retain their holistic character in Canada perhaps a bit more relentlessly than in the United

States, and retention of original languages is easier because of the educational support in the language, the protections afforded such communities by democratic pluralism are obvious and direct. In the United States, because so many immigrants swiftly opt for integration with the rest of the society, and because the effort to learn English is regarded as so rewarding (although not more rapid or widespread than in Canada), democratic pluralism qua community is more masked though not less essential. Nonetheless, every major city in the United States has its 'China town' or its 'Latin section' or its African American enclave. Florida has its own 'little Quebec' with newspapers from Quebec to match. Democratic pluralism allows these communities to interact with one another and with the central government in a way that is comparatively just and efficient. As Lyndon Johnson once said, the United States is a country composed of minorities. That is the true expression of a new and 'created' society. Quebec, as its intellectuals fully admit, is as created as any other.

According to John Kenneth Galbraith, the Scots in Canada were as ethnocentric as any other group. 'But nearly everyone was Scotch. Certainly it never occurred to us that a well-regulated community could be populated by any other kind of people.'[22] The only way such mutually ethnocentric communities can be governed inside a single polity is through a principle such as democratic pluralism. But in many ways both Canada and the United States are prototypes of what many other advanced industrial democracies in the twenty-first century, through the effects of migration and differential birth rates, are likely to become. Democratic pluralism is the principle upon which they must learn to make policy and to govern themselves.

Pluralism As Its Own Enemy

No concept of politics is immune to excess. No concept in isolation, without the qualification afforded by other concepts, can escape excess. No concept can, in the wrong circumstance, avoid becoming its own enemy. So it is with pluralism; if isolated, if wrongly used, if employed to excess, pluralism can become the enemy of itself.

Democratic pluralism is at its best when attempting to facilitate political harmony among ethno-linguistic communities that are territorially based. Harmony means lack of disabling conflict. Such harmony should never be assumed as inevitable. It does not guarantee cooperation, although some degree of harmony is essential for cooperation.

Complementarity (in which each actor contributes that which the other does not possess) is a better extension of harmony because it uses the diversity of the communities to construct a reinforced and overlapping matrix of interaction. Within the democratic framework, each community can contribute to complementarity inside a larger polity without feeling that the duties of the members exceed their rights. Pluralism allows complementarity to flourish across diverse communities.

Where pluralism fails is the situation in which it is used as a justification for expanding the differential rights of individual groups. This expansion may be justified if a group or community has been *denied* rights that other citizens enjoy. Indeed, new rights that all citizens ought to enjoy may become appropriate for the democratic polity to acknowledge, just as from time to time new obligations may become necessary – for example, as technology changes and impinges both positively and negatively upon people. But what is wrong is to attempt to use the concept of pluralism, or the existence of pluralism, as the vehicle with which to try to expand these rights or obligations (beyond that which exists in the polity overall), especially where they redound to a single community or grouping relative to others.

Pluralism should not be used as an excuse for the expansion of rights by single communities. Pluralism inherently is a relative concept. Expansion of rights to a single grouping denies this relative character of pluralism. Indeed to invoke such an attempted expansion of rights for single communities or groups in the name of pluralism is to incur the criticism of those who understand pluralism to be a concept that mediates across groups rather than advances the interest of one group at the possible or perceived expense of the others. If abused as a political notion of singular advancement of group interests, pluralism will collapse everywhere in the polity.

The argument that secession undermines democratic pluralism, when reduced to essentials, is an argument about the failure to reconcile ethno-linguistic or cultural differences between two communities. That these two communities, distinguished primarily by their differences in language or culture or both, no longer want to live together under a single political roof is the problem. Democratic pluralism fails when two communities decide they cannot accommodate each other inside a single set of political institutions.

The impact of secession on democratic pluralism is not primarily about whether there is a lack of sufficient tolerance on either side towards minorities, especially minorities speaking the language of the 'other' community, prior to secession. Nor is the negative impact of secession on democratic pluralism primarily about the effect that breakup could have on the treatment of minorities after secession. These two topics are perhaps legitimate subjects for discussion; but they are not the preoccupations of this study. Nor are they in any way crucial to the conclusion that secession establishes a precedent for the destruction of democratic pluralism when mature democracies must admit that they cannot comprise the political needs of diverse cultural communities within their borders. All the argument that secession puts democratic pluralism at risk requires is the evident failure of mature democracy to reconcile political disputes within its political jurisdiction.

But the harm secession does to democratic pluralism initially damages the prospect for impartiality in the future whenever ethno-linguistic difference impinges, not just in the secessionist entity, but perhaps even more so in the larger state that remains. Through the processes of diffusion, which are now so well studied by social scientists, and via example, the harm done by secession to democratic pluralism extends throughout the international system.[23]

Cultural Identity and Politics

During the past three decades a rich literature has emerged crossing the disciplines of philosophy, anthropology, political theory and political science, and sociology. Its purpose is to reconcile liberal political and cultural value. Yael Tamir, for example, argues that cultural community and political community should not be coterminus; she wishes to delink territory from culture.[24] 'The idea of impartiality legitimates hierarchical decision making,' asserts Iris Marion Young. She believes that perspectives of the 'privileged' gain ascendancy under the guise of impartiality and thereby are held to be more universal than society in reality justifies.[25] Bhikhu Parekh explicitly breaks with the liberal tradition of individual rights as the sole foundation for liberal theory, endorsing group rights.[26] Citizenship, Parekh argues, demands 'obligations of communities' as well as 'rights of communities.'

When each of these conceptualizations is forced to confront the matter of secession, an armful of insights results. Tamir's thesis must recognize, for instance, that the larger, the more densely concentrated, and the more homogeneous a cultural-linguistic community is, the less likely it is to be willing to forgo the territorial identification that she deplores and the more likely such a community is to seek political separation. Democratic pluralism allows cultural-linguistic communities, even those that are concentrated in a single territory, to pursue their objectives of identification, self-expression, and prosperity without having to succumb to 'hierarchical decision making' that Young criticizes and that subordinates the objectives of one community to the objectives of another. Finally, the problem with Parekh's proposal that communities be assigned obligations as well as rights is that once communities rather than individuals begin to assume rights and obligations they begin to differentiate themselves from the polity as a whole, a type of differentiation that often leads quite directly to eventual demands for secession.

Lawrence Cahoone points to a central issue tying together cultural-linguistic identity and the propensity for secession: 'What is more troublesome is utterly thick, hence exclusive, forms of associational identity, which are at home only in homogeneous societies in which the conditions of citizenship, social membership, and cultural identity are fused.'[27] What this prescient statement implies about Quebec, of course, is that if it were less homogeneous in terms of culture and language (less 'thick' in terms of 'associational identity'), it would be less prone to secede. Conversely, Quebec separatists could retort that if the rest of Canada were not so homogeneous in terms of the tendency to speak English (that is, if the rest of Canada were more given to speaking French), Quebec would be less likely to secede. Bilingualism was a proposal to achieve this mixing of languages; the difficulty was that Quebec separatists feared that they would be the ones learning English, but that the rest of Canada would never adequately learn French. Intention is not the same thing as achievement.

Noting that 'integration theorists appreciated this suggestion long ago,' Alexander Wendt reconciles the realist and liberal explanation of cooperation (emerging from the interaction of egoistic individuals under anarchy) with the collectivist view by arguing that 'interaction at the systemic level changes state identities and interests.'

> By engaging in cooperative behavior, an actor will gradually change its own beliefs about who it is, helping to internalize that new identity for itself. By teaching others and themselves to cooperate, in other words, actors are simultaneously learning to identify with each other – to see themselves as a 'we' bound by certain norms.[28]

Cooperation emerges out of the dialogue of opposing interests. Democratic pluralism entails such intellectual honesty and mutual respect at all levels of social and political association among peoples who are culturally different.

Acknowledging 'the increasing divergence between political and cultural identities' in modern societies, Pierre Hassner considers the 'reasonable compromise ... of Anthony Smith's idea of nurturing "families of cultures" ... [wherein] European nations would maintain their respective cultural identities, but would increasingly emphasize their common features.' He warns, however, that the potential political consequences have not been examined. In fact, 'the idea of a European family of cultures' carries with it two grave dangers. It could exacerbate tensions with non-European cultures. Perhaps less likely, but at least as ominous, a European cultural identity could lead to 'a new sense of mission toward the East and South.'[29] In Hassner's view, the contemporary search for homogeneous 'cultural identities' could be antithetical to world order and democracy alike.

The liberal democratic principles of universal civic participation and protection of individual rights seemed to reach their maturity within democratic pluralism. Recalling this premise in a 1998 article entitled 'Europe's Endangered Liberal Order,' Timothy Garton Ash suggests a return to 'Sir Isaiah Berlin's central liberal insight that people pursue different ends that cannot be reconciled but may peacefully coexist.'[30] In their classic work on politics in plural societies, Alvin Rabushka and Kenneth Shepsle posed, and answered in the negative, the central question for all subsequent research on contemporary democracy: 'Is the resolution of intense but conflicting preferences in the plural society manageable in a democratic framework?'[31] But for decades, even as analysts acknowledged that democracy itself may not be viable where ethnic violence is deep and long-standing, others recognized the importance of ethnic and cultural diversity for democracy itself. Lewis Coser, Seymour Martin Lipset, and William Kornhauser, among others, argued that multiple affiliations bind the fate of one individual or group to that of others, so that each would respect the interests of the other in pursuit of the common societal goals.[32] It was never claimed, however, that the task was easy.

In perhaps the boldest effort to deal with the problem of democratic governance in a culturally fragmented society, Arend Lijphart defends the systems of government called 'consociational democracy.'[33] Exemplified by the governmental systems of Switzerland and Belgium, consociational democracy contains four conceptual hallmarks: (1) Grand coalitions broker policy among leaders who represent each political/cultural community. (2) Each community possesses a veto over policies that are averse to its vital interests. (3) Appointments, distribution of financial resources, and allocation of responsibilities are done in a proportional basis. (4) Each community rules over itself in areas of exclusive concern (segmental autonomy). According to Robert Dahl, consociational democracies are rarely successful because most divided societies lack the conditions conducive to, if not necessary for, success.[34] Canada certainly possesses some elements of each attribute of a successful consociational democracy. But, as Dahl warns, 'there are no *general* solutions to the problems of culturally divided countries. Every solution will need to be custom tailored to the features of each country.'[35]

The question arises, however, whether secession is a valid or desirable political option in cases where consociational democracy, or other forms of liberal democracy, breaks down along territorially specific cultural-linguistic lines.

Secession is one of those peculiar political acts that always looks better when recommended to someone else than when applied to oneself. *Schadenfreude*, the joy taken at someone else's misfortune, may be part of the explanation. True empathy for the secessionists' urge for autonomy or self-determination may also play a part. But the analyst cannot avoid noting that France silently approves of Quebec separation while thoroughly rejecting Basque overtures in its own border provinces. Quebec separatists, in turn, favour political independence for themselves but banish the thought that multicultural Montreal could someday opt for independence from an independent Quebec. Moreover, political theorists sometimes like the idea of separation when applied to someone else's country, or in the abstract, but rarely when others seek independence from their own.

Not at issue is whether the outcome of a legal referendum, properly worded and effectively supported by majority vote, will be accepted by other democracies. Realism dictates that if the parties to the agreement to disassociate have themselves accepted the outcome and have based their decision on democratic principles, the outcome stands. Nor at issue is the matter of whether a primary language ought to be spoken and officially recognized whether in the secessionist entity or the larger state. Actual practice will determine which language is predominant despite the ideal that more than a single language may be beneficial and, for many citizens, preferable.

More central is the question regarding what secession along cultural-linguistic lines means to plural democracy, regardless of whether it occurs via a majority vote within the secessionist fragment or via brokered arrangement within a grand coalition of political representatives acting on behalf of the vital interest of each segment of the polity. This book focuses on this more introspective question regarding the permanent effect of secession on mature democracy. Just as divorce in an individual case may appear thoroughly justified and may even be seen as therapeutic, or emotionally plausible, when treated as a larger phenomenon regarding the impact on children, the single-parent family, the welfare system and the quality of education, crime, and human relations in a larger context, the matter of divorce becomes a rather more significant social concern. So it is with secession from the state: the consequence for pluralist democracy more generally is the primary focus of this study.

The act of separation is an act of one communal group cutting itself off from a larger society composed of people of different cultural attributes primarily because of a preference, however rationalized, not to associate with the other group politically. This preference not to associate politically because of cultural difference may be difficult for proponents of secession to admit, if they allow themselves even to recognize it. Nevertheless, secession for cultural and linguistic reasons certainly amounts to a purposeful rejection of association with those who may speak, dress, act, or look different. Of course, this preference for homogeneity may be regarded by some as 'natural' or 'inevitable' because of the desire to interact with those who are most similar.

But this preference for homogeneity may also be construed as quite unnatural in the context of increasing multiculturalism in the twenty-first century. Moreover, the preference for homogeneity is also inevitably an impossibility. Each individual is composed of many attributes, including height, weight, IQ, social background, income, education, and physical appearance, to name only a few. Association based on cultural-linguistic attributes, a very small subset of human attributes, amounts to a demotion of all of the others. Homogeneity based on two or three attributes while ignoring all of the other attributes is not homogeneity at all. For this very reason, political separation of a community for cultural-linguistic reasons is a futile act if it is designed to promote overall homogeneity of a society.

Cultural-linguistic fractionalization must be recognized as an effort to homogenize or 'purify' along lines of language and culture. Such fractionalization cannot be considered in step with the effort to promote greater openness, toleration, and diversity. In fact, a preference for a more homogeneous, closed society is *out* of step with the direction of change in most other multicultural communities – the growth of multi-culturalism is facilitated by the mobility of peoples and individuals.

Bosnia and Kosovo provide troubled examples of the impact of immigration and differential birth rates on homogeneity. In Bosnia, the sizeable Serb dominance of 1961 was replaced by an equivalent Muslim dominance by 1991, and in Kosovo, the ethnic Albanian birth rate was five times that of the Serbs during the same period.[36] The rapid shifts in the population mix caused by the movements of Moslem Bangladeshis into Northeast India, and of Chinese citizens into Russia Manchuria are as equally troubling. Each of these massive alterations of population has spilled over into the political realm and resulted in cultural and political turmoil.

What these huge changes in population composition along cultural lines reveal is that newcomers may be as desirous of separation as are the original inhabitants. The instinct to separate is not limited to the original residents or the predominant cultural grouping. Smaller clusters of ethnic Moslems, Montenegrins, Jews, or Hungarians caught within the borders of a state such as Croatia or Serbia may in their own self-interest mightily resist this push for homogeneity along the lines of a single cultural majority. For them, such homogenization may be the prelude to a threat to survival, since the same impulse to dissociate (or expulse) may ultimately be applied against themselves.

Perhaps the greatest challenge to, and the greatest denial of, the validity of the cultural-linguistic assertion of homogeneity is the willingness of people to ignore these constraints in their marriage preferences.[37] Supposedly, prior to the breakup of Yugoslavia along cultural-linguistic lines, some 30 per cent of the population in Sarajevo had intermarried. It is expected that the large urban centre, with its capacity for anonymity and its larger cosmopolitanism, might show a greater receptivity to cultural diversity than the village or rural community. Where social pressure or communal tradition opposes inter-marriage, as surely must have been the case in Sarajevo, the popularity of intermarriage despite all of its penalties is all the more astonishing. However, a determined political elite fuelled by governmental initiative can reverse much of this interpersonal behaviour.[38] What social pressure cannot prevent, political division can destroy. Promotion of ethnic and cultural toleration is easier to veto than to foster.

But if ethno-linguistic fractionalization is out of step with the twenty-first century in interpersonal terms, why is fractionalization challenging the unity of the nation-state at the communal level? Why in particular is communal nationalism thriving within a local civic community that is so thoroughly liberal, a model of mature liberal democracy? Why is ethnic nationalism, a form of political tribalism, so overpowering in its persuasiveness today?

The Social-Psychology of Divisive Nationalism

At least three complex social-psychological processes are at work within the mentality of contemporary divisive nationalism. These processes are extremely interactive and dynamic. They give the drive to seek political autonomy its energy and continually renewed vitality. For there is something anachronistic about divisive nationalism that seems inconsistent with the moderating character of democracy built on the capacity to compromise. These interactive processes furnish the political impulse that overcomes the atavistic quality of divisive nationalism, making it both more palatable to larger fractions of the disaffected communal population and less subject to criticism by opponents within the larger population of the state. In a word, the processes underwriting the mentality of divisive nationalism are calculated to take away the sting of negativism that is otherwise associated with the breakup of the nation-state.

1. Memory of Historical Exploitation versus Fear of Contemporary Discrimination

For many citizens in a once-subordinate communal group, a sense of historical wrong intermingles in a devastating fashion with the fear of contemporary discrimination. That historical wrong was objective and real and that contemporary discrimination may not be are scarcely relevant to this dynamic interchange between memory and prospective harm.

Historical wrong may stem from the awareness that a communal group is a 'conquered people.' Or, awareness of historical wrong may emerge out of a colonial status that was socially and politically demeaning if not economically unfair. Historical wrong is frequently equated, however, with economic exploitation. Economic exploitation and other forms of social oppression often go hand in hand.

Sometimes the primary relationship of political subordination occurred between the larger state population and a smaller communal population alone. Indeed, the smaller communal population may have historically been socially and politically dominant. Because the comparative advantage of the industrial bases may have altered over time, the once more prosperous communal population may then have entered a long interval of relative economic decline, the memory of which contrasts with an earlier interval of economic success. Contemporary prosperity only reminds the communal group of its historical economic vulnerability and modified fortunes.

But bringing out even more graphic bitterness is the fact that, regardless of the relationship between the communal group and the larger population, within the regionally distinct ethno-linguistic group there may have been a dominant elite of a different cultural orientation, perhaps that of the larger population itself. When this occurs, the regional communal population shifts its memory of exploitation, slights, and subordination to the larger population of the state that broadly shares the same cultural orientation as the original dominant elite inside the communal grouping. The original elite inside the region may have been the source of the subordinate grouping's problems, but the external population of the same cultural-linguistic persuasion gets the blame. They (the outsiders) all look the same to the population of the subordinate communal group.

Likewise the connection between objective historical grievance and fear of projected future grievance can sometimes be very tenuous. Conditions may have changed since the regional communal grouping experienced its past oppression. The chances of future discrimination may not be large. Indeed, the irony is that the communal group may be receiving disproportionate benefits, at least as measured by others in the country, but the weight of history is such that the regional community does not see the benefits as disproportionately advantageous. They see them as acknowledgment of past grievance and therefore thoroughly legitimate. The more that is done from the outside to placate the demands of the smaller ethno-linguistic community, the more it fears that these benefits at some time will be taken away, that it once again will be discriminated against, and that separation is the only way to guarantee a future safe from discrimination.

Future discrimination is made real, not by an objective account of events, either at the individual or the governmental level, but by the memory of historical wrongs that at one time were objective and from whose legacy of feeling the members of the community cannot escape.

Future discrimination is not likely, but to assert this unlikelihood is to invite the wrath of the separatist who claims that only through complete political autonomy can this possibility be effectively negated.

For some, past experience legitimates fear of future injustice. For others, the past is invoked to justify separation. For still others, past wrongs are simply a reminder that the same people who were responsible for wrongs in the past are still in the majority in the larger polity, and that only creation of a separate polity will ensure that the past does not become prologue, regardless of the implausibility of such a scenario. Resentment, wrote Karl Mannheim in *Ideology and Utopia* in 1936, is significant in the formation of 'moral' judgment, and this is perhaps true of the moral sentiment to secede as well.[39]

2. Anxiety over Loss of Collective Political Identity versus Inability to Adapt Fully to an Individualist Political Ethic

Virtually all ethnic linguistic communities of the past were communities that emphasized a collective political identity.[40] The reason for this was that in-group and out-group attitudes became very distinct as the struggle for survival forced upon the members a feeling of group responsibility. Survival meant survival as a group. Survival entailed preserving a language, religion, culture, and lifestyle that in some cases could only be practised in the collective. Religious leaders, for example, had a large social responsibility for everything from counselling to health care to education. Little help came from outside. This meant that everyone in the collective had an obligation to 'pitch in.' The collective identity became synonymous with the welfare of every family and individual living inside the community. Little wonder that for many members of such a communal setting the collective identity of the community became more important than their own individual identities.

Modern communities in an urban secular environment are quite different. They are atomized. Services come from many contributors. Mobility is greater. Urbanization exposes otherwise quite parochial groups to contact with members from different cultural settings. Of course, pockets of parochialism remain untouched. But intermarriage occurs. The sense of the collective is less palpable, in part because the need for group survival is less immediate.

Democracy, especially liberal democracy, places a high value on individualism. Individualism is reflected in the act of voting, which in the end is an individual experience. Individualism is also reflected in occupational choices such as entrepreneur, manager, or worker. Whether liberalism precedes democracy or democracy nurtures liberalism, each is beholden to the individual, to individual decision, and to the mobility of the individual.

Modern societies that find themselves confronting secession often are very democratic in form and sometimes in substance. They are not 'illiberal.' They are liberal in every respect but for their penchant for ethno-linguistic isolation. This very commitment to liberalism sets up tensions between loyalty to the collective on the one hand and aspirations to an individualist identity on the other. These tensions are not easily resolved in the secessionist state.

Alienation from the collective combined with an inability to make the transition fully to the ethic of the individual creates an identity conflict. Nationalist obsession fills the gap between a collectivism that is being left behind and an individualism that still appears unattainable.[41] Nationalism seems to resolve the identity conflict by concealing the faded association with the collective and the yet uncompleted transmigration to the individualist framework. Action accompanying the nationalist impulse seems to resolve all of the contradictions over identity. The warmth of participation in the nationalist cause strips away from the identity problem its more sobering and introspective preoccupations. Nationalism involving secession enables each participant to stand up and be counted.

3. Stress Regarding Preservation of Communal Culture versus Pride in New Nationalist Assertion

Every breakaway province or region worries about the preservation of its communal culture. But strangely, the worry is directed at the larger polity of which it is a member, not against the international system of which it would like to become a part after independence. The worry is that its culture will become folkloric rather than vital.

Yet, quoting John Milton, R.M. MacIver argues (in agreement with our earlier discussion) that 'the well-being of society requires the natural diversity of its members, and that coercive uniformity of morals and manners would spell the ruin and degradation of any people.'[42] Working as the secretary for foreign languages during the time of Cromwell's enforced conformity, Milton understood directly the need for the cultural diversity and liberty of which he spoke.

Loss of language is not an idle concern, however, for the Berbers of

Morocco, for example, or the First Nations Peoples of North America. Beautiful and useful as a language may once have been, as in the case of Yiddish, if an insufficient number of people use it, it will disappear. But oftentimes enough adherents speak and perhaps read the language to keep the spoken language alive and well. (Danish is not in danger of extinction, even though most Danes speak some English, and in 1998 the population size of Denmark was 5.3 million.) This is more true if the language, though a minority tongue in a larger country, is spoken worldwide. But invariably secessionist movements cite preservation of language and culture as an objective now threatened by the present association with a larger polity of diverse culture.

In order to preserve use of language, nationalists in a communal setting often demand that the language be used in the workplace, not just at home. While such mandating of language use in the workplace can have a marked impact, the manner of enforcement can be very controversial, as is the case of English street signs in Quebec. To Americans it seems utterly reasonable, on the one hand, that Quebecers should want French to be the primary language of the province. On the other hand, to it also seems reasonable that, for sound commercial and economic reasons, Quebecers would want their children to learn English as a second language.

Evidence for the argument that there are benefits to learning English as a second language is not hard to find. Ask any international business person. Holding other explanations for trade statistically constant, Shang-Jin Wei shows that 'given two otherwise similar countries, the one whose occupants understood English can expect trading volume divided by GDP to be 17 percent higher.'[43] This is not an argument for giving up French as a first language in Quebec. It is an argument for making English a second language. Moreover, for those inside Quebec who know both languages, the same earnings differential will accrue relative to those who only know French. By working in French at home, but knowing English as well, Quebecers can have the best of both worlds, as most Quebecers are already aware.

At the same time that it presses for cultural-linguistic preservation, secession promotes pride in a new nationalist vision. This nationalist vision is overwhelmingly positive. It touts capacity to prosper and survive on all fronts once independence is declared. Gone is the worry over the extinction of language and culture. Gone is the anxiety that the ethno-linguistic community is being absorbed by its larger affiliate of diverse cultural taste and language expression. Separatism is offered as a solution to language erosion and cultural demise.

It is often contended that traditional language and culture are in danger of extinction within the confines of a broader communal group and that separation will rescue both language and culture by the creation of an autonomous state. Exaggeration probably marks each contention. Neither traditional culture nor use of the language is in actuality threatened by association with the larger population of a federal state. Nor is separation a likely formula for safeguarding traditional culture if indeed it had been threatened. All of the same forces of assimilation – mobility, bombardment by foreign media, and commercial use of English – would remain whether an ethno-linguistic group governs itself or remains part of a larger state. There is no way to isolate a culture or shackle its members into steadfast support for its principles. But strategically this dual exaggeration concerning the peril to culture if a state remains united and concerning the promise of rescue if a fragment secedes has a role in the promotion of divisive nationalism.

In reality, according to cultural anthropologists and historians, above a certain size threshold, concentrated language groupings can survive quite effectively where the will to survive exists. Of the approximately 6,000 languages spoken in the world today, more than half are spoken by fewer than 6,000 people. These languages are endangered, according to Alfred W. Crosby and Frances Karttunen, but not those spoken by millions.[44]

But stress over the effort to preserve communal culture is nicely released by pride in new nationalist assertion. Nationalism is the cathartic to the prior stress. Without fear of loss, there could be little pride in the new alleged gain of cultural protection through national autonomy. Few citizens ask themselves whether their culture is endangered and in fact what such endangerment might really involve. Fewer still reflect deeply upon how the promise of separation actually would rescue a dying culture if such rescue were in reality needed. Instead, the emotional attachments associated with the experience of stress on the one hand, and its release through the promised nirvana of political autonomy on the other, are the stimuli and response that help drive the nationalist program.

The Challenge to Liberal Democracy

For those who contemplate the danger of global warming, the worst fear is that as the oceans become more constant in temperature, the circulation of the waters will slow and some of the deep ocean currents may dissipate, altering weather even more profoundly. For the defend-

ers of liberal democracy, the worst fear ought to be that peoples everywhere will begin to insist on societal homogeneity, and that when this
happens attempts will be made to limit and even eradicate cultural,
social, and political diversity, and thus the positive change that can
come of this diversity, through fragmentation of the polity.

Each polity, from this perspective of cultural homogeneity, 'ought to'
contain a single, monolithic population. In the splintering of the
former Yugoslavia, so-called ethnic cleansing was used to achieve by
force separate regions of supposed cultural oneness. In Belgium, the
Dutch-speaking citizens of Flanders seek to separate from the French
Walloons, who lament the breakup of the state. In Quebec, from time to
time, the Cree have indicated that they would separate from a majority
of French-speaking citizens against the latter's preferences if Quebec
becomes independent. While the means make all the difference,
whether the sword or the ballot box, the outcome may be the same – a
splintering of a country. And while not all cases must be treated identi-
cally, a general pattern of fragmentation is a problem for liberal democracy. For the objective of separation is a culturally monolithic society
within the confines of a narrower, more ethnically based state.

Liberal democracy was founded upon exactly the opposite principle.
Aristotle, the prototypical political scientist, argued that the highest
goal of democracy is liberty. This notion of liberty, however, is
grounded in the idea of equality, an even more fundamental concept.
'The people must be sovereign, and whatever the majority decides that
is final and that is justice. For ... there must be equality among the citizens.' But Aristotle immediately saw one of the flaws in this ideal-type
democracy. This kind of democracy leads to justice based on 'numerical equality, not equality based on merit.'[45] All modern democracies
must thus make efforts to create balancing mechanisms, to introduce
merit, and to offset permanent majorities of any kind that can crush
minorities of varying vulnerability.

In liberal democracy, the equality that prevails is the political and
subsequently legal equality of the individual. If that legal equality of
the individual is absent in a society, whatever other democratic institutions and processes may exist, then it is not a liberal democracy. Democratic thinkers have been good at designing governments, ensuring
that the legal equality of the individual is respected. And, having
established legal equality of the individual, mature liberal democracies
must be ever on guard to make it a societal reality.[46] Consequently, liberty endures and justice ultimately results.

But where modern democracy has not succeeded so well is in ensuring equality of groups, that is, equality of collectives. For example, the United States guarantees equality of each region through the election of two senators from each state regardless of population density or size, which is reflected in the House of Representatives. Canada, on the other hand, neither elects senators nor accords the Senate (much like the British House of Lords) coequal powers vis-à-vis the House of Commons, which is composed of members elected roughly on the basis of population size. Nor is this solution reflective of underlying economic and political equality since these entities vary so much internally in terms of actual size and power – despite the reality that each of the states and provinces, for example, are accorded equal representation. Likewise women's groups or visible minorities that demand equal representation are seldom adequately represented as a collective per se, in part since such representation is open-ended and there are no limits to what can be defined as an interest group. Instead of trying to tailor individual rights to each interest group, ultimately a hopeless and unfair exercise, individuals enjoying the same rights everywhere must be guaranteed that these rights will not be denied if they belong to a group.

Finally, communal representation, especially communal representation involving cultural or linguistic differentiation from a concentrated geographic base, is seldom presented in a fashion inside federal government in a way that satisfies a Scotland, a Flanders, or possibly a Quebec. Each of these equalities cannot simultaneously be represented and balanced in the contemporary polity.

Another way of looking at the problem confronting liberal democracy is in terms of the cleavage between state and society, between the architecture of government and the weight of localized cultural community. Tocqueville recognized more than most the compelling distinction between state and civil society. He noted that 'the principle of equality may be established in civil society without prevailing in the political world.' Tocqueville also saw the trend of power within the state over communal groups. 'From one end of Europe to the other the privileges of the nobility, the liberties of cities, and the powers of provincial bodies are either destroyed or are upon the verge of destruction.'[47] With prescience, he worried about the capacity of the United States to deal effectively in the absence of bloodshed with the emancipation of slaves. What he saw as offsetting such communal difficulties in such situations were commitment to politically unfettered religion and enthusiasm for voluntary association.

But the appeal to localized communal affiliation leading to secession is a political phenomenon that brackets the twentieth century. At Versaille at the end of the First World War, Woodrow Wilson thought he addressed the problem in the Balkans by altering borders and shifting populations. Something of the same happened brutally after the Second World War. But the real pressure to fragment polities came at the end of the twentieth century under a twofold global influence: the end of the Cold War, and the maturation of regional economic integration, which transcended the state and weakened its claim to primary responsibility for the economic well-being of its citizens. Communal fragmentation is not often a problem of equality, in which the local cultural grouping comes out the economic and political loser (although this complaint is commonly heard as well). Rather, communal fragmentation is often a problem of *identity*.

On the one hand, regional communal groups desirous of secession lament an alleged loss of identity and an inability to compete and to cohere against larger ethno-linguistic populations that are said to be assimilationist. On the other hand, these regional communal groups claim that a rise in ethnic group consciousness and political identity drives them to seek autonomy as a separate nation-state, no matter how small. Notwithstanding the conflict between these two assertions of national identity, the one fearful and the other confident, a conflict of political and cultural identity whether tortured or triumphant seems to be at the heart of the present case for secession.

But, by whatever route one comes analytically to the conclusion that secession is a challenge to the workings of liberal democracy, a further conclusion quickly follows. A strategy has not emerged to deal with communal discontents. Tocqueville notes a partial strategy, a strategy that surely is at the centre of the Canadian response to Quebec's secessionist impulse: 'The free institutions which the inhabitants of the United States possess, and the political rights of which they make so much use, remind every citizen, and in a thousand ways, that he lives in society.'[48] Moreover, the society of which he speaks is a country-wide society. The political participation includes all degrees and levels of participation from actual holding of governmental office to enjoying the fruits of patronage. Quebecers have long known this involvement in government at the federal level and have learned to expect such representation and benefit. Identification of community and the architecture of state remain even more as two solitudes as pressures shift and the responsibility of social services – education, immigration, pensions, health care, job training, and taxation – is increased for the communal group and taken away from federal jurisdiction.

Liberal democracy, without a principle such as democratic pluralism, can guarantee neither the sense of communal equality that the substate grouping seeks nor the stalwart cultural and linguistic identity about which the communal entity seems so anxious yet so ambivalent.

If liberal democracy is supposed to enable multiple populations to live in harmony through freedom and equal representation at least at the individual level, then how can liberal democracy accommodate the demands of concentrated communal groupings? Moreover, where does the devolution of authority end as smaller and smaller cultural groupings, arrayed on a geographical basis in ever smaller units, seek their political autonomy? As Alan Hendrikson and Hans Binnendijk assert, 'fragmentation along ethnic lines is now the leading cause of state failure.'[49] Since the concentration and recombination of cultural and linguistic groups within polities will continue, resulting from immigration and differential birth rates, the potential for the fragmentation of the nation-state will scarcely halt.

Democratic theory must find a way to accommodate communal groups within existing polities. Attempting to minimize conflict internal to polities by invariably deconstructing the nation-state only externalizes conflict between countries of differing cultural composition. International relations must then take up where intrastate politics has failed. Internationalization of conflict already has a sorry history.[50] International relations is no more likely to produce harmony and compromise than has the politics within countries.

Hence the burden of imaginative solutions on the architects of liberal democracy is to devise formulas and arrangements that provide harmony amid diversity. An avenue may be to restore the linkage between state and society, to show the advantages to community of association with the larger state, and to revitalize the interactions between cultural communities of sometimes long separate conviction. Liberal democracy deserves help not only from its formal structures but from friendly process elsewhere in the polity.

Why Secession Does Not Support Liberalism

The concept of 'nation' as a unified cultural-linguistic whole (as, for example, expressed vis-à-vis Catalan or Wales or Scotland) is as contrived as the arguments across history that have been used to convince sceptical publics of its necessary validity. Everywhere, as Renan famously asserted, 'the nation' is a created concept that emerges as much out of *various peoples' learning to live together under a single set of political institutions* as out of any prior or historical sense of 'shared identity.' It is the primary awareness of *this sense of learning, of acquiring, and of growing together* that is often missing from the dialogue between the proponents of 'civic nationalism' and the advocates of nationalism as one supposedly homogeneous historically determined, cultural-linguistic 'people' or 'nation.' Despite the rhetoric of advocates of 'national' unity, in an abstract sense all state unity has been 'civic,' because created. Everywhere state unity continues to be earned rather than inherited, conditional rather than guaranteed.

The ideas of civic nationalism and of 'the nation' rest uneasily with each other in the modern debates on secession in advanced liberal democracies. According to Will Kymlicka,

> People decide who they want to share a country with by asking who they identify with, who they feel solidarity with ... Where does this shared identity come from? In nation-states, the answer is simple. Shared identity derives from commonality of history, language, maybe religion. But these are precisely the things that are not shared in a multination state.[51]

But is the answer so simple? Such analysis frequently comes close to that of tautology: Those who share identity retain national unity; those who display national unity possess a shared identity. Perhaps a further answer lies with the proposed 'commonality of history, language, and maybe religion.'

Despite having been on the same side of three prior wars, sharing more than two centuries of history, speaking the same language, and attending the same churches, the American South and North fought a bloody civil war over unity. Germany, often held up as the archetype of the nation-state, was, in 1830, a mere congeries of principalities, divided by religion, without a common language, and disunited in every aspect of a shared culture. Only force and Prussian political and bureaucratic domination changed this. France likewise enjoyed no truly common language until the nineteenth century, no single religion (quite the contrary), and no sense of common history except disputation until the era of Louis XIV. To this day, the embers of restiveness still glow in Brittany and the Basque country (France), and in Bavaria (Germany). Modern America remembers a conflict-ridden past, a multitude of languages spoken by large sectors of its population, and a variety of religions all deeply and divisively expressed.

Are we fooling ourselves that secession in the advanced industrial democracy is not really about a lack of cultural and linguistic tolerance on the part both of those who seek to separate and those who have driven the separatists to do so? Stripped of all the differences of political perspective, of the struggle over power, of the so-called grievances and their alleviation, what underlies the failure to make democratic pluralism work is too often a sense of cultural and linguistic arrogance on both sides that pushes the agenda of separatism – a refusal to accept limitations on one's own cultural preferences or values.

Tolerance across linguistic-cultural, ethnic, and religious communities in North America has been hard-fought. Despite some backsliding, it has on the whole been remarkable in its progress. Indeed, the very fact of communal diversity and political factionalism in the new colonies of North America led to the creation of political principles and institutional structures that enabled democratic pluralism to take root and flourish. Deep respect, not just polite aloofness, must combine with meaningful commercial, social, and political interaction for a shared political culture to evolve.

But what if a shared political culture is given up? Referring to 'any future secession of Quebec from the rest of Canada,' Will Kymlicka writes, 'It is difficult to see why liberals should automatically oppose such peaceful, liberal secessions. After all, liberalism is fundamentally concerned, not with the fate of states, but with the freedom and well-being of individuals, and secession need not harm individual rights.' He then adds, 'However, secession is not always possible or desirable. Some national minorities, particularly indigenous peoples, would have trouble forming viable independent states.'[52] But is the 'fate of states' so divorced from the 'freedom and well-being of individuals'? While secession 'need not' in the abstract 'harm individual rights,' will secession in reality do so in many instances?

While Kymlicka recognized that secession was not in the best interest of the parties involved, he believed the reasons would come from outside liberal theory itself. However, by examining the implications of secession for liberal theory and practice, the full meaning of democratic liberalism itself can be laid bare.

Not only could secession negatively affect the material well-being of individuals (see chapter 6), but to the extent that cultural tolerance on the one hand and the benefits of democratic pluralism on the other are rights, these rights are likely to be directly affected by secession. Inasmuch as the chief distinguishing feature of secession among advanced industrial democracies is cultural-linguistic or ethno-linguistic fractionalization, the issue of cultural tolerance is unavoidably raised. No matter how much protagonists of secession try to characterize secession as 'civic' in nature, that is not what empirical political science reveals. Were tolerance for cultural linguistic diversity present, on both sides, secession would not have been contemplated. Once secession occurs, tolerance of cultural diversity will have been damaged by the very reality that this tolerance has been challenged and has been seen to fail under the weight of secession. Democratic pluralism in the future, not only in North America but worldwide, will have been damaged by secession along cultural-linguistic lines. If democratic pluralism fails in North America, where the political and material conditions for its success are so propitious, then it is likely to have much less prospect of success elsewhere in the world system, where the circumstances are so much harsher and less conducive to democratic practice.

Moreover, the whole notion that the 'fate of states' has no relevance to the rights of individuals living within those states is troubling, a concern addressed at the end of this chapter.

Historically, individualism has most commonly been posed against social class or against vested political or economic interest. Individualism has been championed in most twentieth-century democratic thought as the apex of the utilitarian critique by the middle class against the aristocracy, or against the rural landlord, or against powerful interest groups within the democratic process that can demand special privilege or can blunt social reform advancing the greatest good of the greatest number.

But the argument for individual liberty can as easily be read in terms of the impact that cultural domination has on the individual. Secession based on no evidence of economic exploitation, or of denial of liberties, but only justified on the grounds of the desire to differentiate along cultural-linguistic lines, can readily be interpreted in terms of the liberal idea of the transgression of opinion. 'If all mankind minus one were of one opinion, and only one person were of the contrary opinion, mankind would be no more justified in silencing that one person than he, if he had the power, would be justified in silencing mankind.'[53] If culture is the basis of secessionist impulse, then a situation is created in which culture becomes the one entity with the power not only to separate from a polity composed more broadly, but also the power to silence all other sources of opinion and differentiation. Culture becomes a value superior to all other sources of association, expression, or individuality.

By this logic, a majority culture within any region will always be justified in separating from a larger polity composed of a different (or more diverse) cultural make-up. Culture, and cultural homogeneity alone, will then be regarded as sufficient to determine the political future of whatever regionally specific grouping that culture happens to characterize. This logic is seriously flawed, as Hurst Hannum, an international legal expert on secession, warns regarding claims for ethnic self-determination. Ethnically homogeneous states are neither 'inherently desirable' nor even feasible:

> Even in an environment where human rights are respected, a global system of states based primarily on ethnicity or historical claims is clearly unachievable. Except in the smallest or most isolated environments, there will always be 'trapped' minorities, no matter how carefully boundaries are drawn. Ethnically based states almost inevitably lead to claims of ethnic superiority on the part of the new majority and to a cultural rigidity that creates problems for new minorities.[54]

What is more, 'statehood is not necessary to guarantee the legitimate human rights of groups and individuals to protect and promote their culture, language and tradition.'[55] The secessionist impulse is thus an unnecessary, unworkable, and in the above sense 'inherently undesirable' approach to resolving conflicting attitudes and preferences within a mature liberal democracy.

In the twenty-first century, the final battle of democracy faced by the individual may be the battle for cultural tolerance, that is, for the mature type of political association described by the label 'democratic pluralism.' But having won all of the other confrontations, the individual may lose the battle for democratic pluralism if secession allows cultural identities to silence every other source of political preference as the grounds for political association.

Why Canadian Unity Matters for Liberal Democracy

To argue that the unity of the state is of no consequence or of no concern to liberal democracy is to argue that 1867 was of no consequence for the kind of liberal democracy characterized by the openness, tolerance, and federal–provincial balance that evolved in Canada. To say that there is no correspondence between the unity of the state and the nature of liberal democracy is to neglect history and the role that institutions play in shaping political consciousness. Since Hobbes, democratic political theory takes into account the fragility of the state and the 'opportunity costs' involved with ignoring that fragility in terms of forgone liberty. But in the twenty-first century, theorists of liberal democracy are even more aware than Hobbes of the degree to which the unravelling of the state along cultural-linguistic lines can affect the capacity to govern effectively and with impartiality. Impartiality in governance, especially in cultural-linguistic terms, is key to the legitimacy of political institutions and the acceptance by the electorate of administration and jurisprudence. Impartiality underlies not only the good within multicultural society but the sense of justice that allows democracy to function.

If fragmentation of the state occurs along cultural-linguistic lines, the average citizen will draw the logical conclusion that democratic pluralism is a discarded doctrine, a damaged political good. Henceforward, decisions within the state will be formulated, much as Cromwell thought, according to doctrinal norm rather than representative justice. Partiality according to culturally or linguistically defined truth will replace impartiality based on compromise and pragmatism. When the state shatters according to cultural-linguistic preference, the new norm of consequence will be what is good to promote cultural-linguistic convenience if not ascendancy.

Liberal democracy has a responsibility to support the state institutions that support it. Individualism may be the preoccupation of liberal democracy. The state that breaks up according to cultural-linguistic difference will not only mortgage the capacity to protect the individual in many instances (quite unlike the unusual circumstances of the Norwegian secession), but will also give rise to cultural-linguistic difference as the new standard upon which to base democratic decision. Democratic pluralism and government conducted solely by cultural-linguistic norm are, ultimately, incompatible.

CHAPTER TWO

A U.S. Perspective on Canadian Unity

Both Canadian and U.S. citizens regard what they have accomplished as singular, and how they govern themselves as worthy of emulation. From the outset, this was their mission.

'We shall be as a city on the hill,' said John Winthrop, governor of the Massachusetts Bay Company, in 1629, as he contemplated the future of the North American experience.[1] Freed from political tyranny, that future held the promise of learning to live together politically. The early lesson of this highly conformist society was twofold: it easily created a political tyranny from within and yet it politically accommodated a reality that did not reflect its rigid assumptions. The North American communities, which would eventually include the United States and Canada, mixed a political realism with a stalwart idealism. The New World as opposed to the Old World was a place where many objectives could be accomplished by citizen as much as by government.

While Canada in both its anglophone liberal/tory tradition and its francophone conservative tradition leaned towards a collectivist outlook, and the American colonies leaned towards an individualist interpretation of politics and religion, the Canadian and the American ethos each shared an uncommon mixture of idealism and realism. This was something new in the realm of world politics.

What was new was a mingling of the practical and philosophical legacy of the realists like Hobbes and Talleyrand with the idealists like Kant and Tocqueville. While increasingly wedded to free market ideas, this mixture of liberalism and conservatism, in comparison with the extremes of European political thought and action, was set inside rather narrow conceptual limits and was fundamentally non-dogmatic and non-ideological. So encompassing was the city on the hill metaphor that both a strong liberal like John F. Kennedy and a legendary conservative like Ronald Reagan freely evoked its symbolism. As George Grant remarked, in the United States 'their "right-wing" and "left-wing" are just different species of liberalism.'[2] The roots of democratic pluralism encompass the span of North American politics.

Often the contrast between 'Canadian collectivism' and 'American individualism' is illustrated by the mottoes that distinguish the two countries' approaches to government: 'life, liberty, and the pursuit of happiness' in the United States, and 'peace, order, and good government' in Canada. But the very existence of the United States is a memorial to the Founding Fathers' realization that their great ideal depended on the establishment of peace, order, and good government, while to the Fathers of Confederation those values were arguably nothing more than means to essentially liberal ends.

The city on the hill metaphor implied an internal harmony of interests and purpose among the parts of the city and among its citizens that was essential to the whole. This harmony was not imposed or coerced from above; it emerged from below and was shaped and amplified by good government. It also emerged from the response of peoples who had sought mutual strength in the struggle to overcome the obstacles to survival 'on the frontier,' or, in Canada's case, to survive the rigours of a 'hostile northern climate.' Notwithstanding the very real differences between the two countries, this confrontation between civilization and the frontier, or civilization and a hostile climate, continues to perpetuate an internal harmony within the United States and within Canada.

While embodying a sense of national purpose, and expressing the vision of North American civilization, the city on the hill metaphor was not isolationist in spirit or formation. It was certainly intended to be a beacon to others[3] and, as well, the good fortune of North Americans was to be shared abroad with the materially less affluent. As the polities matured and the role of foreign policy crystallized, this sense of international involvement, later described as interdependence, was considered a justifiable burden. Although there were always strands of isolationist thought and even 'free-riderism' in the policies of each country, these were not the dominant themes of their foreign policy or their domestic political outlook.

The city on the hill also embraced a notion of security, which served the two polities well throughout the twentieth century – through two world wars, the Great Depression, and the forty-year Cold War. Militarily, the city on the hill conveyed a sense of invulnerability. In part, this invulnerability stemmed from a geographically strategic location. Surrounded by three oceans and an extensive gulf, North America combines geostrategically the best aspects of the so-called island maritime state and of the landlocked Continental power. This is reflected in North American defence. Following the Second World War, for example, Canada had the fourth largest navy in the world. But these two states also possessed very capable armies often associated with the Continental power.

Although North America is surrounded by the two largest oceans, the Atlantic and the Pacific, the city on the hill was never a 'fortress' in the way that the proponents of 'Fortress America' had envisioned. Nor was the city on the hill a 'fireproof house,' as Senator Dandurand once called Canada. Their proximities to these oceans required the North American countries to deal with Asia and Europe, Latin America, and other members of the Third World. Even if the architects of the city on the hill had wanted the North American countries to become inward-looking, they could not have achieved this purpose. International commerce, trade, and diplomacy drew the Canadian and U.S. governments into global affairs as well as each other's affairs.

The city on the hill idea came to be associated with multiple dimensions of foreign policy preference and behaviour. In the post–Cold War era, the metaphor reflected a renaissance in the values of democracy and the market-driven economy. The city on the hill came to be associated with all three countries of North America, which now included Mexico, expressing the underlying forces that created of North America a single economy presided over by three sovereign and independent countries. The North American Free Trade Act (NAFTA) epitomized these dimensions of foreign policy.

Several questions come to mind about the city on the hill acting as a counterweight to other North American values that, especially in the U.S., failed to reinforce national harmony. Is the city on the hill metaphor too confining? Is the history of North America filled with more mistakes, backsliding, and social contradiction than the metaphor admits?

To question the honesty of the metaphor is valid. Two great social dilemmas afflicted the United States, one of which in varying ways affected both Canada and Mexico as well. The one common to all three countries was the lamentable treatment of the Native North American populations. What disease did not accomplish, ostracization and discrimination seemed to perpetuate. Slavery, in addition, plagued the first hundred years of the United States, followed by segregation and unequal access. Eighteenth-century war ended for Canada in 'the Conquest' and British North America, and for the United States eventually in the 'Louisiana Purchase.' The first years of the nineteenth century did not go well in terms of amity. Britain, in defence of her dominion, burned the White House during the War of 1812. The United States, in carving out the territory of Texas, invaded Mexico. So the city on the hill was not without blemish and gross imperfection. Yet the idealism never wavered. The beacon was not shuttered.

On the other hand, does the idea of the city on the hill connote what Canadian liberals and a wing of the Conservative Party prior to the Canada–U.S. Free Trade Agreement lamented as 'Continentalism'? The answer is an emphatic 'No!' However plausible it might be to contemporary Europeans, North Americans express no desire to abolish national borders or amalgamate politically.[4] Yet, revealingly, each country is more than willing to try to extract the potential economic efficiencies and reductions of border risk that close interdependence can provide.

Nonetheless, the city on the hill captures the noble spirit of the North Americans, regardless of borders or national and communal differences. Even as his own Puritan community established official intolerance of religious dissent, Winthrop warned Roger Williams of his imminent arrest, enabling him to escape to Rhode Island to set up an alternative city on the hill, which was founded on the principle of tolerance of diversity. The undaunted French explorers Champlain, Joliet, and Duluth charted much of the territory eventually occupied by people of other cultural backgrounds on each side of what became the Canada–U.S. border. The city on the hill metaphor conveys a mutual set of North American aspirations and values regardless of country origin or period of history. In an age of regional trade areas and customs unions, the metaphor perhaps obtains added relevance.

Yet, at this very same moment in history, much more than harmony amid diversity is blurred by Quebec's impetus to separate from Canada. The city on the hill metaphor provides the historical and philosophical context for the U.S. perspective on Quebec's possible separation and its political consequences.

What Underlies U.S. Preferences?

A 'strong and united Canada' is what the United States favours.[5] In one form or another, this is the mantra that covers all official expression of U.S. interest in Canada. Because it is so commonly evoked, the mantra is often examined for the slightest change in wording, almost as though the art of 'Kremlinology' were being applied, out of context and era, to post–Cold War relations between two prominent democracies. The accusation of 'over analysis' justifiably sticks, but the same could be said of the learned interpreters of the mantra.[6] More often than not, a president or a secretary of state gets the wording wrong, not for lack of schooling, or for lack of eagerness, but because he or she strays from the text and stumbles, one of the greatest sins a politician can commit.[7]

Yet for all its tiresomeness, the mantra, like a cliché, is short-hand for substance that is either too complicated or too 'loaded' politically to spell out with care and freshness at each occasion, especially by politicians who have a lot more to think about. But unlike a cliché, the mantra never loses its meaning. The more it is stated, the more meaning and status it obtains.[8] So what underlies the U.S. mantra on Canadian unity?

Democratic Pluralism

In perhaps its singly most poignant message, the city on the hill is a beacon for democratic pluralism worldwide. Democratic pluralism surely was not invented in North America, but it has become equated with the type of democracy that encompasses a variety of ethnic and cultural groupings inside a single, unified set of federal structures. In any major city in North America, there are well-delineated cultural communities that have their own schools, churches, synagogues, or mosques, restaurants, shops, street signs, manner of dress, and language. Yet this diversity of lifestyles and cultural expression is not regarded as discordant or socially troublesome. For the most part, these groups live tranquilly within the confines of interlaced democratic institutions. As indicated in chapter 1, tolerance across linguistic-cultural, ethnic, and religious communities has been hard-fought, mixed with backsliding but on the whole remarkable in its progress.

North America is quite modest about its experiment in social and political harmony. Yet democratic pluralism is not so simple to accomplish. If there is one feature of life in the city on the hill that is worth radiating to the world, it is the practical capacity to make democratic pluralism work. Far from taking democratic pluralism for granted, North Americans ought to recognize how unique and precious is their beacon.

Weight of History

According to Seymour Martin Lipset, the organizing principles of Canada and the United States were very different:

> One was Whig and classically liberal or libertarian – doctrines that emphasize distrust of the state, egalitarianism, and populism – reinforced by a voluntaristic and congregational religious tradition. The other was Tory and conservative in the British and European sense – accepting of the need for a strong state, for respect for authority, for deference – and endorsed by hierarchically organized religions that supported and were supported by the state.[9]

These enduring values also speak to the attitude towards political unity, albeit in different ways on each side of the border.

At first glance, American values might appear quite tolerant of state fragmentation. Voluntarism suggests that political participation is not imposed or necessarily universal but instead is based upon the free-will of the participant. Egalitarianism suggests equal respect for all levels of government and for the degree of political authority that each professes. Populism underlines this preference for decentralization, equal representation at each level of government, and equal counsel from each geographic region.

Voluntarism and populism each reinforce distrust of centralized authority and the sense of formal political obligation. Support for central government in unqualified legal or political terms appears totally rejected. Religious behaviour, so important to the American ethos, mimics the market both in its decentralized voluntaristic character and in the competitive recruitment that so strengthens its popular appeal. Political unity would not appear to find any props among the fissiparous U.S. religious affiliations. Indeed, based on the first fifty years of the nation's existence, these extrapolations of value as they relate to states rights and local autonomy (consider for example the terms of entry of Texas into the Union) do not far miss the mark.

The citizens of the U.S. favour Canadian unity because of the weight of history upon their collective conscience. Although neither paranoid nor hysterical ('passionate' in the current political jargon) on this issue, Americans are wary and cautious. If one seriously wants to get to the bottom of the American distaste for disunity in other polities, their historical experience with disunity at home is the place to start. George

Washington, in the dawn of his presidency, reminded his compatriots: 'It is of infinite moment that you should properly estimate the immense value of your national union ... indignantly frowning upon the first dawning of every attempt to alienate any portion of our country from the rest, or to enfeeble the sacred ties which now link together the various parts.'[10] In the following five decades, 'states rights' continually challenged the federal union and led to one of the bloodiest and longest wars that the United States has ever fought.

The Civil War was a war within and against the polity itself. Long after descendants have forgotten on which side of the war their ancestors fought (excluding many older citizens in Alabama and Mississippi who retain a clearer idea of these matters than their neighbours in Georgia and Texas, for example), they 'remember' the psychological wreckage, the personal ruin, the destruction of community and social structure. Scarred forever by this war, the citizens of the United States rarely think about it, but they feel it. It is a war never to be revisited. But it is a war that led to one serious consequence: states became willingly subordinate to the federal government in Washington. Decentralization could and did take place, but there was no significant 'states rights' movement or festering regional rebellion that challenged Washington's authority. Of course, every politician of stature from the McGovern left to the Reagan right, including George W. Bush in his early campaign, 'runs' against Washington. Politicians critize the president, the domestic and foreign policies. They promise to do more and to do it better. But this is old-fashioned populism, nothing more, just a plain and simple brush-off of federal authority at the level of the individual. It is good fun at the expense of Washington, tolerated and even expected of every aspiring presidential candidate worthy of election to the highest office. Whether that politician follows up on his or her promises is seldom checked, and the promise of political change would certainly not be valued if it meant cutting social programs such as security, health care, or retirement benefits.

Rejection of the political chaos that led to the Civil War is something deeper. This rejection is shared by every American regardless of race or ancestry. Not that anyone actually thinks about the breakup of the country by force or any other means. Rupture is just unthinkable. Part of the reason for spurning the thought of breakup is that the country fought a terrible war that caused tremendous bloodshed and destruction but in the end changed very little. Slavery would have been abolished anyway and perhaps more constructively. The final armistice took place a few feet from where the initial shots were fired.[11] The conflict altered little not already in the process of being changed. However, the Civil War did banish permanently any capacity for disunion. Indeed, out of rejection of the Civil War (as opposed to full acceptance of the Revolutionary War and the Second World War as glorious and necessary) came fervour for unity.

Bias in Favour of Size

Throughout U.S. history, size has yielded benefits. A principal reason the thirteen American colonies could revolt from Britain, whereas the Canadian colonies could and did not, was that the southern U.S. market was large enough to sustain indigenous manufactures that were capable of competing effectively in the world market.[12] The Canadian market was, for a much longer time, not large enough to compete and remained locked into the British system of mercantile trade. The thirteen colonies also had enough freeholder soldiers to throw off the British occupation forces.

Size gave meaning to Washington's admonition in his Farewell Address to the Union. He advised the U.S. to stay out of Europe's entangling quarrels. The United States was militarily large enough to defeat any foreign attempt to dominate it, with the added insulation of two oceans on either side, and therefore until the twentieth century made the need for foreign alliance irrelevant. Size also made possible the 1823 Monroe Doctrine with its heavy strategic responsibility as well as aspirations. Manifest Destiny was likewise a size-driven doctrine, although here Canada was as much a proponent as the United States, since each polity sought to 'fill the Continent' or at least that respective territorial space available to it between the seas. Economies of scale blended with economies of scope, resulting in the first multinational corporations that led the growth of the United States in the twentieth century. These corporations were the institutional equivalent of the huge cargo airplanes and ships that transformed the prior equivalent of a national market into a global market.

Conversely, absence of size has never held much appeal to U.S. citizens. 'Small' has never been regarded as 'beautiful.' Pastoral images of rural life abound as much in the United States as elsewhere in the advanced industrial world. But unlike in Switzerland or Japan, which display the same nostalgia mixed with political self-interest in the rural vote, in the United States the farm keeps expanding. Productivity pushes sentiment out the door. The bigger the shopping mall, the more North Americans approve, as the Canadian builders of the world's largest malls fully understand. Size is efficiency, and efficiency is lower price, higher quality, greater availability, and wider choice. For the U.S. citizen, often the target of ridicule by allegedly more perspicacious consumers in Europe and Japan or their self-appointed representatives in the media, size does equate with value.

Given this barrage of size-biased beliefs, Canadian wholeness could only be taken for granted by U.S. citizens as a 'good' even if unity is questioned in Quebec or elsewhere in Canada.[13] Most Americans are not concerned with whether Canadian unity is a value shared or challenged in Canada. But these same Americans know what they believe about size and why it holds such a towering place in their library of preference.

Distaste for and Fear of Chaos in Explaining Societal Ethnicity

A final reason for the values that explain why U.S. citizens automatically seem to prefer Canadian political unity to separation is the innate fear that chaos would emerge should their own society break down in its ethnicity. An external observer might quickly attribute this fear to guilt, guilt over America's past as a slave-owning society.[14] This fear then would be a projected fear based on a historic sense of wrongful action that is displaced to present-day society. But for a number of reasons, that judgment, no matter how plausible on its seeming merits, can scarcely be supported by its contemporary manifestation.

If it were a sense of guilt about historical slave ownership that troubles contemporary America, then one might expect the greatest remorse in those geographic regions that were most directly responsible for that ownership, and in those social strata and those industrial divisions such as modern plantation agriculture that were most directly involved with slavery. Of course, there is nothing of the kind. Moreover, we might expect the segments of society that are the least responsible for slavery, such as descendants of the past victims, to show the least concern about the possibility of future societal chaos over ethnic division. Again, this interpretation is not validated by the evidence.[15] African Americans are as concerned as other Americans about the possibility of some type of future societal division or tumult. In fact, apprehension over this social problem, however hypothetical, is shared by all segments of the society. Purported guilt about the past is not the reason the U.S. prefers Canadian unity.

Instead, a society that is multiethnic and multilinguistic always contains the thread of discord within the opinion of each member.[16] If this awareness is used positively, it is a source of unity and confidence. All will take the steps necessary to control themselves.[17] Therefore the society remains peaceful and integrated. But there is always some background anxiety that this integration will not go far enough, that some members will feel short-changed, or that crime and drugs will drag down the sense of common social purpose and will erode cohesion.

Where languages differ and where races differ, there is inevitably a degree of social suspicion that must always be overcome by the educational system and wise government. The United States is cognizant that black–white relations are less than perfect. It is aware that English–Spanish language issues arise in some parts of the country even though the Hispanic population is not unitary. An ethos of the 'melting pot' shapes thinking and being in America. But sometimes the contents of the pot do not melt or take a long time to do so.[18] In a society with a very high immigration rate, the melting process is continually started anew. Poverty, always a problem even in rich societies, worsens the differences between linguistic groupings and between ethnic groupings of uneven average income. Regardless of race or ethnic background, U.S. citizens are familiar with the tensions, the successes, and the failures on an individual as well as on a collective societal basis.

Given all of this political and social consciousness, the fear that fragmentation of Canada would set a precedent for other countries is not unreasoned, despite the continuing strength of unity in a country like the United States.[19] Americans, of whatever cultural or linguistic orientation, cannot be blamed if their own social ethos warns them that a breakup of Canada could mean extenuating dangers for other advanced-industrial countries, however different in cultural make-up they may appear to be.

The Economic Claim to Wholeness

FTA, NAFTA, and Beyond

North America does not quite know in which direction to move. The impulse towards North American regionalism began with the U.S.–Canada Free Trade Agreement (FTA). This historic departure for Canada resulted from two important developments.

First, Canada and the United States were part of a single North American market that was inextricably linked. Notwithstanding the initiatives of the Trudeau government to try to establish a 'Third Option' in economic terms, fostered by a 'contractual link' with Europe for example, the trade figures with the United States just kept climbing.[20] No one in policy circles in Canada was willing to take the steps necessary to force diversification of trade and investment. This would have meant severe government intervention in the economy. In the absence of this direct action, the Canadian economy grew on the back of export trade to the United States.

Canada alone among the advanced industrial countries had immediate access to the U.S. market, and that access created a boom for Canada. In the 1990s, for instance, Canada continued to improve its trade surplus with the United States.[21] In the doldrums during the 1990–6 period, Japan had a lower growth rate than Canada, as did most of the other countries belonging to the Organization for Economic Cooperation and Development (OECD). Very few firms in Canada were willing to substitute such high economic growth with its contingent 'liability' – closer trade and investment ties to the United States – for the possibility of a much lower growth rate and diversification of commercial ties outside North America. Very few individuals so prized the notion of 'economic autonomy' that they were willing to sacrifice industrialization, with its attendant increases in jobs and income, for an attractive but much more ephemeral goal of alleged increase in foreign policy 'autonomy.' Thus Canada recognized that its economic future lay in North America.

Second, with the advent of the highly visible and financially important softwood lumber dispute, Canada recognized that its trading relationship with the United States had changed.[22] No longer was the old State Department adage correct that if the United States targeted Canada with a so-called trade remedy, it would 'shoot itself in the foot,' the argument being that it would legitimize such unilateral trade actions by other countries against itself as well. Now the United States seemed ready to shoot itself in the foot on a regular basis. Consequently, Canada's Liberal Party and the ruling Conservative Party decided that a new set of trade policies with the United States had to be initiated. The era of 'free trade,' or freer trade, with United States had begun.

Underlying freer trade was a primary and well-understood objective: Canada needed 'guaranteed access' to the U.S. market. But guaranteed access was not an easy goal. As the much smaller trading partner, Canada had to count its bargaining chips carefully. Formation of a free trade area with the United States, a previously unthinkable 'Continentalist' action, was big enough and bold enough to get Washington's attention. But only in the last hour of bargaining did free trade carry with it the promise of access, partially guaranteed through an elaborate and pioneering mechanism for the resolution of trade disputes. Although seldom discussed in this way in political circles, quick, inexpensive, and effective trade dispute resolution was not a 'win' for either country alone, but was rather a way of taking trade disputes, often linked to narrow industrial/labour interests at the expense of the consumer, out of the misplaced forum of the national political process.

Thus Canada opted for regional free trade because its commercial interdependence with the U.S. was too close and the only way it could safeguard its trade interests was to move still closer to the U.S. Through formalizing a regional trade area, Canada could better control its economic relationship with the United States.

In contrast, the North American Free Trade Agreement (NAFTA) was not a Canadian invention. It was not even a U.S. invention. It was basically the invention of President Salinas, the Mexican head of state, who already had the outlines of FTA expansion in mind when he came into office. NAFTA was an unlikely creation, unlikely and bold because for the first time in the history of regional integration it brought together less-developed and developed countries.

Canada was not an early proponent of NAFTA. Many in the Canadian policy elite wanted Canada to keep special access to the U.S. market to itself. Japan, after all, had informally inquired whether the same terms offered to Canada would be offered to it, and had quietly been told by Washington that the United States had 'too much on its plate' at present to think of extending the agreement so soon. Very quickly, however, Canada saw the merits of inclusion in NAFTA.

To be left out of NAFTA was technically possible even after three-way negotiations began, since the terms agreed upon between the United States and Mexico were that any two partners could continue with the negotiations, in the absence of the third, if that third party chose not to proceed. Canada acknowledged that to be left out of NAFTA was to open Canadian economic relations to the existence of a 'hub and spokes' model, with the United States at the hub and each of the smaller trading partners at the other end of separate spokes.[23] This model would place Canada or Mexico in the unenviable position of having to trade through the United States to reach the economy of the other party. While Mexico did not seem to worry much about this model, Canada did. Perhaps the much greater trade dependence of Canada made it feel all such difficulties more readily. In any case, Canada quickly became a stalwart backer of NAFTA, and NAFTA itself systematically moved through the last stages of negotiations.

Passage in Canada was assured, but not because of the conservative government's parliamentary majority or the Canadian tradition of strong party discipline in terms of parliamentary voting. Rather, what assured passage was the primary desire not to be left out and the broad national recognition that, given the small absolute amount of trade between Canada and Mexico, most of the economic adjustment would be felt by the other two trading partners, especially Mexico.[24] Given its form of government and its early enthusiasm for NAFTA, Mexico was not likely to have much political difficulty with passage. Most of the uncertainty rested in Washington, and here a very strong though belated push by President Clinton, in the face of majority opposition by his own party, led to a victory for the tripartite regional trade and investment arrangement. NAFTA became the defining focus for a trade arrangement that was truly regional.

Economic Integration and Political Fragmentation

Can economic integration proceed in the midst of political fragmentation? That is a question too seldom considered in academic, press, and policy realms. The problem is essentially this: When political boundaries are established, there is a tendency to raise economic barriers as well. In previous eras, an old adage had it that 'trade follows the flag,' meaning that when the colonial powers like Britain explored new territories, and established political outposts there, trade relations usually followed. In the modern context, when new polities are created, by whatever means – devolution or evolution, peaceful cooperation or force – there is a tendency that economic barriers will be created as well.

One explanation lies in the effort of special interest groups which claim that they need protection to survive in a now more competitive, more vulnerable local marketplace.[25] Facing a smaller market and greater border risk and because a smaller and weaker government will have less power in trade and investment negotiations to defend them, these firms and affected labour unions are likely to demand special subsidies and other forms of protection to help them survive.

When a new polity is formed, however, economic protectionism need not arise. This is especially true when the new polity is the member of a larger regional economic grouping in the way that an independent Quebec, for example, would be inside NAFTA. The norms of the regional trade arrangement would militate against the establishment of new trade or investment barriers by the recently created independent state. Indeed, were that new polity to raise obvious and contravened economic barriers, the regional trade arrangement would react. In the case of NAFTA, an independent Quebec that tried to raise trade or investment barriers would be subject to the dispute resolution mechanism at the very least. This set of norms does not appear to create much of an opportunity for a newly created political entity that is a member of a trade grouping like NAFTA to launch new economic barriers of its own.

On the other hand, one of the attributes of overall sovereignty is economic sovereignty. Rejection in December 1998 of the *Multilateral Investment Act* by the Organization of Economic Cooperation and Development, with strong French and Canadian approval, is a measure of this reality. Firms that are suddenly subject to a new set of competitive forces are likely to urge 'their' government to help them. An independent Quebec would be no different than other countries and might plead the argument that as a newly created state it ought to be eligible for a 'development bonus,' namely, the opportunity to use some forms of protectionism for an extended period so as to adjust to the necessarily greater competition that its industries would face. Given that the industrial structure of Quebec, fostered by much government-led support, is quite different from that in the United States, the major competitor for an independent Quebec's industries, the newly separate country would face major economic adjustments towards openness. How all of this adjustment would occur, and when, is not entirely clear.

While an independent Quebec would certainly not enjoy automatic admission to NAFTA, the presumption is that after making a commitment to the necessary adjustments, an independent Quebec would accede to NAFTA. From the U.S. perspective, this inclusion of Quebec in NAFTA is strongly desirable.[26] No hole or rent in the North American fabric of economic integration is attractive; rather, all of North America ought to be woven on the same skein. This is the tenor of

NAFTA and this is the North American orientation towards Quebec, whether inside or outside Canada.

Yet Quebec should be under no illusions. The temptation to raise economic barriers to match political barriers will not wash with the other NAFTA partners. Adjustments, even if phased in and graduated, will not be easy for a small, vulnerable polity to accept. Individual interests will put great pressure on Quebec City for continued protection and increased support, albeit a more subtle or non-tariff-oriented support.

Political fragmentation of North America does not guarantee a loss of economic integration. Much depends upon how routinized and how vital NAFTA is. But at the same time, political fragmentation may not readily accommodate the rules of economic integration. From the U.S. perspective, the proof of what will actually happen will come not in prior promises but in very careful subsequent observance of both the letter and the spirit of the NAFTA codes and of the problems of integration.

First Deepen, then Widen

In the jargon of the European Union, 'widening' means the addition of new members, 'deepening' means further harmonization of policies among the existing members of a trade arrangement.[27] These concepts can be as easily applied to NAFTA. Whether one widens or deepens or both, and when, will make a great deal of difference to the kind of trade area that eventually emerges. This decision also reflects the kind of preferences the members hold concerning their own future association. The U.S. claim of an economic wholeness for North America is thus, to some extent, a product of the trade-off between widening and deepening.

Although the debate over U.S. entry into NAFTA or the Canadian entry into the original U.S.–Canada FTA may not reflect this facility, addition of new members to a trade group is a relatively easy exercise. This is particularly true as the trade area grows larger. Increasingly, most of the adjustment falls on the marginal entrant. Original members obtain the benefits of economies of scale and of enhanced negotiating prowess without having to yield very much. Because the original members set the tone of the arrangement in terms of the kind of industrial structure that will have primacy, there is also a reward to initial entry. Subsequent entrants must adapt to the framework that was originally negotiated.

Moreover, the opportunity costs to belated entry continue to increase as time wears on. Both trade diversion and investment diversion add sharply to the costs of staying outside the trade area for proximate countries within the region, especially relative to goods that have large shipping costs or tastes that are similar to those for products already produced and consumed within the trade area.[28] The upshot is that there is a premium on joining a trade area early and a large penalty for attempting to remain outside a regional group, as Switzerland has done vis-à-vis the European Union.

But in any case, widening as a process diminishes both economic and political difficulty for the original members of a trade arrangement. Widening creates a feeling of momentum, looks good at election time, and creates comparatively few negotiating trouble spots for the members of a trade group as the size of the group increases.

Conversely, deepening is a much more demanding process, at least for the initial members of the trade group relative to the burdens placed on it by widening. Deepening requires further mutual concessions among the original members – concessions that may be unpopular at home and may transform not only the respective industrial bases of the countries but also their administrative policies, institutions, and laws. In addition, deepening often involves aligning tax policies; attempting to create a single monetary union; eliminating differences in terms of product standards; smoothing or eliminating customs rules and requirements; adopting similar environmental and energy procedures; making health and technical standards conform; and opening up borders to the movement of labour as well as capital.[29] Much of this is equivalent to moving from a formal trade area to a common market, in which all of the factors of production are allowed to move freely and where there is a single external tariff to eliminate the administrative cost and confusion of dealing with rules of origin problems and multiple domestic content requirements. But none of this change comes easily to a society or government long accustomed to doing most of these things in its own parochial way. Fear of dominance by a powerful central actor also cools the ardour for such change by the smaller members. Fear of being overwhelmed by the flow of goods, services, capital, or people likewise reduces their enthusiasm. Not surprisingly, politicians would rather widen than deepen. Even when deepening will produce much greater benefits to an individual member and to the economic grouping as a unit than will widening, the political response will often be to widen because it is politically less painful.

A further reality emerges over time concerning the dynamics of regionalism. As a regional group becomes larger, greater diversity occurs within the group. Diversity causes conflict, that is, political disagreement over goals and over strategies to reach those goals. Thus a paradox emerges, the paradox of *declining opportunity for integration*. As a particular regional group becomes larger, and therefore structurally and behaviourally more diverse, it finds it much more difficult to make compromises and lacks the will to make the tough choices associated with genuine integration. Conversely, if the group had remained smaller and had thus enjoyed the advantages of less diversity and greater homogeneity while deepening, it would have made much faster and surer progress towards effective economic integration. Part of the problem is trying to decide what the architects of integration really want. Do they want a large, shallow form of increased economic cohesion, and will they be satisfied with that kind of arrangement in the future? Or do they want a deeper, tighter form of economic integration with all of the benefits such an arrangement can bestow?[30]

A full implication of the paradox of declining opportunity for integration is that sequencing of efforts to widen and to deepen is very important. Effective integration is much more achievable when the group deepens first and widens later. Gaining agreement for the tough choices involved with deepening is much easier among a few members than among many. Once a high degree of integration has been achieved, *then* new members can be added. The bargaining will be much easier because the terms of adhesion will already be in place and new members will know what to expect. Phased adjustment is always possible. Incentives for membership will remain as strong as ever. But the ultimate level of integration will be on a much higher plane than if widening had preceded deepening or if they had been pursued simultaneously.

Of course, if widening is foregone but nothing happens in the interim, then the paradox of declining opportunity for integration does not apply. The reason it does not apply is lethargy on the part of governments not capable or willing to either deepen or widen. Ironically, from the political perspective, this latter possibility of paralytic inaction is all too likely.

In sum, North America faces a decision. It can either proceed rapidly towards deep and meaningful economic integration, or it can proceed with systematic widening by the addition of new members. Chile ought to have followed the original three members of NAFTA. Chile's industrial structure is sufficiently similar to that of the original members, and its small economic size and congenial outlook towards integration would not slow down commitment to serious deepening. But the difficulty in getting 'fast-track' authority in the U.S. Congress to permit accession of Chile – largely because of the failure to get the business community fully behind what was falsely regarded as a 'minor' matter – indicates how difficult it is to coordinate trade liberalization.

The real decision is this: Does North America see itself as a distinctive region upon which to build economically, defined by common interests and problems, or does it see itself as essentially part of the Western Hemisphere?[31] If the latter is the case, the level of eventual economic integration is likely to be much lower. With the latter option, Canada, the United States, and Mexico will be buying into a large trade area, not much more. The progress towards such a goal will be much less arduous than with the effort to create a tighter North American common market. Also, the economic benefits in the long run are likely to be much less significant for the original three countries.

Regardless of the long-term strategy, whose elements ought to be examined with considerable attention, the movement towards devolutionary fragmentation in North America looks to Americans to be out of sync with the evolutionary objectives of these broader integrative strategies of deepening and widening. From the U.S. perspective, Quebec separation is fragmenting the trend towards increased integration and greater cohesion.

Of course, Quebec separatists, starting with Jacques Parizeau, have always made it plain that they favour further economic integration and insist that they must be included in any such effort. They ought to be taken seriously in their assertions of commitment. But perhaps neither they nor the present members of NAFTA fully realize what challenges lie ahead in attempting to mesh political separation with economic integration. The idea of sovereignty is caught in the middle.

Sovereignty is divisible. But in the end, if the commitment of the *indépendantistes* is as strong as they allege in favour of economic association with the rest of North America, and is not just a bargaining ploy to get Quebecers to join the bandwagon in favour of separation, a tension will emerge within the notion of sovereignty itself. Those who strongly believe in economic integration will try to drag sovereignty in their direction. Those who believe essentially and rather exclusively in political autonomy will attempt to drag sovereignty in that direction.

How sovereignty will look ultimately for Quebec, and for the present members of NAFTA, is not yet clear. But sovereignty as a general concept cannot amount to two things at the same time. It cannot both increase and decrease with integration. Decisive shifts towards economic integration will mean an overall decline in sovereignty for all states in North America.[32] Even for a Quebec that perhaps has just separated itself politically from the rest of Canada to enhance its sovereignty, economic integration with the rest of North America will entail an actual reduction in sovereignty.

Defence of the North American Continent: The Security Claim

In the post–Cold War world, defence looks to North Americans like a tired subject. Defence against whom is the often-asked question. Defence appears to some to be a free good. But as the basis of prudent policy, that all-too-easy response faces three difficulties.

First, Canada and the United States have many interests that could be affected by aggression abroad, beginning perhaps with instability on the European periphery or in the Asian heartland. A continuity of the energy supply from the Persian Gulf is always problematic.[33] Canada and the United States cannot wait for someone else to safeguard their own interests. Since 1945, these two countries have been in the forefront of maintaining order, not because they wanted to but because their interests and their stature dictated such a role in foreign policy.

For the first time in the history of the modern state system, financial, trade, and commercial relations are global. The capacity to initiate aggression is also global, so that security is imperiled not only by an immediate neighbour, but also by a country half way around the world that may be a territorial enemy.[34] The old European adage that 'my neighbour's neighbour is my friend,' implying that my immediate neighbour is an enemy, is wrong in two respects both in Europe and North America. Not only can one's neighbour be a friend and ally, as is concurrently true on these two continents, but very distant countries can do mortal damage to one's national interests, such as to the continuity of energy supply and, via nuclear weapons and missilery, terrible destruction to a population and military installations.

Second, North Americans would lose their security edge by neglecting the military preparedness reflected in technological sophistication.[35] If North Americans fail to remain competitive in the operation of space-age systems, for example, other countries will erode the advantage that currently makes diplomacy relatively easy. As the late and distinguished Canadian diplomat John Halstead warned, all diplomacy must be backed by the capacity to use force in order that force will not have to be used. In the twenty-first century, 'force' is not so much the number of troops or ships at a country's disposal, it is the more sophisticated capacity to monitor, command, and control weaponry. Space-age technology is not limited to anti-ballistic missile systems or the deployment of highly developed space stations; space-age technology can involve something as simple as personal reconnaissance pagers that operate out of satellites to let the individual soldier know his or her exact location on the battlefield anywhere at any time.

Third, there will eventually be challengers to the power positions of the North American actors. How the North Americans react will be crucial and may not be the simple dyadic pattern that many theories of international relations predict. Rather, North America will likely join with the European Union and Japan to protect their interests within a central system that contains the North American polities, the European Union, Russia, Japan, and China. The United States is likely to remain 'first among equals' for a very long time, giving more precise meaning to multipolarity. Rules of diplomacy, the principles of maintaining order, and the limits to foreign policy implementation will change and security will become increasingly pressing once again.[36]

North America is experiencing an *interim of reprieve* before these major shifts occur. This reprieve will look like a page of history, much like the interval at mid-eighteenth century before the Napoleonic Wars, or like the peaceful interval from 1815 to the revolutions of 1848 shepherded by Metternich. How Canada and the United States use this interval will determine how well defended and prosperous they are in the subsequent and more difficult period of global statecraft.

What Fragmentation Endangers, and What It Does Not

At the simplest level of analysis, fragmentation of Canada would not endanger continental defence if both (or all) of the resulting units continued membership in NATO. That is a 'boiler-plate' response to the question of security effects, and in the aftermath of the Cold War, such a response is often considered to be sufficient. Since Quebec separatists have formally committed themselves to staying in NATO should they prevail, and since English-speaking Canada presumably would remain a NATO member, most analysis stops here.

No strategic missile emplacements lie on Canadian soil. No anti-ballistic missile facilities are envisioned for Canada, although technology is a determining factor in what will become necessary and what will not.[37] Nor does Canada possess crucial port facilities or training areas that could not be replaced. Hence, in a strict inventory sense of what fragmentation might do to operational or planned strategic defences of North America, the response is not particularly negative.

Canadian participation in NORAD has been very close and very effective. It is difficult to identify two military command structures working closer together in operational terms where such a high level of trust and competence is essential. Fragmentation would endanger this cooperation. There is a limit to how many parallel decision structures and fail-safe mechanisms one can put into place in the advanced nuclear age. In practice, fragmentation of Canada would accelerate a trend that technology itself perhaps is driving towards greater centralization of decision making in strategic matters.[38] History has witnessed a reversal of the trend in the requests for greater Canadian participation. The trend, largely for technical reasons as the manned bomber is phased out, has gone from the United States demanding Canadian inclusion to Canada demanding its own inclusion. Fragmentation of Canada would surely speed this transfer of roles and functions.

Air space and undersea space remain important matters of shared concern. Not only has the end of the Cold War made these matters less pressing, however, since patrols are less common or cancelled altogether. Monitoring networks are less significant, at least in the traditional land-based mode. Yet physical access to the air space and undersea space involving both territories continues to be of theoretical value. Fragmentation of these spaces would not be helpful if the issue of access were in any way compromised. But since compromise involves the capacity to enforce limitations on access, the concern may once again be minimized by analysts.

In short, in the absence of any profound alliance revisions, fragmentation of the North American air and sea space is not likely to hamstring strategic defences. In fact, such fragmentation is likely to speed up trends, which are already occurring for technical reasons, away from the close coordination between militaries that had taken place in the past. This is not attractive from the Canadian perspective. Continued cutbacks in defence spending and some uncertainty as to overall mission are further eroding the Canadian capacity to participate fully. A breakup of Canada would just about finish the strategic partnership that has characterized U.S.–Canada relations for more than half a century. These functions would all migrate to a single centre of decision making.

Canadian Participation in NATO

Canada's effective as opposed to titular participation in NATO is under siege. This is understood very well by the Department of National Defence, less well so in other areas of the Canadian government. After years of financial cutbacks, deferred maintenance, downsizing of the forces, and postponed equipment expenditures, Canada's military is in a sorry condition.[39] Scandals and bad luck have not helped. All of these setbacks caught up with Canada in its European deployments. If a political decision to withdraw from Europe had not been made, the inability to service and supply its small military contingent there would have done the job as thoroughly.

Long summarized as 'keeping a seat at the table,' Canada's role is quickly dwindling. A proud organizer of NATO and a defender of Europe's liberties in the First World War and at different level of involvement in the Second World War, Canada is slowly sinking to the bottom of the NATO hierarchy. From one perspective, this decision is conscious. After half a century, why should Canada subsidize Europe to do what it is rich enough to do for itself, that is defend itself, especially in the aftermath of the Cold War when the Red Army is no longer on hair-trigger and in easy striking distance of Berlin? On the other hand, whatever the mission of NATO, Canada must in its own interest be ready and able to take part. It can no longer provide significant assistance in Europe without depending to an extraordinary degree on other allies for logistics and transport capacity. Training and equipment cannot be far behind on this declining growth curve.

Canada in its own interest must decide whether it really wishes to drop out of the inner-decision circle. As new members of NATO are added through enlargement, an inner circle and an outer circle within NATO will develop. Having a seat at the outer table in terms of influence and even access to information is virtually like having no seat at all. Canada may prevail on the United States to bolster its case with the principal European allies, but what the United States needs is not a dependent North American ally but one that can on occasion take a lead on its own within the NATO ranks. This is what Canadian political figures say they want. An example of this was Canadian Ambassador to the United States Raymond Chrétien's November 1996 peacekeeping initiative to Rwanda and Central Africa. It is this stature that Canada, by its declining expenditure and other decisions, seems to be relinquishing. Brilliance of diplomacy is not enough. If all the military substance to back up that diplomacy seeps away, so goes an effective seat at the table as well.

Peacekeeping and Peacemaking

Canada virtually invented the notion of peacekeeping.[40] Mike Pearson came to the rescue of the international system during the 1956 Suez Crisis with a timely formulation of peacekeeping as a precondition of the withdrawal of British, French, and Israeli military forces from parts of the Sinai. Since that time, Canada has participated in virtually every major peacekeeping expedition fielded by the UN. In total numbers, this is a substantial amount of personnel and equipment deployed to trouble-spots worldwide. Canada rightly can take great pride in these international accomplishments.

Peacekeeping, however, is not becoming simpler or smaller in size. Peacekeeping is often mixed with the notion of peacemaking, such as in Bosnia. Contrasts between the deployment of a few thousand Canadian peacekeepers under U.N. leadership in Bosnia, and more than sixty thousand personnel under NATO, reveals the advantages of a larger force when active hostilities are still ongoing but the effort to squelch belligerency is thought to be necessary and feasible. Peacemaking is riskier and costlier, especially where smaller deployments are used to stop a hot war from spreading prior to the effort to keep belligerents apart. Canada will face two problems in its peacekeeping roles should it experience a fragmentation of the country.

First, would a fragmented Canada possess the military base from which to train, equip, and deploy peacekeeping as well as regular armed force units? The answer almost certainly is that a splintered Canada would not. Such a Canada would have to choose between a regular military role and a peacekeeping role. Although the multiple parts of Canada might want to cooperate in the field, it is doubtful that these parts would be willing to specialize in a fashion that would both safeguard the Canadian regular army, air force, and navy traditions and continue to perform a peacekeeping function as well. One or the other standard military function would disappear and peacekeeping would probably replace the regular military units as the Quebec and English Canada military contribution abroad.

Second, given the changing nature of peacekeeping, the increased number of demands for peacekeepers and peacemakers, and the greater attention devoted to this mode of order-maintenance by the

United States, Britain, and France, a fragmented Canada might find that the contribution of its parts was less than the contribution of the whole.[41] As peacekeeping becomes more dependent on sophisticated command and control and on logistics capability as well as on large numbers of trained personnel, a fragmented Canada would become more a follower and less a leader. It simply could not coordinate and manage as large an operation as the country now does. The contribution to UN peacekeeping by the respective subunits of a fragmented Canada hence would often come in the form of material and money rather than as organized units with an adequate number of personnel.

The fragmentation of Canada would tend to gut the one major military function for which Canada has become recognized on the world stage. Not only would this be a pity in terms of the loss of Canadian status and self-image, it would also be an even greater loss to the world of diplomacy and order-maintenance. The United States, in its effort to promote order-maintenance, would be among the first of the members of the central system to feel this loss of support and experienced counsel. Regardless of good feeling among its prior regional components, a decentralized and fragmented Canada could not meet the peacekeeping and peacemaking requirements of the twenty-first century.

Why Canada Is Important: City on the Hill, Interdependence, and Cohesion

Given the U.S. attitude towards democratic pluralism, size, economic integration, and international security, how does the possible separation of Quebec affect the image Americans hold of themselves in North America? In particular, is that image compatible with a fragmentation of sovereignty in North America? State fragmentation certainly jars the image of emergent harmony of interests and purpose implied in the 'city on the hill' metaphor. Careful reflection suggests that the metaphor, and the reality of fragmentation, may strongly be at odds in an even deeper sense.[42]

As top Parti Québécois leaders in the past have reminded their listeners, in the struggle for independence after a referendum, if the United States did not act immediately to recognize Quebec sovereignty, Quebec would reach out to other governments to do so, thus putting pressure on the United States. The United States is not without the political means to contend with such a situation. But this proposed separatist strategy is a classic balance of power strategy, drawing in a third powerful actor to challenge another government for the purpose of altering that government's policies. An analogy in the business world is to employ the so-called loose brick strategy of inviting another firm to penetrate a given market.[43] In world politics, things always look different from the perspective of another state.

From the perspective of the United States, this proposed use of the balance of power to alter its game plan is exactly what the United States would find unsatisfactory from a Quebec that was independent. How far could it trust such a government? Instead of threatening the balance of power tactics based on a hypothetical future contingency, perhaps Quebec would do better to reassure the United States of the commonality of viewpoints under all future circumstances. In the absence of such assurances, the United States is likely to lose further confidence in separatist intentions. Indeed, an effort to maintain the balance of power would merely drive the United States into a frame of mind that more strongly supported whatever position an English Canadian remnant was likely to hold. From the U.S. perspective, harmony is desirable whatever the outcome of another referendum on separation, should that referendum ever be called. But attempted balance of power politics would surely poison the atmosphere for such harmony.

If Americans require a lesson 'closer to home' in this problem of assailability during secession, they need only look at the practices of Great Britain during the U.S. Civil War. Britain, despite official opposition to slavery, contemplated siding with the South and would have done so if the war had tilted in the South's direction. Britain sought to bolster the South through additional trade in manufactured goods (which, but for the credit required from a comparatively poor credit risk during war, was just good business) and in war material. But more than this, Britain attempted to weaken the United States as an emerging rival, which secession would cut down to size.

Thus secession elicited from an apparently otherwise friendly state policies calculated to undermine and weaken federation or the return to federation. At a time when Washington was unable to respond, British behaviour was not helpful, although it was not unique. Britain was not more perfidious than other actors capable of exploiting political insecurity. Moreover, the Civil War is only one of many diplomatic examples of similar propensity to erode the foundations of a powerful rival when and where it is weakest. European powers did this to China in the late nineteenth century. China did the same to Taiwan during the 1997 Taiwanese presidential elections. Political temptations to exploit such a strategy are endemic to statecraft.

Second, the city on the hill metaphor contains within it a concept of invulnerability from external challenge or attack. In an interval of history where U.S. security looks so uncontested, the very idea of territorial security is difficult for some to comprehend. Questions are raised as to why expenditures on military defence are even made. The world seems so benign that some regard Harvard political scientist Joseph Nye's idea of soft power as free-standing or self-sufficient rather than, as Nye intended, a complement to hard power, the essential ingredient to the maintenance of world order. Soft power alone cannot stand, and hard power alone is insufficient. As an addendum to hard power, soft power provides additional influence and global reach. Together hard power and soft power will provide international security for North America in the future.

But regardless of how well the United States and Canada use their hard and soft power, a fragmentation of the jurisdictions, whose sharing has been so carefully nurtured since the end of the Second World War, is worrisome. Nothing exemplifies the harmony of the city on the hill in military terms like the cooperation between the United States and Canada in NORAD. Quebec secession would surely undercut this cooperation, not because Quebecers would be less talented than their partners but because the Canadian remnants would now be too anaemic to fulfill the responsibilities of NORAD partnership.

Likewise, Canadian fragmentation would destroy the armed forces since the economies of scale necessary to mount an appreciable military effort would dissolve with secession. Not because of friction between a Canadian anglophone military outfit and a Quebec francophone unit, but because of size difficulties that leave each polity beneath a feasible start-up threshold, the respective remnants would lose all military effectiveness. More than any other ally, the United States would lament this loss of military coordination, including contributions to peacekeeping.[44]

Moreover, the problems posed for the North American city on the hill by airspace jurisdiction and undersea jurisdiction would multiply. As the claimants to the seabed and to the above-territory airspace and asynchronous orbit expand in number, there is no guarantee that all will see the occupation and even the defence of these areas in the same way, or in the way that present day Canada, Mexico, and the United

States see these jurisdictional matters. While the United States would remain as economically and politically dominant as ever, the propensity for a dissatisfied smaller participant might be to draw in outside allies or bidders to enhance its weight at the bargaining table. Such balance of power tactics probably would fail. But the task of administration for the United States at a minimum would increase. More seriously, it might begin to experience rivalry for jurisdiction within the very boundaries of the city on the hill.

Third, from the U.S. perspective, the city on the hill is a base for internationalism.[45] More than a beacon for others to see and perhaps to emulate, the city on the hill is a place from which to reach out to the international system, not to build an empire nor to threaten the interests of others, but to interact with them, to trade, to construct commercial linkages, to evolve international regimes that actually protect the rain forests, for instance, or limit the spread of weapons of mass destruction. The city on the hill is not isolationist or inward-looking. It is interdependent with many other such cities that occupy other hills across the globe.

The essential concept that underlies this flourishing of external contact and openness associated with the North American city on the hill is impregnability. It is safe from internal disharmony, secure from external domination or incipient erosion. That the North American city on the hill is unassailable is the key to its prudence and caution in diplomacy, since it never is obliged to act in haste or anger. Likewise, the city on the hill is able to form coalitions with other partners and to extend an umbrella of world order because it is so invincible in purpose and material being at home relative to other potential challengers abroad. But without the local invincibility and ease of administration and governance, the global reach of North America would surely be foreshortened.

Perhaps a real-world analogy will catch the relevance of this observation about comparative invincibility at the local level. Today, North America is a city on a hill; in many ways the comparable union of European states is not.[46] Where lies the difference? In population size, wealth, cultural richness, economic size, and potential for military defence, North America and Europe are proportionate. Yet Europe continues to be an importer of security; North America is an exporter. Europe struggles to achieve a single voice on internal economic policy; North America, despite the disputes in 5 per cent of its bilateral trade, is already more integrated. Europe strives to generate a sense of soft power; North America radiates soft power to every corner of the world system. North America exercises leadership regarding such matters as NATO expansion and a resolution of the Bosnian conflict on the European doorstep. Europe itself is not yet sufficiently unified politically to decide much of anything in terms of a common foreign or defence policy. The only thing prominently different about the two regions is that, relative to North America, Europe lacks cohesion and a common strategic vision.

Whether Europe will ever achieve what North America already possesses is open to speculation.[47] But what North America dares not chance is slippage towards the condition from which Europe is trying to escape. In other words, why would North America place the unity, harmony, and self-confidence it currently enjoys in a lottery in which any of these precious attributes were more at risk?

This tends to be the United States perspective regarding the North American ethos and its own attitude towards political fragmentation. When one considers the unique aspects of Mexico's own developmental experience, it is not so surprising that Mexico seems to share this attitude. The metaphor of the city on the hill can serve Canada, the United States, and Mexico well as they contemplate the role North American countries must play in the twenty-first century.

Underlying the U.S. perspective towards Canadian unity treated in this chapter is the background preoccupation with the preservation of a set of norms, however much modified over the years, that have served each country well since their foundings in the seventeenth century. This set of norms with respect to the rules for public order were especially urgent for a young country like the United States, or like Canada, composed of many different regions and ethno-linguistic groupings. Almost by experience rather than by design, the norms of democratic pluralism emerged to shape the way each country sought to govern itself.

As the analysis reveals, each of the assumptions that reinforces the U.S. perspective towards Canada is totally compatible with the idea of democratic pluralism. The preference for size, economic wholeness, a cohesive security outlook, interdependence politically, economically, and in security terms with other like-minded polities worldwide drive the American preference for Canadian unity and stem from the notion of democratic pluralism. Indeed, if the analyst were to try to derive the policy statements of the U.S. government on the Canadian unity issue from an underlying political philosophy of governance, that philosophy would be summed up in the notion of democratic pluralism. Democratic pluralism epitomizes the North American worldview regarding itself and regarding the world outside.

Hence when Canada and the United States look at world politics, they inevitably do so through a lens that has been ground and polished through the struggles to sustain democratic pluralism. When they think of what they modestly might have to offer other fledgling democracies in terms of example, all of the elements of that example can be traced back to what they have attempted to achieve politically through a practical application of the norms of democratic pluralism. So omnipresent are these norms that almost no U.S. citizen, or Canadian, would need prompting to express the values encompassed in them. Nor do they think much about the norms; North Americans merely take them for granted. Thus when asked what the U.S. perspective on Canada involves, the answer is inseparable from the unspoken commitment to the preservation of democratic pluralism.

CHAPTER THREE

Will Quebec Secede?

Quebec is unique unto itself, but it is also uniquely North American. It is often said that English Canada needs Quebec to fulfill Canada's authenticity. A North American Quebec likewise needs an amiable English Canadian counterpart to bring out Quebec's richest tradition, to preserve it from unremitting inwardness, to attain its loftiest fulfillment as a people and as a nation.[1] Quebec and English Canada are, in many ways, dependent on one another. But the dependency could be broken. Quebec could separate. Quebecers for the most part will themselves decide, but they alone will not be affected. All of North America will feel the bite of divorce or the balm of reconciliation.

How Three Social-Psychological Processes Fan Quebec Nationalism

There are three complex social-psychological processes that underlie the question, Will Quebec secede? First is the counterpoint between the memory of historical subordination and manipulation and the fear that it might occur again or is somehow occurring now. There is still fear that every federal action is a conspiracy by the old, now much weakened, Montreal Anglo elite to take advantage of the Quebec francophone. Second is the anxiety over loss of collective identity, which, when combined with suspicion that the type of individualism found in the United States is to some lesser extent found in English Canada, tends to leave the modern Quebecer adrift between two powerful kinds of political and social identity. In a society that is changing so dramatically, the identity conflict is sharply real. It is little wonder that the solution for many young Quebecers is to cling to nationalism as though it were a raft in a turbulent political sea.

Third is the worry over the durability of Quebec culture, a culture of which Quebecers are justifiably proud. The survival of Quebec society and culture is one of the great stories of North American perseverance and courage. Yet, Quebec separatists claim that Quebec nationalism is so robust that independence is a self-fulfilling prophecy. Which is it? Is Quebec culture frail and vulnerable? Or is it so strong and vital that it will automatically spill over into statehood, dragging doubters and the less-than-committed along with it? Quebec culture cannot be both under siege and ready to assail the castle walls at the same time. The answer, of course, is that it is neither. It is durable but not passionately supportive of national autonomy. Caught between fears of cultural and linguistic vulnerability on the one hand and the hopes of statehood on the other, Quebec culture is being used for strategic purposes to motivate a political agenda.

These three social-psychological processes are interactive. The historical versus contemporary discrimination feeds the problem over identity crisis. The identity crisis keeps the trade-off between cultural vulnerability and cultural pride boiling and unresolved. Since Quebecers alternate between excessive pessimism to assert their language and culture and excessive nationalist pride, the need for confidence in their present political identity and in their capacity to disentangle themselves from the burden of history could not be more relevant or needed.

In short, each process acts as a catalyst for the others. When one is incomplete or without resolution, the others cannot find satisfactory answers. Quebec independence becomes the short cut that can provide solutions to all these problems at the same time. This is why the search for the single factor that will settle the Quebec quest for greater political autonomy is so frustrating. There is no single factor. This is why an analysis of Quebec nationalism is fascinating and worthy of examination. The explanations are complex, deep, and intertwined.

Nationalists All, Separatists Some

Not to be a nationalist in today's Quebec is either to be outdated or to be less than relevant. Notwithstanding Jean Chrétien's federalism, all political party leaders within Quebec identify as nationalists. Many francophone schoolchildren think of themselves as a Quebecer first, a Canadian second.[2] To be a Quebec nationalist is to be au courant and politically correct.

But every Quebec nationalist is not a separatist. At the beginning of the 1995 referendum campaign on separation, Lucien Bouchard took the sting out of the word 'separatist' by calling himself a separatist and saying he was proud of it. Before that, in Quebec one was an '*indépendantiste*' perhaps, or a 'sovereigntist' surely, but only covertly and hesitatingly a 'separatist.' In a single speech, Bouchard made the term respectable, for some even fashionable. Yet by no means are all Quebecers strict separatists. The margin that determines the swing vote towards or away from independence is influenced by many factors inside the province and over time.

Until only a few years ago, while a Quebecer may have been a confirmed separatist in his or her heart, when considering the economic costs and risks, that same Quebecer usually identified as a federalist. Upon hearing this distinction between rationalism and romanticism applied to Quebec, Lis Bissonette, distinguished novelist and former editor of *Le Devoir*, said that while this distinction may be valid, in the present-day Quebec heart and head are growing ever closer. She proved to be right.

Two Strategies

Late premier and great political tactician Robert Bourassa made a tongue-in-cheek distinction between the two strategies for dealing with Ottawa that were then playing themselves out. The first was separation, which he disdained. The second, which he called 'profitable federalism,' was a complex strategy designed to press Ottawa as hard as possible for benefits, especially economic benefits, without slipping into a kind of defiance that would unalterably alienate English Canada. It was a commitment to federalism that possessed financial strings. This was a strategy that carried an appealing ring in Quebec and avoided upsetting Ottawa.

But, he warned, the strategy was also very subtle and difficult to implement. If English Canadians became too aware of the nature of the strategy, they would likely balk, thus destroying its efficacy. If Quebecers were led to believe that the strategy was only about economic benefits and did little or nothing about other declared grievances, they would discredit the strategy regardless of its actual success. A vulnerability of the strategy in Quebec was that its proponent, or at least one less gifted than Bourassa, could easily be seen as 'unable to deliver,' especially as the expectations for performance mounted. Finally, the strategy was all process and said little about outcomes.

Underlying these two strategies, separatism and conditional federalism, lay a common ideal of Quebec nationalism. Outsiders often confused nationalism with separation and therefore, ironically, confused the politics that Robert Bourassa favoured with those intended to break up the polity. Hence Bourassa was often deeply misunderstood throughout Quebec and English Canada, and was distrusted. That is perhaps the political price the true liberal politician must pay for advocating 'middle-of-the-road' policies.

Facing the analyst of Canadian unity is a great question. Towards which end of the nationalist spectrum is Quebec drifting – towards continued use of conditional federalism or towards outright secession? Doubtless Quebec leaders of the calibre of Bouchard do not yet know. The answer lies in the Quebec body politic, not within a single political party, not in the hands of a single leader. The challenge is to discern what the direction of the political forces shaping the strategy of Quebec governments is likely to be – a sustained commitment to conditional federalism or a lurch towards unqualified separatism?[3]

Factors Contributing to Separation

There are four feasible approaches that the analyst studying the roots of Quebec nationalism, especially its most extreme form of secession, could follow. First, the analyst could study the efforts, at least since the early 1980s following patriation, to reform the constitution so it meets the concerns of all Canadians. This would entail a careful examination of the constitutional talks at Meech Lake and Charlottetown and the Calgary Declaration, the raising of expectations and the plummeting of these expectations when attempts at proposal and compromise failed. But this analysis has already been undertaken by such scholars as Peter Russell, Alan Cairns, Charles Taylor, Richard Simeon, Guy LaForest, and Kenneth McRoberts that one hesitates to retrace this ground. In addition, the prospect of further initiatives for constitutional renewal on the past scale seem rather dim.

Second, the analyst could examine Quebec's demands for change, reform, and a redistribution of power and note the response of the federal government and of the other provinces. This approach has the merit of focusing directly on Quebec and on the strategy involved. But it too has already been undertaken.[4] Moreover, this analysis is filled with its own type of frustration, since much of the debate is explicitly between Quebec City and Ottawa and is very dependent upon the specific identity of the political parties in power and on the personality and tactics of the players. While documenting specific demands regarding control of immigration, language policy, educational initiative, cultural policy, and workforce training is simple, finding a 'bottom line' is not. In this highly dynamic negotiation process, a summing up of the individual demands and responses does not bring the analyst any closer to the roots of contemporary Quebec nationalism.

Third, the analyst could examine two policy changes originating from outside Canada that may have a bearing on separatist attitudes in Quebec: the sense of international security provided by the U.S. nuclear umbrella and NATO, and the advent of regional integration offering broader economic opportunities.[5] But there are also problems with an analysis of these policies, though they may have some background relevance. The security explanation long preceded the upsurgence of contemporary Quebec separatism. Likewise, the specific emergence of FTA and NAFTA does not correlate with increased secessionist sentiment. Effect precedes alleged cause. Worse, the fact that a separate Quebec would not automatically negotiate its inclusion in FTA or NAFTA, and the reality that it would likely pay a price in terms of foregone per capita income growth (see chapter 6), could undermine the regional integration explanation. Still, the existence of international security and regional economic opportunity may explain some of the static if not dynamic effects that stimulate the separatist impulse.

A fourth approach, and the one chosen here, is to consider the historical sociology of attitudinal and behavioural change towards separatism in Quebec. By trying to ask the 'right questions,' as Aron, Carr, and Dehio long ago recommended, the analyst can look for patterns and shifts within Quebec society that have influenced the specific preference for growing nationalism. No single event or issue accounts for the emergence of the separatist impulse. Instead, this impulse arises from the complex set of social, economic, cultural and political forces inside and outside Quebec that can intensify nationalism. An advantage to this approach is that it stresses continuity, and allows that nonlinear change and backsliding will inevitably occur, without attributing design and purpose to any future outcome.

Memories Retained

It is not by accident that the license plates of Quebec automobiles still bear the phrase 'Je me souviens.' The meaning that the phrase evokes to Quebecers, according to Thomas Barnes, a historian at Berkeley, is not so much that they remember as that 'they never allow themselves to forget.' What they supposedly remember is the Conquest – the military defeat of Montcalm's forces by Wolfe's English troops on the Plains of Abraham above Quebec City in 1759. In fact, what they remember is domination by the British government, and subsequently by the English-speaking business elite within the province. They remember the past slights and the obstacles to promotion inside the ranks of the army officer corp (an army that is now more truly bilingual and more fairly representative than perhaps any other institution in the country), or within the banking system. Banking was once synonymous with the Scotts, and lawyering and the priesthood with the francophones.[6] 'I remember' really means remembering the stereotypes and discrimination, real or imagined.

The problem for Canada is that many francophones are still fighting psychological battles inside Quebec that, in turn, are projected outward towards English Canada. Hence the calls among purists for French-only signs (despite what businesspeople know their customers may want and despite that which will maximize sales). Hence the struggle of Premier Bouchard to discourage the demand to create a 'unilingual' province. These struggles have gone on long after their relevance for contemporary policy. It doesn't matter that discrimination no longer exists against francophones inside Quebec or indeed inside the federal government, or that francophones may, in some cases, have a disproportionate advantage to promotion inside certain bureaucracies. There is often suspicion that discrimination exists and the belief that only complete political separation will undo past wrongs.

One problem with a collective memory of discrimination is that there is sometimes a temptation by a few of the majority to impose on the present-day minority the same exclusion from opportunity that they, the dominant group, experienced in the past when they were the minority group. This temptation has led to bitter exchanges, for example, between the Montreal Jewish community, part of which is itself francophone, and the majority francophone community.[7] Often the francophone leadership attempts to shield the minority anglophone or allophone communities from the unreasoned actions or statements of a few francophones. This shielding can be misunderstood in each of these communities, especially in the dominant francophone community, making the administration of policy inside Quebec difficult, even politically precarious.

Political memory is often partial and sometimes even wrongly biased, at least in terms of current social and political realities. Yet political memory is a factor in all political situations, especially during elections. The English-speaking Quebec community may say that it is now paying an unfair price for past wrongs, but it cannot easily correct or compensate for those wrongs. All too readily a few members of the francophone community can demand policy initiatives that respond to a past sense of grievance, even if that governmental response would not be in the long-term interest of the province, and even if the political leadership of each political party knows the initiatives are detrimental to the prosperity and image of Quebec in the future.[8] But heading off mistakes is not simple, especially for the Parti Québécois, which is officially dedicated to separatism.

Population Distribution along a Narrow Band

The Canadian population stretches for more than 3,000 miles (4,828 km) in a narrow band, which is seldom more than a 100 miles (160 km) wide, along the U.S. border.[9] Punctuated by long distances of prairie and forest or sparsely populated farm land, this band is subject in these protracted segments to intense cross-border contact. Regionalism and the North–South pull flourish under these circumstances. The capacity of Canada to 'hang together' under these geoeconomic conditions is all the more remarkable.

But the geopolitical tension between Quebec and English Canada on either side of the Quebec border is greater because of this population configuration. If the band were wider and not so long, it would not snap so easily. The Quebec segment can be cut out of the longer band rather precisely. But such surgery would put the rest of the band in peril, making internal population contact less direct, and making other segments of the band subject to further fragmentation.

If Canada had been settled differently, say in the fashion where six million French-speaking Canadians had located randomly from Halifax to Vancouver, then Quebec separation would be moot. Territorial concentration in Acadia, however, has led to a very different form of identity in New Brunswick. Francophones can correctly claim they were the 'original Canadians' only if one discounts the similar claims of the million or so First Nations peoples scattered around a much larger territorial area. Moreover, from the legalist perspective, according to Paul Romney, the only reason francophones can claim to be the 'original Canadians' is that they are descended from people who called themselves 'Canadiens,' so that 'the claim bears no rational relation to claims of status within the territorial unit called Canada, or within the territorial unit known as Canada in the eighteenth century, let alone within present-day Quebec.'[10] From this legalist perspective, such claims must rest on privileges accorded by the lawful governments of those territories to the group of persons known as Canadiens. Neither history nor geography alone lends credibility to some Quebecers' demand for separation.

But if in fact historical settlement, with its heavy concentration of French-speaking peoples in one geographic area, does fuel the separatist impulse, it is the impact that such an impulse has on other peoples in Canada which could have the greatest long-term consequence for wholeness. The greatest consequence of Quebec separation may be the loosening of bonds between the First Nations and all of Canada. A rise in the national consciousness of Quebecers may in the end transfer to a rise in the cultural and political awareness of the First Nations.[11] Dispersed over wide and sometimes less habitable areas in the far North, the First Nations may use this historical episode to claim their own 'national' autonomy. This demand could take many forms – the creation of the territory of Nunavut being only one – but at its most meaningful it would irrevocably transfer to the First Nations resource and mineral rights (always claimed as their own) which, while not exploited immediately, could in the future be worth extraordinary value. As technology improves the capacity to extract resources such as petroleum or natural gas from wilderness areas with minimal harm to the environment and without interfering with habitat or ancestral ways of life, even the most committed traditionalist might have a hard time objecting to development. At stake is the prospect of demand for far greater autonomy, although expressed or concealed in a dozen different arguments, across generations of Canadians and across peoples within Canada.

The narrow band of settlement by English-speaking and French-speaking Canadians invites the question, Who owns Canada, or which subgroup of Canadians is likely to lay claim to exclusive control of some section of territory that is now unqualifiedly pan-Canadian?[12] Moreover, the historical pattern of settlement encourages Quebec separation because, despite the presence of perhaps a million French-speaking people outside Quebec and some three-quarter million non-French-speaking people inside Quebec, Quebec has come to represent the place in Canada where French is spoken.

Regionalism

Canada is a polity composed of regions. Canadian regionalism can be observed, albeit incompletely, in the diversity of its regional cultures, architectures, and lifestyles.[13] Every country experiences regional differences, especially very old (or conversely, recently combined) countries, including the United States. But Canada's regions seem to be, by North American standards at least, quite prominent. Yet it is probably a mistake to believe that regional fractionalization is either a profound political weakness for Canada or the predominant source of cleavage within the polity.

First, as poll results reveal, Canadians invariably share affiliations between their province or region and the country as a whole. With the exception of francophone Quebec, and despite substantial regional loyalty, for example, in Newfoundland, Alberta, and British Columbia, Canadians feel greater attachment to Canada than to their own locale. This multiple affiliation across lines of cleavage is symptomatic of the effects of fractionalization on Canadians.

Second, regional affiliation is further split in terms of new and prior residents. Because of immigration, the so-called new Canadians now outnumber their counterparts in the largest cities, but also in areas of priority immigration such as British Columbia. Of course, the new Canadians themselves are not homogeneous. Sikhs, Haitians, Armenians, Chinese, and Vietnamese, who have emigrated to Canada within the last decade, compose significant portions of local populations.

Third, there is an increasingly important division in the Canadian population, matching that elsewhere in the industrial world, between youth, middle-aged, and retired populations. This age difference affects political preferences and public policy decisions. In Quebec, for example, this age split is as important as any other for determining federal preference. The effect of the age split on regional preferences is to 'wash out' or offset much of the influence of parochial geographical preference. As the Canadian population ages, concerns about federal support for pensions, health care, and other social services will tend to amalgamate the retired cohort and the politically most active cohort, and diminish the influence of regional identity. Older citizens will increasingly look to Ottawa to safeguard their retirement funds.

Regionalism, on the surface such a strong force in the lives of most Canadians, tends to collapse as an explanatory variable in the face of divisions according to age, wealth and education, immigrant status, and other linguistic or cultural preferences. Canada is not as weakened politically by regionalization as the evident split in federal/regional preferences might otherwise indicate. Regionalism in Quebec may reinforce both historical and ethno-linguistic delineation, but it is also undercut by the other types of cleavage within the province that are cross-cutting and of broader scope. To say that Canada is a 'country of regions' is to miss the political implications of Canadian regionalism for future Canadian political unity.

The intense regionalism of Canada ought to reinforce understanding of the Quebec position. But that is not what seems to be happening. The West seems to take just the opposite position. Why should they acknowledge Quebec society as distinct, and thereby as worthy of special treatment, when they view their own regional identity as being just as distinct and just as worthy of privilege?[14] To recognize one form of regional identity as authentic but not another seems to discriminate against those that are not primarily ethno-linguistic in composition. Beneath that assertion is also fear – fear that regionalism is growing faster than pan-Canadianism; fear of what regionalism may do to the fabric of Canada; fear in the end that they themselves may be contributing to the fragmentation of Canada by clinging to regional preference.

This may sound like *Weltschmerz*, but it is the situation in which modern Canada finds itself.[15] To some extent, Belgium, the United Kingdom, Hungary, Spain, and Italy all face analogous conundrums.

North-South Geoeconomic Pull

The purpose of the North American Free Trade Agreement (NAFTA) was to enhance the efficiency of the North American marketplace by increasing the capacity for economies of scale and by eliminating investment and other barriers to economic exchange, as well as to increase the security of market access by creating a binational dispute resolution mechanism modelled after that in the old FTA. However, NAFTA's political effect may have been somewhat different – the political effect may have increased the relative strength of the North–South pull on particular regions of Canada.[16]

Of any of the provinces, Quebec was one of the most enthusiastic advocates of freer trade with the United States, on a par with conservative Alberta. Yet Quebec was far from conservative. Nor were its domestic economic institutions and its strategy of economic development, so dependent upon interventionist policies, especially compati-

ble with free trade.[17] Rather, advocates of Quebec separatism saw that
greater certainty of access to the U.S. market through NAFTA reduced
the economic risk of secession from the rest of Canada. NAFTA could
be seen as the Trojan Horse of Quebec separation inside Confederation.

On the other hand, the benefits of greater economic growth for all of
Canada and of greater assured access for Canadian goods and services
to the U.S. market could be regarded as a shield against the challenge
that Canadian Confederation was not working well, was not productive, and was not capable of generating jobs and income.[18] A richer and
more economically vibrant Canada could be seen to be a stronger and
more united Canada. Furthermore, given the direction of U.S. trade
policy following the initial strains of the softwood lumber episode,
Canada could be regarded as having no other meaningful choice than
to improve its comparative trading position through a regional trading
agreement.

Regardless of how compelling these latter arguments were, and they
did carry weight, the simple reality was that NAFTA also fit into the
plans of Quebec separatists. Again and again, 'automatic' accession to
NAFTA was held up to Quebecers during the 1995 referendum campaign as a beacon for future Quebec economic prosperity after independence.[19] Whether the arguments of guaranteed access to the U.S.
market were merely instrumental, or whether they were actually
believed by proponents during the referendum, is scarcely the issue.
These arguments about NAFTA were used in Quebec in favour of separation.

Regional free trade, while essential to the economic competitiveness
of North America vis-à-vis offshore competition worldwide, tugged on
confederation in another way. East–West trade within Canada, at least
for heavy goods, was always at a disadvantage to the North–South
markets in the United States. By eliminating tariffs and other barriers,
Canadian regions could become closer to these natural North–South
markets.

There was one further problem concerning the North–South pull.
According to the original MacDonald Commission, a new economic
free market *inside* Canada was supposed to emerge after signing the
NAFTA agreement.[20] Indeed, in the minds of some, NAFTA would
prod Canada into doing what was economically best for itself, namely,
reducing intraprovincial barriers to trade and investment. These barriers had, for example, limited the beer production of individual breweries to the size of the province's market. Breweries could not expand

and were too small to be efficient. (Microbreweries have proven that such a niche can be very profitable, although the markets remain too small for the big low-cost, high-volume beer producers who retain the largest share of North American markets.) The problem was that the resistance of provincial interests everywhere in Canada proved difficult to offset. Barriers did not come down in many sectors. Subsidies, preferential hiring practices, procurement rules, and a host of non-tariff barriers continued to plague the Canadian economy internally. Not that many of these same barriers were absent among the states, but the American market was ten times larger than the Canadian market and, however damaging, these interstate barriers often did not hinder trade and investment as severely as they did their Canadian counterparts.

In short, without the elimination of intraprovincial trade and investment barriers, the North–South pull, accentuated by the elimination of North–South restrictions, tended to place increasing strain on the Canadian marketplace. An indicator was the increasing strength of North–South trade as measured by the per cent of Canadian trade involved with the United States.[21] As more and more trade shifted from the East–West axis to the North–South axis, predictably more strain was placed on the federal institutions in Canada. The struggle to maintain a Canadian economy became ever more difficult because of the dual effect of the North–South influence and the breaking up of the internal economy that was not subject to immediate policy correction.

Economics does not drive politics, nor is it irrelevant to the evolution of political institutions and practice. Over time, the failure to eliminate economic barriers inside Canada will add to the strains on the Canadian polity and will be used in arguments in Quebec to bolster separation. The answer is not to give up economic efficiency or to try to persevere under the old, bankrupt procedures. The answer is two-fold. First, clarify exactly what the terms of Quebec accession to NAFTA would be.[22] Negotiation, not automatic accession, is the reality. Second, reopen the intraprovincial trade and investment barrier debate and create a true Canadian common market in all sectors so as to strengthen the East–West Canadian economy to its maximum. These are the valid responses to a set of forces that in the past were dismissed as 'Continental' but that in fact are part of a larger world trend towards rationalization of the marketplace along global lines and maximum technological change.

Growing Passion for Quebec Nationalism

Three hundred and fifty years after the founding of New France, finding the source of the Quebec desire for separation in terms of historical
sociology is not so difficult.[23] The analyst may ask why now, why so
many decades after the Conquest, after the rebellions of 1837–8, after
the bitter memories of the two Conscription crises, after the implanta-
tion of bilingualism in English Canada, after the actual success of the
Quiet Revolution itself?[24] Of all these experiences, the unfolding of the
Quiet Revolution is the most revealing explanation. Among other
things, why did the shift towards separatism come long after the
period of greatest discrimination and discontent in Quebec?

Contemporary nationalism has many origins, which will differ from
country to country. Part of the explanation for the present nationalist
impulse is surely international (see chapter 5). Take away the preoccupation of the Cold War, with its overweening consciousness of East–
West ideological discord, and all of the reasons for communal difference rise to the surface, reasons previously weighed down by the
issues and instruments of the Cold War. But however satisfactory this
explanation is for much of the world's nationalist turmoil, for example
along the Russian littoral, it does not fit the situation in Quebec very
well. Quebec's nationalism is both older (prior to 1945 the great enemy
was '*l'américanisme saxonisant*') and more recent, less affected by what
lies outside North America and more contingent upon the stage of
political development in which Quebec finds itself today. Quebec
nationalism is for the most part home-grown.[25]

In five short decades, francophone Quebecers lifted themselves out
of inferior social status, leaving the farm, entering the university,
embracing business, celebrating their language and culture. The clergy
that had saved Quebec from the neglect of Louis XV and his court, and
from the hardships of survival in a rough land, now became a burden.
A Catholic faith that had provided the social cement for the colony, as
well as the solace from fear and from societal and job exclusion for its
members, became an embarrassing reminder of a past that everyone
wanted to forget. In discussing Quebec and other 'collectivities' with a
Catholic cultural background, Charles Taylor notes the importance of
religion as an element of identity: 'And modern peoples, that is collectives that ought to be agents in history, need some understanding of
what they are all about, what I call political identity, some sense of
what bonds them together. In these cases, being Catholic was an
important part of political identity.'[26]

Modern Quebecers had much material and social success. But while exhilarated by the release from rural bonds, they also inadvertently felt much uncertainty and angst.[27] Revenge of the cradle' sounded mocking in a society that went from one of the highest birth rates in the world to one of the lowest. Rapid social mobility and a contemporary education provided no certain answers. A void emerged. Pride in culture and language did not fill the vacuum, which was only worsened by the anxiety over relative decline in population and in suspected societal loyalty. Anxiety plagued the consciousness of the collective in a North American setting that lauded only the individual.

Transfer of Identities and Rebellion

Anxiety arose because, to be modern, the Quebecer had to turn against Mother Church, the institution that had succoured and protected them but that now condemned their materialism. The Quebec Church was the institution that stayed with Quebecers when the French elite abandoned them after the Conquest, that helped defend them against the depredations of the 1839 Durham Report (that proposed to assimilate them), that cared for their sick and educated their children, and that provided cultural continuity across three centuries of difficult survival as a people. Yet under the umbrella of the Quiet Revolution this was the institution against which they rebelled.

Why did they rebel? This is the story waiting to be told, but can only be touched on, in a few short paragraphs. They rebelled because the Church was coercive and controlling. For the most part, it strengthened the most conservative elements of the society. Ironically, its control came to resemble the control exerted commercially by the despised English-speaking elite. But its greatest sin was that it stood for the anti-modern. It resisted the upward mobility and the urbanization and industrialization that contemporary Quebecers yearned for or hoped that their children would participate in. In the end, the Quebec Church represented the last bastion of an old world Quebecers were in a rush to leave behind. They had to flee it. As the seminaries and monasteries emptied in the aftermath of Vatican II in the mid-1960s, the Quebec Church shattered, almost destroying itself. In a word, the Church for most Quebecers became a social and political embarrassment.

This is a problematic thesis to argue because it invites mischaracterization. Those with some familiarity with the history of the province and these institutions may confuse this interpretation with the erroneous claim that the allegiance of Quebecers to their state institutions is

identical in type and motivation as to the Church in the earlier era; that
nothing has changed in the interim; that politics remain as conservative and undemocratic today as before; that the state exacts and gets
the same unqualified loyalty as the Church did a century before. Such
confusion would be a great pity, for it covers up the monumental difference between this thesis and that of the much popularized Louis
Hartz thesis.[28]

According to the Hartz thesis, Quebec is the ultraconservative fragment of feudal France, untouched by either the American or the French
Revolutions and unable to identify with the Tory conservatism of the
English Canadians. Like other 'fragments' in the Middle East and elsewhere with no hereditary aristocracy against which to rebel, it is
impossible to develop a radical left because there is nothing to resist
and nothing upon which to build. Hierarchy, statism, and backward-
looking social institutions in the Hartzian view were the results for
modern-day Quebec.

Here is where the analytic work of Seymour Martin Lipset becomes
so important. Lipset shows on issue after issue, through careful empirical delineation, how contemporary Quebecers have broken with their
controlling institutional past, how they often espouse values even
more liberal than those of the Americans or of their English Canadian
counterparts, and how they express all of the behaviours and attitudes
of a modern, liberal, democratic, urban (and urbane) society. Lipset is
the corrective to Hartz; he explains, in terms of the value differences of
a later age, why allegiance to the Quebec government cannot be identical to the historical allegiance to the Catholic Church. Yet more than
formal similarities remain; so do subtlety and complexity.

Despite its authoritarian rule, the Church in many ways was benevolent. (From the Ursuline Sisters who nursed both Montcalm's and
Wolfe's wounded back to health, to the struggle of Archbishop Char-
bonneau against Duplessis, a balanced story of the Catholic Church in
Quebec, despite its objectionable sometimes ultramontanist character,
has not been told and probably will not be told for some time.) Hence
the modern Quebecer is turning away from an institution that historically was responsible for saving Quebec society from obliteration. This
is no mere rejection of religion or old-fashioned thinking. This is a
monumental and traumatic dispelling of something that is existential,
that is part of the personality, the education, the value structure of
every Quebecer. This is tantamount to personal rebellion, and such
bold defiance exacts a high social and political price. Such rebellion

creates a repressed anger that somehow must be displaced, and the anger creates a single-minded drive to assert one's autonomy.

Does this mean that contemporary Quebec is backward-looking, irrational, or illiberal? Does this mean that today's Quebec is heavily 'Catholic-influenced,' 'chauvinistic,' or subject to 'xenophobic French-Canadian nationalism'? These are the criticisms that have been directed at the Louis Hartz thesis. But they surely could not be applied to the analysis and findings supplied by Lipset. Nor can such comments be applied to the interpretation provided here. Modern Quebec has slipped the bonds of its rural, clerical, ultraconservative past and in the twenty-first century shares many roughly similar values with all other advanced industrial, democratic communities.

Modern Quebec is a liberal society. Its financial assistance to hospitals, notwithstanding the pressures of hospital amalgamation, is above reproach and is even-handed, irrespective of whether the hospital provides French-speaking or English-speaking care. Quebec provides funding not only to public but to religious schools. Whether the instruction is in French, English, Hebrew, or another language, financial support has been forthcoming in a way that would make schools in many other countries quite envious. Quebec's newspapers are vital, diverse, and capable of expressing strong opinion. No religious group in Quebec can claim discrimination. In short, on many indices of behaviour and public policy, Quebec receives highest marks for its liberal programs.

All societies have gone through much of the same secular and metropolitan evolution. The pattern itself is not unique. It is called industrialization and political modernization.[29] But all societies have not done so as quickly. Nor have most societies fled the dominance of so omnipresent an institution and life-experience as the Catholic Church in Quebec. Scarcely a francophone Quebecer born in the 1940s or earlier does not have a story to recount, a childhood memory to dispel, a personal metamorphosis to relate. This is not political modernization as witnessed in the Thirteen Colonies or in English Canada. It is more like that of nineteenth century Italy, compressed into one-half the interval, projected upon a people anachronistically, one century late. (Not coincidentally, historical and contemporary attitudes towards religion, a very politicized religion in each case, are quite similar.)

What has transpired, as religious belief has been jettisoned, is belief in a new secular ideal. Quebec culture has replaced religion as a nonmaterial value to revere. But culture could not adequately supplant religion as a thing in which to 'believe.' Culture was not a sufficient absolute. After all, culture itself looked like it was under siege.[30] Culture and language therefore had to be protected, for in the rapid ascent of the Quiet Revolution, culture and language, no matter how seemingly vulnerable, were the only legacies of the past with which the modern Quebecer could still identify. Nationalism thus superceded culture as the ultimate faith. Understandably, anti-religion correlates with separatism.

In the latter half of the twentieth century, the state replaced the Church as the guarantor of personal economic security within Quebec. In a society that is very interventionist in terms of governmental programs of all kinds with a heavy commitment to social expenditure, the state is far more visible than in either English Canada or the United States. This is not a historical accident. Even though much has changed in terms of education and public wealth, social dependence and patronage still exist. The government 'minister' is the substitute for village priest. Faith in the caisse de depôt replaces faith in the basilica. Even though a kind of social emancipation has occurred for rural francophones, the overwhelming power of the government follows the overwhelming supremacy of the Church. This does not mean, as critics of the Hartz thesis justifiably have warned, that the society is 'atavistic.' Rather, the society is quite comfortable with a heavy degree of governmental involvement that leaves the individual Quebecer dependent on centralized institutions, perhaps not in contrast to much of Europe, outside Britain, or to Mexico (though that is changing) but certainly in contrast to the rest of North America.

A paradox results. Never was Quebec society and culture so visible and ebullient, but never was that sense of culture so anguished and troubled. In its greatest hour of victory, the Quebec language was interpreted to be more threatened than at any time in its prior 350 years of evolution.

In the present day, a strange combination of anxiety over language and culture mixes with an almost unshakable optimism about the benefits that complete state autonomy will provide. Insofar as Quebec separatism is actually assessed as to cause and consequence, separatism bridges the gap between gnawing pessimism about current personal and cultural security and collective optimism about the fruits that future undivided sovereignty is expected to bring.

Quebec nationalism, always strong, has now merged with a growing conviction that independence can guarantee unqualified protection to culture and language. Assimilation by American values and culture after independence is looked upon as less a danger than manipulation by English Canada under present institutional arrangements. Ironically, nearly as many Quebecers and people of Quebec descent live in the United States as live in Quebec, in various states of assimilation, happily as far as anyone can tell, a fact virtually overlooked by official Quebec assessment. English Canadian culture is thought of less as an ally against common bombardment than as an untrustworthy sentry at the gate.

Access to the huge market south of the border opens up a confidence in Quebec that its present strategies and institutions can provide the same kind of market penetration in the future as at present. But that all might change after independence. A thought not often broached is that NAFTA, a shining light for most separatists, might not offer the same deal in the future, after extended negotiation, that Quebecers now receive under the auspices of federation.

Thus the question 'Why now?' for the urge to separate requires a historical sociological explanation. Only in this organic, historical context is Quebec nationalism understood in analytical and policy terms. Government replaces the Church as benevolent defender. Quebec nationalism is at once a personal and a collective Act of Contrition. Nationalism fills the void of lost faith. Nationalist passion is rapidly replacing cold electoral and economic calculation.

Quebec Nationalism: Ethnic or Civic?

A paper published by the Bloc Québécois in October 1999, 'At the Heart of Sovereigntist Thought,' exposes an incontrovertible dilemma that Quebec separatists face. Although it attempts to make the case for an inclusive concept of Quebec separatism, it invariably returns to the idea of 'incompatibility,' so strongly stated in its conclusion:

> Quebec does not want to hinder Canadians in reaching their goal of building a nation that corresponds to their needs and values. *In fact, however, Quebec citizens' social, economic, and political choices are not compatible with Canadians's choices.* Both Quebec and Canadian citizens, then, are called upon to answer a critical question. Would it not be preferable to abandon this arduous, costly battle? Should we not build ourselves parallel countries, neighbouring nations, sovereign partners? Although Quebec citizens want to maintain economic and political recognition as a

nation, after more than 40 years of constitutional failures and fruitless endeavours to obtain *recognition as a people* within Canada, the time has come for Quebec to seek *this recognition* internationally, by becoming a sovereign nation.[31] (Emphasis added.)

This section examines why separatist 'thought' cannot resolve this contradiction at its very 'heart.'

Clearly, what is happening for some Quebecers today is that nationalism is 'taking on a life of its own.' This is not to claim that Quebec nationalism is 'atavistic' or 'regressive,' to use the language of the Hartz thesis critics. Quebec nationalism for the most committed separatists, however, is entering the sociopolitical realm of romanticism where economic costs are not felt to be worth calculating, and where visions of recognition as an independent nation-state are replacing the customary, practical, Quebec estimation of individual political gains and losses (or choices).

It is this Quebec estimation of individual political gains and losses, for which Quebecers are justifiably so well-known, that has made democratic pluralism work, indeed that makes liberal democracy work. The secessionist urge, asserting incompatibility of social, economic and political 'choices,' overwhelms individual political calculation and thereby puts democratic pluralism at risk.

Is Quebec nationalism predominantly ethnic in impulse or is it civic in nature? That is the question many have asked. Since a majority of francophone voters support the Parti Québécois and a majority of non-francophone voters oppose separatism and the PQ, can one say that all those voting for (or against) the Parti Québécois are voting along ethno-linguistic lines? No, one cannot. There are many cross-cutting issues that may cause a voter to choose the PQ, just as there are many issues that would encourage a voter to choose either of the other two parties. Supporters of the PQ, for example, may have a civic view of nationalism despite, in effect, assisting the separatist cause. Yet if a strong majority of francophone voters supports separatism and a large majority of non-francophone voters is opposed to separatism, this effect is not likely to be 'washed out' easily by other voting preferences. In such a situation, there is a strong predisposition to assume that the nationalism underlying a separatist vote is ethnic nationalism. Certainly the 'No' of the one group is 'incompatible' with the 'Oui' of the other. Therein lies the problem for the separatist.

Separatists would like to reach out to minorities to make separatism a truly Quebec-wide movement, yet minorities are not attracted to the sovereigntist program. Quebec separatists are puzzled by the indifference, indeed the mutual opposition, of not only the anglophones but also the allophone minorities who do not identify with the rhetoric or symbolism of the separatist enterprise. This puzzlement suggests that they do not entirely realize the contradiction in the Parti Québécois and Bloc Québécois program that is so obvious to francophone federalists, minorities, and outsiders.

The secessionist leadership appeals to minorities to participate in the common enterprise of setting up a new government, but at the same time, it notes that 'Quebec citizens' social, economic, and political choices are not compatible with Canadians' choices.' For 'Quebec citizens' choices' read the 'francophone separatists' choices,' which are not the choices of all francophones and certainly not the choices of the Quebec minorities who identify much more with Quebec federalism. The dilemma for the separatists is that the minorities cannot identify with their objective of 'becoming a sovereign nation' because it requires that minorities abandon the opportunities they believe are associated with Canada-wide membership.

The goal of Quebec independence, as so far defined and promoted, thus gets in the way of minorities participating in the PQ and BQ who might otherwise participate in a program of 'good government.' No amount of rhetoric will cover up the contradiction that shows how these parties put emphasis on differences in language and culture while appealing to the more general attitudes and interests of the non-francophone minorities. But might this assessment misrepresent secessionist thought?

Let the separatist voice speak for itself. In the very section claiming an 'open, inclusive concept of democracy,' the BQ paper states: 'The Bloc Québécois does not endorse an exclusively societal model that would submerge Quebec's Francophone majority in a sea of political sanitization.'[32] It explains: 'an exclusively societal, or so-called post-national, model is not appropriate to Quebec's particular situation.' Here, 'societal model' is a euphemism for *civic* model. While asserting the role of minorities in the sovereigntist process, the BQ makes clear that its principal objective is to preserve the rights and privileges of the francophone majority, who are after all its overwhelming source of electoral support against 'a sea of sanitization.' The term sanitization has an oddly similar sound and connotation much like the word 'cleansing,' which is used infamously elsewhere in the world. The choice of words cannot be accidental and is meant to bring out in the Quebec francophone population a fear of being sanitized or of being cleansed by the English-speaking population in Canada. The impact of the cultural-linguistic divide and the handling of political issues is just too prominent to ignore either in electoral terms or in terms of opinion data.

The existential primacy of this cultural-linguistic divide is even more clearly expressed in *The Main Proposal*, the official statement that outlines the Bloc Québécois' goals for sovereignty:

> There could be no Quebec nation if a national majority of Francophone Quebeckers with a specific language, culture and history constituting the basis of their common public identity did not live within Quebec's borders. This common public identity is also consistent with the express recognition of cultural pluralism within Quebec society, since English-speaking Quebeckers, Quebeckers of all other origins and Aboriginal peoples, in short all Quebec citizens, have the opportunity and *duty* to take part in the preservation of this language, in the transformation, mixing and dissemination of this culture and the pursuit of this common history.[33] (Emphasis added.)

In other words, the civic role of all non-francophone Quebecers is, according to the BQ separatists, the 'duty' to preserve the language and culture of a single privileged group, the francophone majority.

Hence, regarding the question whether Quebec nationalism is civic or ethnic, much depends upon how 'civic nationalism' is defined. If it means merely that any person living in Quebec can become a Quebecer just as she or he can become a Canadian, then the Quebec notion of citizenship is surely civic, as is the notion of citizenship of virtually every other democracy in the world.[34] But this definition of 'civic nationalism' is so broad that it spreads over and submerges 'ethnic nationalism' beneath it, rendering the latter category meaningless. If, on the other hand, 'civic' is to connote that each citizen of the province of Quebec must think like those who vote separatist because that is the true measure of being a Quebecer, then of course the test of 'civic nationalism' in Quebec, in terms of inclusiveness and tolerance, would fail.

After castigating those mostly anglophone Canadians who would deny Quebec the status of a distinct society under the claim of provincial equality (whatever their other justifications might be), and after rejecting racism as the basis of the remark by the premier of Quebec on referendum night about the role of ethnic voters and money in the outcome, Charles Taylor perceptively probes, beneath the surface, the implications of the Parizeau statement:

> But it does reflect a blind and almost obsessive commitment to the Jacobin model, according to which 'ethnics' are considered Quebecois to the extent that they vote for 'our' national dream. Their only role is to sing along in the chorus with those whose ancestors have been tilling our soil for four hundred years – while adding a bit of folkloric spice to our culture.[35]

Here, in the Jacobin model of nationalism, the idea of 'civic' yields to a particular variant of ethnic nationalism. Inclusion is determined by whether an ethnic voter is willing to, 'sing along.' Taylor worries that the 'refusals to share identity space' by those who nonetheless think of themselves as 'wonderfully generous and welcoming to diversity' will create a deepening xenophobia and intolerance that cannot be stopped or reversed.[36]

No longer submerged and now clarified further for Quebecers, the Jacobin model was outlined in its nationalist implications by the former premier of Quebec in his October 2000 reflections about how Quebec ought to act in the future toward those who did not support the 1995 Referendum. As reported in *The Globe and Mail*, Mr Parizeau admonished that, in contrast to earlier claims to protection, a sovereign Quebec now had no obligation to 'offer airtight guarantees to the anglophone minority by promising that hospitals, schools, and post-secondary institutions would be protected in a sovereign Quebec.'[37] The Jacobin model of nationalism puts calculated pressure on anglophone and allophone in Quebec to 'sing along in the chorus' of separation or to lose their rights. But does this not also put calculated pressure on English Canada elsewhere in the country to respond with similar pressure on francophones? And so, democratic pluralism in both Quebec and the rest of Canada is gradually put at risk.

As observed earlier, many Quebecers who have voted 'Oui' do not agree with all of the PQ or BQ program and have responded to other cross-cutting issues. But, and this is the core of the argument presented here, once separation occurs, it will occur along cultural-linguistic lines. Once separation occurs, it will not matter why a voter supported the party that brought separation into existence. Separation will be a reality and democratic pluralism will have failed in Canada. Across Canada, ethnic nationalism will in effect have undermined the long-held principle of democratic pluralism. This will be true even if the resulting fragments of Canada continue to practise basic liberal policies as independent polities. Liberalism's goal of political harmony across diverse languages and cultures, which preoccupies democratic pluralism, will not have been achieved. Whether the conditions for secession exist and whether secession is an option is the dilemma that all modern democratic polities, not just Canada, will face in the twenty-first century.

Sources of Resistance to Disunity

Effect of Three-party Politics inside Quebec

Quebec is essentially a two-party system, made up of the Liberals and the Parti Québécois. But the presence of the Action Démocratique, electing only a single member to the National Assembly, gives the appearance of a three-party system. In this electoral system, a dynamic is set up that polarizes most issues and creates political 'turf' that an opposition party must defend if that is all the governing party has left it.[38] The Quebec Liberal Party is the defender of Quebec nationalism but, perversely for some, from the perspective of federalism. The Quebec Liberals also possess a constituency that is more solidly federalist, especially after the defection of Mario Dumont to the Action Démocratique. Yet, even if they did not, the political 'turf' left to the Quebec Liberal Party by the ardently nationalist and separatist Parti Québécois, with its own radical wings, is that of opposing separation. If the governing PQ supports independence, then the opposition Liberals must resist the separatist impulse.

Of course the more the governing party moves towards the centre of the issue, in this case separation, the more difficult is the task of the opposition party. It, too, must move over, so as to distinguish its position from that of the governing party. But this causes the opposition party to lose some of the crucial support in the centre and pushes it into more extreme positions than it would otherwise favour. Moreover, the governing party has all the advantages of incumbency, including guaranteed press coverage and the legitimacy of the Office of the Premier. So the opposition party must make up for its disadvantages either by being more wily and opportunistic or by resorting to stridency. Stridency usually fails. Cleverness is usually not a tactic that is in great supply, nor is it a commodity that the opposition leadership will necessarily be able to monopolize. Hence, in a two-party system, the leadership of the governing party usually 'calls the shots.'

Lucien Bouchard, Quebec Premier and Leader of the Parti Québécois, was fully able to exploit the advantages of incumbency. He has in fact played out the role of the governing party with great skill. In public statements, he has minimized the long-term PQ interest regarding separation, thus quieting fears of the more conservative, pro-federalist electorate in Quebec. He has concentrated on the importance of governing and deficit reduction, two natural targets of criticism for the opposition Liberals. At the same time he has held together his own party, despite the unpopularity of suppressing the issue of independence and focusing on the unpopular issue of deficit reduction, with the more radical youth wing. This tactic left the Liberal Party Leader Daniel Johnson and his successor Jean Charest with less to work with politically, and it invited criticism of 'weakness' and 'inefficacy' when the real problem was the dynamic of the three-party system (provincial level) and the inherent advantages associated with incumbency. Jean Charest, sagacious and dynamic, faces some of the same difficulties in opposition as did his predecessor.

But there is a situation that could alter all of this abruptly.[39] This is the situation in which either time or a sudden external shock could alter the foundation upon which political battles are waged. Time usually generates a lot of 'political baggage,' scandals, and other unwanted burdens that an incumbent (witness Bourassa in his first term of office) cannot shake. External shocks can occur unexpectedly. In Quebec, separation has held appeal despite quite a high level of unemployment by North American and indeed Canadian standards. But despite this high support for separation in the midst of high unemployment figures, a downturn of the business cycle could decisively alter conditions of support for separation. A plunge of the business cycle, following a modest boom in the Quebec economy (a boom modified by shortage of investment funds and the exodus of businesses and a talented workforce) could alter the political landscape as well. Hard times could make the Liberal Party message under Jean Charest, who understands the market, far more palatable to the average Quebecer.

A consequence of the 1998 Parti Québécois victory is that the matter of Quebec separation could be put off for perhaps another decade. Many things could happen to the composition of the electorate in so long an interval. The key reason this postponement of 'separation D-Day' could take place is the dynamic of a system that allows the opposition to capture the likely disaffection of the electorate. Such disaffection will come from the governing party having been in power too long, thus accruing the scars of office, and the effect of external shock, especially that of an economic downturn, causing the electorate to look elsewhere for political leadership. In this situation, separation is swept aside in the face of more pressing economic concerns.

Some analysts will be tempted to interpret the November 2000 federal election results in Quebec as an indication of a softening of support for separation. The BQ went from forty-four to thirty-seven seats. The federal Liberal Party won 44 per cent of the popular vote as opposed to a mere 40 per cent by the BQ.[40] Yet considering that the election involved five federal parties, the loss of only seven seats was an indication of how concentrated the BQ strength still remains. Prediction of any kind of a trend in political opinion within Quebec, based on the 2000 election alone, is probably unjustified.

Economic Costs of Separation (Discounted)

If the political opposition were to make clear the short- and long-term costs of separation to the Quebec electorate, the secessionist impulse could be deterred. This conclusion entails that at least three conditions exist: (1) there are short and long-term costs, (2) the economic costs of secession were not sufficiently articulated in either of the prior referenda, and (3) such explication of costs is possible in the future and will be successful. It is worth determining whether all of these conditions exist.[41]

A full-fledged study of the economic costs of separation to Quebec (there would of course be costs to English Canada and to the United States, although these would be less significant) has never been undertaken, at least in the public domain. That in itself is surprising. There have been small isolated studies that have caught the attention of the press and academics.[42] These studies tend to be partial, and some are self-serving. If a firm that handles portfolio investments in Canada does the study, for example, its own self-interest in good news may get in the way of its reporting. On the other hand, an institution or government agency opposed to separation could as easily come up with a biased set of results.

The most immediate and most obvious economic cost is the two-fold loss that has been going on for years: loss of domestic and foreign investment and loss of a talented workforce. Surely the economic opportunity costs have been high in terms of foregone economic prosperity throughout Quebec, most visibly in Montreal. Uncertainty has driven out almost one-quarter million predominantly English-speaking Canadians from Quebec. The head offices of prominent multinational firms such as Sun Life, the Royal Bank, and the Bank of Montreal have moved to Toronto. What makes the analysis more difficult is that this economic migration to Ontario is substantial with or without the threat of Quebec separation. Montreal needs all the help it can muster to hold its own against this westward exodus. Separation makes the job of enhancing the status of this great North American city all that much tougher.

The more prolonged the separation drama, the higher the costs in terms of 'brain drain' and loss of capital.[43] The higher the political shock of separation, the more sustained these losses during and immediately after the event.

An index of how the danger of breakup is negatively affecting Canada is the plunge in the value of the Canadian dollar.[44] Money that would otherwise have entered Canada, or money self-generated in Canada that would have stayed there, is not available to bolster the currency. A weaker Canadian dollar may bolster exports, but it increases the price of needed imports that are essential to the manufacturing and service industries. This cost is shared throughout Canada.

Trade with Ontario and with New England has undoubtedly been damaged by the uncertainty associated with the threat of secession. Commerce thrives on certainty and cannot abide anticipated uncertainty. Trade remains constrained under these circumstances, however sizeable the foundation for that trade. Ironically, just the kind of trade in goods and services Quebec might most like to attract, namely, high-tech firms and new, aggressive middle-sized companies, are the ones that can least tolerate added risk, especially at the border. They will dismiss Quebec as an unattractive investment and export location.

Related costs involve the tax base of Quebec and what the province could otherwise do for its transportation network, its educational institutions, and its social benefits. The costs will be seen directly in terms of wages and salaries, at least those not disproportionately favoured by a separatist government able to redistribute income towards supporters. All of these costs are relative to a standard that would be significantly higher in the absence of separatist uncertainties.

Some costs would emerge after separation only. Quebec dairy and poultry interests now benefitting from high preferential barriers would find their markets outside Quebec cut off.[45] It is not likely that a heavily burdened independent Quebec could afford to make up the difference in agricultural receipts through additional subsidies. Likewise, the Montreal clothing and needle trade industries would face loss of markets in the United States after a renegotiated NAFTA.[46]

A successful NAFTA round of negotiations after separation would be key to whether companies like Bombardier would remain predominantly in Quebec or would move to the United States or elsewhere. Since, according to the rules of NAFTA and according to the U.S. Congressional mandate, NAFTA would need to be renegotiated, Quebec would not have the weight of English Canada in Ottawa to defend its interests.[47] It would be alone. Without question, various economic interests in the members of NAFTA – Mexico, Canada, and the United States – would take the opportunity of a renegotiated NAFTA to improve their positions. Cultural industries both in Quebec and English Canada would come under much more scrutiny than was true under the first round of NAFTA negotiations.[48] This does not mean they would lose all of their subsidies; it does mean that those Canadian media corporations, for example, making as much or more of their income in the United States as in Canada will not be allowed to shield their investments in Quebec and in English Canada while their U.S. and other foreign counterparts are economically discriminated against in Canada.

In the long-term, the picture is far more complicated. Using conventional linear methods of analysis, the results seem to indicate that the Quebec separatists are right when they say that size and economic growth do not seem to be correlated.[49] This is a great conundrum for economic theory. If size and growth are not correlated, then why, for example, should Europe opt for access to the greater size of the European Union and North America for the supposed benefits of size offered by NAFTA? The answer must be, assuming everything else is equal, that size is very important for the economies of scale it affords and for attracting investments.

The reason this conclusion has long been obscured in the debate over Quebec unity is that neither the theory of economic integration nor the empirical economic analysis has been sufficiently examined to come to definitive conclusions about whether separation is likely to hurt long-term economic growth. Little wonder that Quebec sovereigntists and federalists seem to have been talking past each other. A more definitive discussion of this important question of whether separation hurts economically is undertaken in chapter 6.

The answer to the second question – why the 'No' forces failed to articulate economic cost sufficiently in each of the prior referenda – is quite political. In a personal interview, Robert Bourassa, an architect of one of the 'No' campaigns, said, 'I cannot emphasize the costs to Quebec of separation, because my remarks will be perceived as negative.'[50] Bourassa was much more concerned about the image projected than about the substance of the argument itself. This suggests several things about the nature of the debate over sovereignty in Quebec.

Cost discussions are highly complex, even for trained economists. It is easy to get lost in the argument. Moreover, the argument is inevitably hypothetical, and unlike academics, politicians hate hypotheticals. A focus on costs could easily be turned around by the pro-sovereignty forces and characterized as denunciation rather than ernest argumentation. News media often characterize cost discussions as negative rather than as a positive contribution to the political debate because of the complexity and open-endedness of the arguments.

This all says something about the psychology of the Quebec voter during a referendum, especially the 1995 referendum. It suggests that many more voters had actually made up their minds to support separation than was revealed in the polls prior to the last week of the campaign. These 'convinced voters' did not want to be troubled by facts and a 'negative sort' of speculation that would interfere with their preferences. Hence Bourassa understood that the debate had already passed into a sphere of fantasy where ardent oratory more than mere numbers was needed.

While a great deal was made of the notion in the referenda that the 'No' forces were not convincing enough, nor charismatic enough, the reality is that such matters as the economic costs of separation, so compelling to outside observers, could not easily be brought into the campaign. For this reason, the criticism that the opponents of separation failed to justify their position in terms of the economic costs of independence is a criticism that does not grasp the difficulty that inside Quebec voters were willing to disregard economic analysis.

Perhaps in the future, if the cost argument were based on different data and information, backed up by serious and responsible analytic studies, and dramatically presented to a sceptical yet increasingly emotional set of voters, the opponents of separation could benefit from looking at what separation is likely to mean financially for themselves and for Quebec. The problem is that numbers and statistics do not speak for themselves. Worse, they lie with vindication when they emerge from the wrong mouths. Moreover, the dullness and abstractness of economic considerations must be overcome in public debates. Surely whatever shock value the cost argument has is apparently long gone for Quebecers. What is evident is that the proponent of the cost argument must overcome a negative image. Perhaps the way to make the cost argument work is to turn it on its head. Instead of decrying future economic costs, the proponent must stress how much better off financially the province will be with federation. Instead of showing losses, the proponent of the cost argument must show future gains from partnership with the Rest of Canada.

Finally, the risks associated with a renegotiation of NAFTA are real. Unless these are brought into the argument about future Quebec economic well-being, the debate over sovereignty will forever assume a mood of fakery and artificiality, which even the most romantic defender of the new order will want to eschew.

In sum, if the costs of separation are as real and as high as demonstrated by sound studies and careful analysis, if these arguments have not been presented in a convincing fashion in past referenda, and, if a new way is found to explicate the cost argument in positive and dramatic terms, the economic cost of separation could become a major deterrent. Both for the individual Quebecer and for the province as a whole, financial costs of separation and potential self-sufficiency are genuine and worth stressing.

Vexing Doubts Caused by Partition

Public opinion polls reveal that the one issue stemming the separatist tide is the prospect of the loss of territory.[51] No separatist delights in the thought of a shrunken Quebec. Historically aware Quebecers know that Rupert's Land in the North was only acquired by Quebec proper at the turn of the twentieth century through a grant from Britain. Even the less knowledgeable observer senses the fissiparousness of the villages along the Ottawa River and of the English-speaking areas of Montreal such as Westmount, or the differing attitude towards independence of the Eastern Townships. Demands by the Cree and the Inuit, among other Native Peoples, for greater autonomy have become more insistent by the year, inspired by some of the bargains recently struck in British Columbia. In both anglophone and francophone Canada, rumours articulate that a separate Quebec would need to provide a land bridge between the Maritimes and Ontario that would somehow involve the Eastern Townships. Quebec rings with the threats and counterthreats of partition. Governing such a polity after independence is not likely to be an easy task for any leadership intent upon keeping modern Quebec whole.

Of course partition is only one of many curses that an independent Quebec would face. How likely that risk is, is something the Parti Québécois leadership might tend to discount. Some part of the impulse towards partition is mere bluff, just as another part is probably genuine commitment, even actual plan. Independence is a high-risk strategy. Undoubtedly the less risk-averse leadership will ignore partition as a commonplace bluff designed for the consumption of the naive.

For the federalist position, one danger of partition is that it is only bluff and that it would not occur.[52] The other danger, however, is that it could occur. Between this Scylla and Charybdis lies contemporary Quebec. If the Parti Québécois leadership called the bluff of these communities, bought them off, acted resolutely with the outside world, and declared itself independent perhaps after sheering off the most anti-separatist and troublesome elements of the population, Quebec might become independent abruptly. The problem is that neither the threat of partition nor its actuality would halt Quebec separation. Oppositely, partition could occur either before or after Quebec separation, creating a separate Cree or Inuit state or creating small city states that could generate problems of identity and cohesion as well as political uncertainty. But if the threat of partition is credible, and the menace does not become real in terms of actual fragmentation (which would cause subsequent political problems for Canada and the United States), partition can discourage separation. No government in Quebec City will want to suffer an actual major loss of Quebec territory for the promise of independence. Nor do Quebec voters want to give up territory for the privilege of Quebec independence. Thus the unactualized threat of partition is a deterrent to secession even if the concept itself is not as simple or troublefree as some proponents might envisage.

In sum, the dynamic of two dominant political parties that shifts the impetus for separation towards unity, the effect of economic cost considerations, and, however discounted, the threat of partition, all have some influence on the probability of Quebec separation.

Background Trends Affecting Quebec Nationalism

At least four background trends of societal change in Quebec are likely to determine the outcome of the next referendum on separation, if there is another referendum as Premier Lucien Bouchard has promised (although qualifiedly). Politics itself vacillates around a mean of preference that varies with the epoch and the issues of each election. The first trend is the effect of young voters entering the electorate, their values, and outlooks.[53] Second is the retention of nationalism by each age cohort as that temporal grouping of voters ages.[54] Third is the effect of immigration on the voting population.[55] Fourth is the effect of outmigration, especially the exodus of English-speaking Quebecers.[56]

These trends operate independently. Each is a process, social and political by nature, that has its own origins. One may be much more important than the others in determining how Quebec votes. But all of these trends must be considered together in judging whether Quebec will eventually separate.

1. Young Voters

In general, young francophone voters in Quebec are more prone than their forbearers to support Quebec independence. The earlier discussion can provide a guide to a causal explanation of this political preference. Natural reasons for the breakup of the Canadian polity operate equally on all age clusters and ethno-linguistic groupings. Reasons such as the historical settlement pattern of French-speaking and English-speaking citizens, the thin band of population density, the impact of regionalism, and the North–South pull, operate equally on every citizen regardless of age. While these reasons facilitate breakup, they do so irrespective of the age of the voter.

Conversely, the factors that tend to hinder breakup seem to be more age-sensitive. For example, the extent to which younger voters tend to support the Parti Québécois and older voters the Quebec Liberal Party has an effect on each party's policies towards separatism. Likewise, the reality that younger voters tend to discount the economic costs of independence more than older voters, who perhaps worry more about retirement and job security, helps explain the disproportionate enthusiasm of younger voters for separation. The greater willingness of younger voters, though still hesitant, to ignore the threat of partition, with its attendant loss of areas now occupied by anglophones and allophones, also affects their preference for independence.

Based on a comparison of three polls taken in Quebec between October of 1995 and March of 1996, for example, approximately one-half of all respondents in the eighteen to twenty-four age group indicated that they would vote 'Yes' in the next referendum on 'Sovereignty-Partnership.' Only 25 per cent in the age group fifty-five and over said they would vote 'Yes.'[57]

But the key explanation for the preference of younger voters for separation is the dynamic of the Quiet Revolution. Older voters felt at one with the Church, with the more conservative political parties, with the existing anglophone-francophone social hierarchy despite its unpleasant aspects, and with membership in Canada as the 'original Canadians.' The older Quebecers did not feel the dislocation of rapid social mobilization to the same degree as their younger counterparts. They had not rebelled against their traditional religion and did not feel a loss of values to the same degree as their children did. They did not feel to the same extent the hollowness of materialism and its eroding effect on cultural self-confidence. They worried less about the survival of the language since they were less exposed to the urbanization and industrialization that seemed to place the French language in peril. Finally, older Quebecers, unlike their children, placed less confidence in the Quebec government to solve their problems and to protect them as citizens – their parents were a product of a more self-reliant and Church-reliant society, which the modern 'welfare state' had not yet penetrated.

In short, younger voters are more enthusiastic about Quebec independence because they feel more alienated from the older values, including the values of Canadian unity, because they feel more insecure socially and culturally than their progenitors, and because they profess a greater self-confidence in the new machinery of state and in the modern welfare reforms that contemporary Quebec offers. At once more rebellious of older norms and more trusting of the new, younger voters are natural proponents of the promised political and social order after Quebec independence.

2. Retention of Nationalism

As each age cohort matures, composed of members of a single generation relative to the generations before and after it, the age grouping tends to retain much of the earlier enthusiasm for independence displayed during its more youthful days. As each generation of voters ages, it seems to preserve support for Quebec separation rather than shedding it. Instead of discarding the impulse, as occurs with so many other youthful fantasies, why does each succeeding generation hold onto the desire for Quebec autonomy? The answer must be that preference for Quebec independence is not just a function of youth versus maturity. This preference is imbedded in the historical process of Quebec modernization itself and is time-bound, that is, it is unique to each generation and historically determined.

This means that each succeeding generation in Quebec gets a little more nationalistic than the generation it replaces. Nationalism then drifts towards a preference for separatism. Votes aggregate in favour of Quebec independence. Retention of nationalism by succeeding generations of voters helps account for the increase in support for separation – between 1970 and 1995 preference increased from 15 per cent to approximately 50 per cent of the electorate. The creation of the Parti Québécois spurred the desire for independence by institutionalizing a route to separation.

3. Immigration

Following the 'Revenge of the Cradle,' Quebec governments of whatever political stripe all agreed that immigration to Quebec had to increase, that Quebec City needed more control over the reins of immigration, and that immigration to Quebec had to come from French-speaking countries. Otherwise the Quebec population was in danger of dwindling and with it the critical mass necessary to sustain its language and culture.

After much struggle, Quebec did gain greater control over immigration and sustained its flow. But the search for French-speaking immigrants proved difficult. Haitians did not always adjust easily to the rest of Quebec society. France itself offered few emigrés. This forced Quebec to select so-called allophones, namely, those whose first language was not French but who spoke French. More than twenty thousand Jews from Tunisia, fluent in French, came to Quebec. Italians, Greeks, and Lebanese joined the influx.

But the problem in all cases was that these new Quebecers developed a very unreliable attitude towards the French language. Though they spoke and worked easily in French, they believed that for their children 'the more languages, the better.' The first additional language they learned or wanted to learn was English. English for the children of these allophones guaranteed entry to the rest of North America even if they continued to live in Quebec. They feared that Quebec statehood would cut off their physical entry to English Canada.

For the purists of the language cult in Quebec, this learning of English was detrimental to the ethos they wanted to promote – essentially, dominance of the French language throughout Quebec, including Montreal. The purists wanted a language revolution in Montreal, and the allophones were not cooperating. As the then Premier Jacques Parizeau described the situation after the last close but unsuccessful referendum, 'the Ethnics' and money had defeated separatism.

Immigration and language policy in Quebec are critical to understanding the dynamics of nationalism. If immigration policy had been more successful, the pressure would have been taken off language and education policy. Proponents of independence would not have felt so strong a compulsion to be vigilant about language and education. Growing numbers of French speakers would have greater confidence in the survival of their language and culture. But since immigration was not very helpful, the full brunt of concern about survival was felt on language and educational procedure, a situation bound to create tensions, even in an educational system that by U.S. standards was very liberal and supportive of diversity. That religious schools in Quebec, including Protestant and Hebrew schools, for example, continue to receive state aid is surprising by American standards. Immigration was not seen as holding its own in the struggle to expand the use of French.

From the analytic perspective, however, what happens to immigration is crucial to the independence vote. If immigration of committed French speakers increases, separation is abetted. If immigration of those who work in the French language falls off, or if immigration of English speakers increases, the cause of Quebec separation is harmed. Rate and type of immigration significantly affect the prospects for Quebec independence.

4. Out-migration of Anglo Voters

Between 1970 and 1995 more than one-quarter million English-speaking Quebecers migrated to Ontario, the West of Canada, and the United States. Relative to the size of the voting public in Quebec, depending upon turn-out (94 per cent in the 1995 referendum), this number could amount to as much as 7 per cent of the total vote.[58] Seven per cent of the vote would easily have transformed the 1995 referendum into a rout for the 'No' forces.

Conversely, with an estimated 1,000 Quebecers leaving Quebec every month since the last referendum, most of them English-speakers, another exodus of some 100,000 pro-federalist voters will have occurred within the decade. This group could easily represent the crucial 2 to 3 per cent of the vote needed to oppose a majority in favour of separation. Bilingual anglophones and allophones earn more than unilingual anglophones but much less than unilingual francophones. While motivated by economics, their exodus carries great political significance. English-speaking Quebec citizens are literally voting with their feet. Ironically, the vote they are registering, by leaving, is a vote in *favour* of Quebec separation.

Together, then, the effects of these four trends will determine the outcome of the next referendum. Over the last three decades the effects of young voters entering the electorate who are more nationalistic than their parents the retention of nationalism by each age cohort have been predominant. Immigration has been a disappointment to the separatists because the allophones, though fluent in French, have not been reliable supporters of Quebec independence. Overall, immigration of French-speaking people has lagged. In the short-term, the most important trend is the out-migration of English-speaking Quebecers. Indeed, this out-migration may itself be a bellwether of societal tension.

Unaccounted-for Trends and Surprises

No model, no matter how complete, can predict the future nor eliminate the impact that surprises will have on voter outcomes. Anticipation and the open-endedness of human behaviour make true predictions in the social sciences impossible. The effects of trends can indicate variations in Quebec voting behaviour and improve random guessing, but unaccounted-for trends ought to be examined as well.

Urbanization and Increased Education

One would expect that urbanization and greater education would fuel the nationalist impulse.[59] Intellectuals, bureaucrats, the press, teachers, labour union heads, all have strongly supported the nationalist urge. So the conclusion might be that as the Quebec population becomes more urban, it will also become more nationalistic. Surely, a time-series analysis over several decades would support this conclusion, since the trends of urbanization and the impulse to nationalism move in the same direction. Yet such analysis, taken alone, is very misleading.

Some of the greatest strongholds of Quebec separatism are in small towns and rural areas that are heavily French-speaking. Montreal, with its mixed population, is also, even in its French-speaking sectors, more open-minded about options and more pragmatic than many of the rural areas. So urbanization and education affect the propensity for Quebec nationalism in a complex and perhaps non-linear fashion. But over time, the consequence of urbanization and education cannot be left out of judgments about the future of the province.

Outlook of the New Business Elite

On the one hand, the new Quebec business elite is composed of Quebecers who are proud of their culture and language and proud of their ascension as spokespeople for their society.[60] They are aware of the financial power they wield and the impact this power has on the outlook and sense of political direction of other Quebecers. They are primarily committed to the professional responsibilities entailed in business management, but in a period of history that is abundant with opportunity for them and their enterprises yet also full of risk, they are not afraid to speak out on issues. Many of these young businessmen and women in francophone Quebec are prepared to accept life in an independent polity. They know where the lines of finance and power cross at the top of their society.

On the other hand, these Quebecers are extremely sophisticated and cosmopolitan. Invariably they work in both the French and English languages and send their children to universities where the next generation will speak English without an accent. They know that business in North America means doing business in English because they cannot count on Americans or English-Canadians to learn French well enough to work in it. Most of their enterprises will have operations that one day will make as much or more money outside Quebec as in. So the young Quebec business elite is pragmatic, optimistic, and performance-oriented. They know what is best economically for Quebec and for their own commercial enterprises, even if they have not admitted this view publicly.

What this francophone business elite knows most clearly is that the delay in making a decision about Quebec's future is bleeding the province financially. They grieve over what is happening to Montreal, a city most of them love. They do not approve of the flight of capital, jobs, and a talented workforce. They are frustrated over the lack of investment capital and the toll the referenda on separation has taken on all

aspects of life in Quebec. In a word, this business elite wants the decision of Quebec separation to be made soon and with finality. They can
live with whatever outcome occurs. They cannot continue to live and
prosper with the degree of political and economic uncertainty they
have experienced in the 1990s.

Politics of the Canada–U.S. Business Cycle and Quebec Nationalism

When the business cycle turns up, Canada traditionally acts more
feisty, more capable of autonomous initiative, more nationalistic.
Under the same economic circumstances, the United States is more
open and conciliatory. When the business cycle turns down, Canada
acts more cautiously, more congruently with the policies of its large
ally and neighbour. The United States, in contrast, tends to be miserly
and even mean-spirited towards other nations such as Britain, France,
Germany, or Japan. Each country is ironically out of sync with the
other. This differential foreign policy behaviour defines the politics of
the Canada–U.S. business cycle.[61]

What does the politics of the Canada–U.S. business cycle hold for
Quebec nationalism? The answer is two-fold and is relative to English-
speaking Canada and Quebec. If historical patterns are a guide, a
down-turn in the business cycle is likely to mollify otherwise intense
antagonisms between the West, the Ontario Centre, and Quebec. In
hard times Canada has learned to turn inward and to exploit its own
political and economic resources more effectively. Perpetual quarrels
are shelved temporarily. Regional differences are appeased. Ottawa
becomes a source of financial inspiration even in a deficit-conscious
age.

But even if the direction of this tendency is correctly estimated, the
strength is something very difficult to gauge. This effect may be strong
or mild, broadly shared throughout Canada or asymmetrically distributed. The basic point is that really difficult economic times may scare
Canadians enough to start them thinking as a nation again. Ottawa has
very few options in dealing with Quebec when English Canada cate-
gorically refuses to bargain, as it did immediately following the close
outcome of the 1995 Quebec referendum.

The lesson here is not that federalists should wish for bad economic
news. Bad economic news has a way of coming around all by itself at
the trough of a business cycle, on average every seven to ten years. A
smarter conclusion is that the next time the business cycle turns down,

federalists in both Ottawa and Quebec City ought to have an agenda in place that offers Canada a different political menu than what they have been consuming during the prior decade. Politics of the business cycle suggests that neither Quebec nationalism nor the response to it follows a simple, linear course.

Leadership

For most of the post-1945 era, Canada has been governed by very talented francophone politicians. St Laurent, Trudeau, Mulroney, and Chrétien have been an extraordinary group. No less impressive have been the leaders of the province of Quebec, including the PQ leadership under René Lévesque, Robert Bourassa, Jacques Parizeau, and Lucien Bouchard. Jean Charest and Mario Dumont represent the new aspirants to Quebec leadership waiting in the wings.

Leadership can make quite a difference in the next and perhaps final referendum, if and when it is scheduled. Leadership can certainly bring people to the election booth. It cannot so much change the voters' minds as reinforce their convictions to the point of causing them to vote. What is more, as many as 20 per cent of the electorate is open to persuasion, depending upon the survey question asked. With the resignation of Lucien Bouchard in January 2001 as Premier of Quebec and head of the Parti Québécois, some of the logic of the foregoing analysis in this chapter has played itself out. With the likely ascension to the leadership of the PQ by Bernard Landry at this writing, the politics of nationalism in Quebec will have entered a new phase, although passage of a referendum on independence looks no more nor less likely than in the past.

At issue in the 'final' referendum is the matter of the substance of the question put to the Quebec people.[62] Despite much assertion to the contrary, the federal government has a rather small role in determining the wording of the referendum. The PQ, as always, will determine that. But the opposition leadership has a large responsibility in communicating the meaning of the wording. Federal politicians are banking on the importance of clarity to persuade undecided voters not to support the PQ. What should be remembered here is how quickly Lucien Bouchard transformed the notion of 'separatist' from a pejorative word to a political asset. How much room there is for clarification, even by a very astute, energetic opposition leadership that exists in Quebec City and Ottawa, is something not to exaggerate.

Leadership itself cannot easily be persuaded; politics puts on too many shackles to leave any room for manoeuvering. But politicians surely can be alienated. Perhaps the fear of alienation is why the United States, in dealing with matters of Canadian unity, has been so circumspect.

No Bottom Line, No Willingness to Budge

From outside Canada, there is a common problem to the dual strategies of secession and 'profitable federalism' that have dominated relations between Quebec and the federal government since 1945. There is no bottom line to whichever strategy is pursued by Quebec. Secession by definition leaves no room for bargaining: It is a fait accompli. Profitable federalism, which pushes Ottawa as far as it will go to obtain political and economic advantage, is now recognized as a hollow strategy, because the unilateral benefits distributed to Quebec must come at the cost of some other region of Canada. Those regions are now all too aware of the nature of the strategic game.

The battle over the notion of Quebec as a 'distinct society' illustrates this point.[63] Any schoolchild knows that Quebec is distinct (or unique, as expressed in the Calgary Declaration) in terms of its language and culture in North America. Such an obvious designation ought to be immediately and automatically recognized. Moreover, the designation ought to be imbedded in the constitution where it is not as susceptible to political change as in a parliamentary action. Quebecers have a right to expect this. Not to admit the 'distinct society' character of Quebec is to infuriate those sectors of Quebec that are extremely proud of their ethno-linguistic difference in comparison to the rest of the continent. Such outrage plays into the hand of separatist strategists who use it to promote attitudes favouring independence. Ultranationalists in Quebec undoubtedly would declare 'distinct or unique society' as insufficient were it to be granted today.

To offer 'the distinct society clause' without safeguards, however, is to open up the Canadian constitution to perpetual challenge. The court system could be used to provide every sort of special benefit to Quebec not enjoyed by the Rest of Canada. This is not fantasy. The Parti Québécois leadership is fully aware of the legal possibilities, but so is the political leadership of British Columbia and Alberta. Western political leadership is extremely sceptical of any action calculated to enhance the distinctiveness of Quebec society if that action has any possible legal validity.

Quebec wants a clause in the constitution that on the surface looks plausible and harmless, but the Rest of Canada fears that clause as an open door to special privileges for Quebec. Quebec will not accept anything less than full legal validation for the notion of its exclusiveness. Much of English Canada will not yield on anything that is of more than benign, symbolic value. Constitutional extremists on both sides want all or nothing arrangements. What is obvious becomes impossible, and what is impossible becomes obviously inflammatory.

The problem therefore is that there is no bottom line to Quebec demands. For some this is strategic and intentional. For others it is based on prudence and fear of foreclosing necessary opportunity.[64] But the consequence is the same. If English Canada has no way of knowing what the ultimate demands posed by Quebec are, it has less reason to offer concessions.

On the other hand, English Canada is quickly entering a bargaining zone characterized by unwillingness to budge on any issue of substance for fear that all such federal and provincial issues are strategic traps and endless.[65] The counterpart to the failure of establishing a bottom line is answering every invitation to negotiate with a rigid 'no,' a response initiated by the federal government. English Canada is in danger of seeing Ottawa as part of the problem instead of the interlocutor to a solution.

Appearing unwilling to budge is a good bargaining ploy unless the bluff is called. Then the argument is turned around in Quebec and sounds like this: If English Canada is unwilling to budge, Quebec must shift to the ultimate weapon, secession. Absolutism invites absolutism.

As Ottawa well knows, the next years will be occupied by attempting to make bargaining positions less absolute. But at the same time, Ottawa must try to make bargaining terms more concrete. It is thus caught between the extremes of too vague a negotiating position and too specific a position, too open-ended a set of demands and too close-ended a set of terms.

Meanwhile, the real locus of debate over secession remains inside Quebec itself. For it is ultimately Quebecers, and no one else in North America, who will determine their own home and political preference. They will decide whether they are indeed the 'original Canadians' and proud of it, or whether they now are Quebecers who are distinct, separate, and 7.5 million strong on a continent of 380 million foreign voices.

CHAPTER FOUR

Could English Canada Unravel?

If Quebec secession occurs, might English Canada, splintered geographically, be able to cohere politically? Exploring the reasons for the dismaying possibility that perhaps it could not, the analyst finds plenty to worry about. There are a number of natural obstacles to continued unity that the Rest of Canada (ROC) would be required to overcome. Issues involving the impact of economic inequality and the likely end to transfer (equalization) payments must be resolved. The inherent unevenness of political power between Ontario and the other provinces must get sorted out. 'Western alienation' and its subordinate demands will require more serious attention than in the past. Idiosyncratic problems and aspirations associated with the Atlantic provinces as a group and with the individual provinces of Alberta and British Columbia require airing.

Such an analysis leads the observer outside Canada to believe that, in the event of Quebec secession, English Canada will likely need to reconstitute itself politically. Whether the ROC would have the will and the political momentum to do this is the overwhelming question. A speculative case can be made that political reconstitution will be difficult and may not even be attempted by certain dissident provinces.

In that speculative case, North America would be left with the unattractive expectation of further fragmentation. It would be left with the possibility that the United States would be forced to contend with a number of small, weak, and fissiparous polities along its northern border. Fragmentation of English Canada, and the accompanying impact upon the economic, political, and security interests of the United States are a daunting hurdle for a country long accustomed to thinking of Canada with a sense of confidence and even impervious assurance.

Quebec separatists sometimes argue that political pluralism would not be affected if Quebec separated. All that would change is that there would be two polities instead of one. They also claim that just as minorities in Quebec are now treated liberally, so they would be after separation. Even if all this were true, however, democratic pluralism would face two large challenges.

First, the only reason Quebec would separate is to mollify those who want to distance their own culture from that of English Canada. This act is an overt challenge to democratic pluralism in North America, since democratic pluralism seeks to allow each culture to flourish in harmony within the federal framework of a single democracy. Second, by separating, Quebec could destroy the remainder of Canada inasmuch as English Canada itself might succumb to excessive strain. Thus political pluralism would once again suffer a terrible political blow.

But if these thoughts are troubling to Americans, equally troubling to Canadians is the thought that Americans are thinking these thoughts.

In the *Washington Post*, Howard Schneider noted that, with the publication of 'Will Canada Unravel?' in the fall 1996 issue of *Foreign Affairs*, 'U.S. academics have begun divining the not-necessarily-rosy look of post-separation Canada.'[1] In *The Chronicle-Journal*, Bogdan Kipling called the essay 'a bone-chilling article on Canada's likely future if Quebec separatists succeed.'[2] 'For Canadians,' explained Graham Fraser, former Washington correspondent for *The Globe and Mail*, 'this kind of discussion is unnerving. As in any family fight, one prefers not to have the neighbours holding meetings to discuss what separation and divorce might do to property values on the street.'[3]

Indeed, according to the Canadian Press, the *Foreign Affairs* article was a factor in precipitating the September 25, 1996, Congressional Committee hearings on Quebec separation.[4] Andrew Phillips of *Maclean's* attributes to the sponsor of those hearings, Congressman Tom Campbell (Republican, California), the worry 'that if Quebec separates from Canada, the North American Free Trade Agreement might be put in jeopardy – and the United States might see its most important trading partner disintegrate into a string of weak and squabbling states.'[5] Anthony De Palma of *The New York Times* recognized that the strong reaction of Canadians to the Congressional hearing was nonetheless ultimately positive for the country. 'Having the unraveling of Canada laid out in a Washington hearing room, Professor Watkins [of the University of Toronto] said, made Canadians pay attention in a way they never would have if the same arguments had been made in Ottawa.'[6]

In fact, some of the Canadian reactions only proved the validity of the questions raised. Fern Callan responded on line to the article on 'Globe: Canada's National Web Site,' published in the *National Issues Forum*, in which he asserts, 'I believe strongly that the Western provinces would balk at membership in a new Canada, half of whose population would be located in Ontario.'[7] George Bain, in *The Globe and Mail*, interpreted the article for Canadians with an ominous spin:

> Having lived in the United States for many years, I can read between the lines in Prof. Doran's article. He says clearly that if Canada breaks up, no overseas third parties will be permitted to destabilize U.S. security interests in the region; that Canada had better get its act together and realize that, inevitably, the rules will change; and that what the U.S. put up with previously in relation to independent Canadian international political moves will change. It would be better for the remaining parts of Canada—the Rest of Canada (ROC)—to work out a sensible political and economic system to deal with the situation, including trade, security, political and economic relations with the U.S. under a new system of regional affiliation. If that can't be done, the U.S. will accept applications for statehood from a few provinces and the rest can go fish on their political and economic own.[8]

Outside Canada, from the *International Herald Tribune* to *Die Frankfurter Allgemeine*, and from *The New York Times* to *The Washington Post*, 'Will Canada Unravel?' was weighed, dissected, and examined. Inside Canada, in some twenty newspaper articles and nearly as many talk shows on Canadian radio and television (in addition to quite a number of news shows in the United States), the *Foreign Affairs* piece was digested and scrutinized.[9] By scrutinizing the arguments of the article, Canadians could finally confront the question they understandably did not want to ask.

In a vigorous response, Thomas d'Aquino, president of the Business Council for National Issues, Canada's association of large national and multinational firms and banks, argued that Canada could prosper and remain fused even after Quebec separation, though secession was held to be of extremely low probability.[10] In contrast, 'the essential problem Canada would face if they tried to keep their country going without Quebec,' said *The Globe and Mail* Ottawa correspondent Jeffrey Simpson, is the so-called Ontario problem, that is, what to do with the overweening size and power of a single province among the remaining eight.[11]

Columnist Gordon Gibson saw the theme and purpose of the article as a 'wake-up call' for Canada, to roust the polity out of complacence.[12] A wake-up call it was, but it and the subsequent Congressional hearing were also something else. From the American perspective, Canada's former Ambassador to the United States, Allan Gotlieb, perhaps got to the heart of U.S. concerns most directly: 'One cannot fault U.S. policy-makers,' he said, 'for exploring these issues and seeking to prepare the U.S. for what some may view as an increasingly likely outcome.'[13]

This chapter examines the proposition that if Quebec secedes, Canada would need to reconstitute itself. What issues could strain the continued political integrity of the rest of Canada?

Geographical Isolation of the Atlantic Provinces

If Quebec secedes, the Atlantic provinces will feel a sense of geographic and psychological isolation that they perhaps cannot now imagine or envision.[14] A foreign country will separate them from the rest of English Canada. While Quebec would probably be quick to honour all treaties with its new neighbours, and would facilitate transportation and communication across its borders, residents from the Atlantic provinces would nonetheless need to cross a foreign country to reach Ontario. This would mean, at a minimum, customs and immigration checks, separate rules for taxes and currency usage, and a host of arrangements to fly over or drive around Quebec if it chooses to exercise its autonomy in various, plausible ways. But would geographic isolation necessarily lead to a thorough-going sense of social-psychological isolation?

West Berlin lived for four decades removed from West Germany. Canada itself separates Alaska from the 'lower 48.' Various island groupings around the world are divided from mainland counterparts by wide oceans. Surely the sense of social-psychological isolation in these instances was or is sufferable. Perhaps the Atlantic provinces, after being severed from the remainder of Canada, would experience no greater trauma than have these entities.

Yet the difficulty of identifying countries whose territories have actually been physically divided by the secession of a subunit with a different language and culture is an indicator of how rare such a political occurrence is. At present the international system is composed of more than 180 countries. Only a few of these countries have divided territories. There are no examples of countries in which a newly created territorial subunit emerges as a separate polity, thus shearing off one section of a country's territory from that of another.[15]

Countries are like atoms. They obviously are for the most part 'hard, irreducible units.' States cohere around territory and a population. They do not break up easily. When atoms break up, or fuse, they tend to do so explosively. States, like atoms, may break up according to the rules of a peaceful, stable 'chain reaction.' But such a process requires a facility or framework in which to contain that reaction. The stable process of break up for the state requires that 'machinery of government' be in place both for the subunit leaving the polity and for the divided remnants of the polity that must struggle to hold together.

All of this suggests that the Atlantic provinces must overcome any crisis of identity that might result from a sense of territorial isolation after Quebec secession. Of course Quebec is likely to quickly shore up communications and transportation links, and would likely try to miti- gate the sense of territorial isolation felt by the Atlantic provinces. But the reality of physical estrangement from Ontario and the rest of English Canada could not be easily erased or banished.

At a minimum, the Atlantic provinces would face customs rules and passport restrictions, differing tax and currency regulations, and per- haps for a time requirements on content and rules of origin on goods and services that cross Quebec territory.[16] The odds are that Quebec would become disenchanted with the policies of the Bank of Canada and opt for its own currency. All of these actions would tend to remind the Atlantic provinces of their 'loss.'

Loss is at the heart of the difference between the situation in which the Atlantic provinces would find themselves and the situation that Alaska, for example, experiences today. Alaska always was isolated, territorially and politically. The presence of Britain and subsequently Canada did little to accentuate that isolation. When Alaska became a state, something was added, not subtracted. It still remained physically distant from the main body of the United States, but politically and psychologically Alaska was now a full voting member of a polity. Hence much of the strain of separation was actually overcome by state- hood. Alaskans felt no loss, only gain. In contrast, after Quebec seces- sion, the Atlantic provinces would likely experience little gain.

Notwithstanding the violence that took place in the division of East and West Pakistan, this situation provides an example of the difficulty involved in administering a territorially divided polity. The problem of administration stems in part from the fear, by the entity on whose territory the governing authority does not reside, that the more isolated entity will be slighted or even abandoned politically.[17] Conversely, the isolated remnant may feel oppressed or weighed down by an absentee government, as was true for East Pakistan (Bangladesh). The location of the English Canada government would therefore make a great deal of difference to the Atlantic provinces. Yet they could scarcely expect that the government would be located so far eastward as Nova Scotia or New Brunswick, in one of the smaller remnants at that. Apprehension over the location and nature of government in English Canada might create foreboding in the Atlantic provinces.

The Special Case of Newfoundland

How the Atlantic provinces cope with their sense of detachment from English Canada after Quebec separation will be very much affected by the attitude in Newfoundland. Newfoundland is a special case for a number of historical and *sui generis* reasons.

First, Newfoundland joined Confederation quite late, indeed after the Second World War. While individually every Newfoundlander is as loyal to Canada as every other Canadian, the feeling of collective loyalty may not be as great since the tradition of association is not as long.[18] Not as much time has elapsed to develop those symbols and outward expressions of nationhood in comparison to other Canadian provinces, including the three Maritime provinces.

Second, Newfoundland is not among the richest provinces. Its industry is quite narrowly based. Recent problems with the cod fishery seem to be spreading to other fisheries as well.[19] These difficulties give Newfoundlanders fewer 'degrees of freedom' to tolerate uncertainties. Isolation for Newfoundland carries with it a heavy anxiety about economic well-being not experienced to the same degree by other provinces. While commercially viable oil discoveries in the Hibernia fields, for example, or new hydropower developments in Labrador could turn the per capita income situation around quickly, the plunge in the real world price for energy since 1982 reveals the variability of price and the uncertainty of its benefits.[20] Newfoundland remains economically vulnerable, and this vulnerability may cause it to act differently than would its neighbours if Quebec chose to secede.

Third, Newfoundland has always had a perceived affinity for association with the United States. As many as 30 per cent of the voters at the time of Newfoundland accession to Canada preferred admission to the

United States.[21] This same imagined affinity with the United States stands out in contemporary survey results. This attitude on the part of a significant portion of the Newfoundland population is the more remarkable since it has been neither in any way encouraged by Washington nor grounded in any real evidence of political feasibility.

For all of these reasons and more, Newfoundland remains different. How these differences would play out after Quebec separation is very difficult to estimate. But a too-ready assumption that Newfoundland would act just like any other province in English Canada is not supported by contemporary evidence or analysis. Newfoundland could well join the other Atlantic provinces in a common strategy to safeguard the interests of the region. Or, Newfoundland might choose to go its own way, comfortable in the awareness that its situation is unique and therefore that its approach to strategy must be unique. Only one conclusion seems quite well-established based on contemporary polling data and knowledge of the province: Newfoundland is not likely to opt for independent status as a separate polity.

Could the Atlantic Provinces Reconstitute Themselves?

This absorbing question invites both a direct and an indirect response. The direct response is that not only could the Atlantic provinces reconstitute themselves as a single political unit representing the entire region, but such reconstitution could take place with or without the spur of Quebec separation. Although the pride in provincial autonomy and identity is deep in the Atlantic provinces – the history of these affiliations predate Confederation, having their roots in the decades of British colonialism – the people of the Atlantic provinces are also political realists. Given that Prince Edward Island, Nova Scotia or New Brunswick could enhance their bargaining power with Ottawa and with the rest of Canada, the notion of political reconstitution has its defenders. Deep disagreements among these provinces do not exist and hence do not hinder such speculation. Common goals and common vulnerabilities indeed drive the Atlantic provinces to think of themselves as a counterweight to Central Canada and to the West, whether in coalition or as a single political entity.

But the propensity to reconstitute, catalysed by the fear of the aftermath of Quebec separation, is also problematic. Herein lies the indirect response to the proposed question about reconstitution. That such reconstitution is politically possible does not guarantee that it will simplify the task of union after Quebec leaves. As a more powerful, self-confident entity, the Atlantic provinces would demand more of Central Canada. Greater demands would lead to tougher bargaining and more concessions by Ontario and the West. While this outcome might be deemed good for the Atlantic provinces, would the outcome lead to eventual harmony or to greater political conflict within English Canada itself? Much would depend on the mood for compromise. But an angry Ontario and an acrimonious West would not assist the process of compromise, especially in a situation where, reconstituted, the Maritime region now held considerably more bargaining power.

Thus the simple question whether the Atlantic provinces could reconstitute themselves politically leads to a complex answer: It all depends. If a Maritime union did not include Newfoundland, the cause of a united English Canada would not be advanced. Willingness and the capacity to create a single large bargaining unit encompassing all or most of the Maritime region will force the remainder of Canada to take the eastern-most provinces more seriously.[22] But this greater bargaining power for Eastern Canada will not in and of itself lead to harmonious solutions for English Canada or to a way out, if the dreaded day of Quebec independence actually arrives.

'Transfer Payments' Would End

Transfer payments, or equalization payments, are not unique to Canada. Germany has used such payments to foster unification with the former East Germany, although in truth the Federal Republic of Germany has long used such payments inside its own federal structure.[23] Italy, in one of the more famous examples of ongoing one-way transfer payments, has distributed wealth from the Milan-Turin-Bologna triangle of the industrial north to the poor, more agricultural south, the Mezzogiorno.[24] Japan pursues a policy of equalizing many social investments in roads, bridges, and education, often raising the wrath of citizens – they question what plausible outcomes could be obtained on some of the islands where the population is slight and their needs might be described as less great than those in Tokyo. The United States itself possesses a federal policy of redistributing tax proceeds to the states, either as block grants or more specifically, in a pattern of distribution that favours the poorer areas.[25] So Canada is not alone in advocating transfer payments.

In many countries, the efficiency and results of transfer payments seems to be coming under criticism. The effect of this criticism will not eliminate these payments, for that is politically difficult, but will effectively constrain them to the point of irrelevance. Surely the rebellion in Germany over higher taxes for the purposes of subsidizing the 'Osties' is a good example. But even earlier on the question arose whether subsidies to Hamburg and Bremen really did much for reindustrialization in those areas. In Italy, according to Jean-Marie Guehenno, 'the rich Lombards no longer want their tax monies to be wasted in Naples.'[26] Americans are trying to shift the burdens of welfare and education to the states, thus reversing a policy of federal leadership and redistribution first established by Franklin Delano Roosevelt in the 1930s. Critics are asking if the redistribution of funds along geographic lines has resulted in lasting growth and industrial benefits.

As one prominent Toronto banker explained, the problem goes deeper: The problem is that massive transfer payments 'cause corruption.' It is necessary to assess the meaning of this phrase in more detail. By corruption, this head of one of the largest banks in Canada did not mean corruption in the petty, personal sense often attributed to politics and politicians. He did not mean that such redistribution of funds could be used to bribe local officials and undermine public confidence in government. What he meant was a much broader and deeper economic and sociological notion of corruption. For the economists, the problem with transfer payments on a grand scale is that they take money away from areas of greater productivity and give it to areas of lesser productivity, thus slowing the increase in output and overall growth. For sociologists, the problem is that by removing income from areas of greater productivity generated a disincentive to invest in individuals, communities, and firms who might invest wisely and productively according to the signals of the market and do so with vigour and creativity. Most transfer payments end up in consumed income, in projects that are commercially unworkable or that are often not needed (i.e., the famous road to nowhere).

Canada has often touted the distinction between its 'social democracy' and the brand practised south of the border. In the United States, public policy dictates for the most part that people must move to where the jobs are, and they do. The United States is geographically a highly mobile society, as the Sunbelt can attest. In Canada, money is moved to where the people are.[27] In public policy, this assures that people do not abandon frontier areas of development because of loss of social services. While in the abstract each approach seems functional, the human reality is that the former approach, that of the United States, can be harsher and less 'kind.' But conversely, the latter approach is more economically wasteful and less likely to encourage an entrepreneurial spirit.

Transfer Payments as the 'Glue' of Federation

Despite what theorists of social policy may think of transfer payments, these payments have become the glue of federation in Canada. They help hold the country together. It does no good to argue that if such massive payments had not been geographically dispersed, Canada might have evolved an even stronger economic foundation for federation. Canada did not pursue that course. Use of transfer payments is the route that Canadian governments, federal and provincial, have chosen to foster unity. For better or for worse, Canada is now stuck with this preferred instrument of public policy and social integration.

For an external observer, one of the remarkable characteristics of Canadian elections is how shameless voters are in making demands on politicians for dispersements from public funds.[28] Actual lists of public projects are sometimes drawn up and published in local newspapers. On the one hand, this 'upfront' mentality that demands public funds and public services shows that transparency prevails. On the other hand, demands for roads, schools, bridges, subsidized housing, and even the requisite transference of entire industries, suggests how deep the feeling is that people have the right to demand financial benefits from government, and that if a politician resists these attempts, the proper thing is to 'turf him or her out' at election time.

The logic of the transfer payment is then extended to the logic of further political uses of the public purse. In particular, subsidies for the location of firms and public procurement contracts become very politicized in Canada. Ultimately, many of these subsidies and contracts are not won on the basis of low bids or productivity, but on the basis of which community shouts the loudest and can make the greatest claim to make a politician yield. Quebec has established a successful record in these competitions, often very visibly at the cost of the West, which has made its disenchantment with the process audible.

Canada, as well as the western Germans, northern Italians, and southern Americans, has become vocally unhappy with the broad-based use of transfer payments, and the program has come under scrutiny. If net transfers are no longer given to Quebec after separation, the financial cost of transfers might be somewhat lower. For the first time, discussion is taking place, if not about the legitimacy of the transfer process in a social democracy (admittedly a label that is itself challenged by some), then about the comparative size and purpose of the financial transfers overall.

Disincentives to Continue after the Collapse of Confederation

Put very directly, the average citizen living in British Columbia, Alberta, or Ontario may willingly allow himself or herself to be taxed to help others living in Saskatchewan, Manitoba, or Newfoundland under the present need to foster Confederation. But if Confederation collapsed, this same generous citizen might feel quite differently about perpetuating a process that has led to the loss of very large sums of investment monies locally and regionally. In other words, the worldwide trend that is forcing governments to reassess their policies of geographical financial transfers might hit Canada very hard after Quebec secession. Looked at as a justifiable cost of holding Confederation together, financial transfers could become an unacceptable accounting entry once the alleged purpose of those transfers disappears.

But, a critic might object, after Quebec secession the citizens of the ROC, traumatized by the break up of Canada, might be prepared to sacrifice even more for unity than before. Without the transfers to Quebec, the overall bill for transfer payments would decline a little. The departure of Quebec might be just the thing to get the rich provinces to transfer even more money to the poor provinces on behalf of the goal of unity for English Canada. They might. But based on prior experience with this type of attempted unification by public finance, the rich provinces might question the value of this nation-building strategy. Driven by the conservative fiscal attitudes of many in Central and Western Canada, and aware of the broader global re-examination of geographical transfers within polities, English Canadians might by themselves decide to drop the transfer payments altogether.[29] Operating federalism on the basis of 'every tub (province) on its own bottom' could lead to a new sense of self-reliance within English Canada, and a new sense of economic promise for its citizens that would spur economic growth and entrepreneurial initiative for its firms.

Alternatively, English Canada might let transfer payments slide, not so much by collective decision but because those who pay are unwilling to continue under the old rules since the potential of Confederation is unproven. The argument is that transfer payments did not stop Quebec from leaving Confederation. Indeed the critics of the transfer payment scheme will assert that Quebec actually exploited the arrangement for its own advantage, citing Bourassa's 'profitable federalism' tactic as evidence. Yet, they will say, Quebec broke with its Confederation partners anyway.

In reality, transfer payments did provide glue for federation, and that glue may have been quite helpful to hard-pressed policy-makers trying to find some sort of leverage to promote political integration. The tactic may simply have been insufficient, though probably not counterproductive to the goal of unity. Yet those who have to pay may not see the issue this way. They may quite gladly allow the financial transfer idea to sink under its own weight. For those long accustomed to operating social democracy under the rules of transfers in English Canada, this outcome could be devastating to plans for a union of the English-speaking provinces.

Impact on the 'Poor' Provinces

Whether the transfer payment approach dissipates under the pressure of evidence in Italy, Germany, and France where it is not working, or whether after Quebec secession financial transfers are simply dropped by collective fiat of the rich provinces, the consequence could be the same for the poor provinces. They will find themselves in a new commercial and social world that will be less supportive of the services and benefits citizens have grown accustomed to enjoying. Since less satisfied citizens are likely to make their anxieties felt at the ballot box, governments will begin to look around for alternative ways to appease the electorate. Some of these alternatives may involve options other than continued membership in the Rest of Canada.

It would be unfair to accuse the poorer provinces of materialism instead of patriotism. They have grown accustomed to a system of 'equalization' and have come to think of the arrangement as an entitlement, not as a 'perk.' When an entitlement vanishes, bitterness lies in its wake. Provincial governments will feel justified in trying to appease their citizenry in any way they can. These governments will not measure membership in Confederation purely in economic terms, but they will feel exonerated by circumstance if they look for other options once federal transfer payments are withdrawn or slowly disappear.

This scenario suggests that the most loyal provinces to the federal idea are the poorer ones. They have the most to lose from a breakup of Canada. If the transfer payment approach to government erodes, for reasons that may be understandable in economic terms, the political cost could be high.[30] The poorer provinces may be among the first to register their displeasure. If their voice does not yield political results, they may respond with their feet.

Impact on the 'Rich' Provinces

If some of the rich provinces are looking for an opportunity to leave Canada, and that is by no means arguable at this time, transfer payments will be one of their major excuses. They will have economic logic on their side, namely, that transfers move money from potentially more productive (lucrative) locations to less productive locations and uses, but given the experience with Quebec (even though by 1995 the net effect of payments received to taxes paid was ever closer to even for Quebec), they may question whether the political benefits to nation-building are as evident as the proponents of transfers have claimed. If the rest of Canada insists that transfer payments continue, some of the rich provinces may balk. They may use the insistence of others favouring equalization as a justification for 'going it alone.'

No one should underestimate the shock to Canada of Quebec secession. All the standard assumptions about governance will be, like a new deck of cards, thoroughly reshuffled. Some of the rich provinces may, as a condition of their further participation, force an end to equalization. This debate in itself could spawn a crisis. But the more serious crisis would involve the actual decision either to end or not to end the practice of financial transfers. While money as opposed to political principle is divisible, the mood at the time when these matters will have to be resolved may not be particularly supportive of compromise. Some of the rich provinces may decide simply that they have had enough of executive federalism and its main instrument, the equalization payment. Because of their size and wealth, the rich provinces will not only have considerable power with which to make their arguments, but they will also possess the commercial and financial ability to succeed if they decide to pursue more adventurous routes.[31]

Scepter of Disintegration

On the heels of a seriously torn Canada, the Rest of Canada may face a dilemma fostered by the increasingly contentious issue of transfer payments. On the one hand, if English Canada succumbs to economic logic and to the depressing evidence from abroad that the transfer approach is a failure, and allows the transfer approach to dissipate, the cost will be felt most immediately by the poor provinces. Like loose bricks in a well-mortared wall, the poor provinces may for this reason, in combination with other reasons, tumble out of Confederation.[32]

On the other hand, if English Canada refuses to consider ending transfers, some of the rich provinces, now seemingly exempt from the accusation that their action was the cause of the breakup of Canada, may decide to seek alternatives to a confederation of the English-speaking provinces. Ironically, the harder the proponents of an English-Canadian union push, the more reluctant some of these more conservative provinces may be to accept the argument that a continuation of transfer payments is good for the ROC. During such an intense debate, the hesitant provinces may decide to remove themselves from the pressures of having to resolve yet one more contentious matter. They may simply opt out.

Caught in this dilemma of transfer payments, a dilemma going to the very heart of governance in a social democracy, Canada ought to examine the alternatives in advance so as to forestall an outcome that no one in North America outside Quebec wants to visit. Otherwise such an outcome, for reasons that hurt the poor provinces or compel the rich ones, could lead to further unravelling.

Effervescence of 'Western Alienation'

Myth lives in the public mind. Like news, bad political myth travels faster and lasts longer. This appears to be so for Canada. Canada has a rough time creating and perpetuating good, helpful political myth. But a myth such as that of Western alienation seems to generate itself.

Western alienation is social symptom for a lot of ills, some real, many imagined, that are experienced, believed, and mostly felt by Canadians living from Winnipeg to the Pacific. Cosmopolitan Winnipeg itself may be somewhat exempt from this malady, though surely rural Manitoba is not. Hence Winnipeg is identified more with Central Canada than with the West, per se. But as a Winnipeg resident once explained to me, Western alienation is all about the reality, and perhaps more about the fear, of being skimmed and exploited.

The villain in this melodrama is Central Canada, explicitly, Toronto. The victim is quintessentially the prairie farmer but has since become anyone living in the Western region. To comprehend Western alienation, one must delve into the tradition of prairie radicalism that produced the short-lived Progressive Party and Social Credit, the CCF (the forerunner of the NDP), and the Reform Party (now the Canadian Alliance).[33] To capture the nuance fully, one must distinguish, for example, the right wing of the NDP that is fundamentally Western and agrarian from the left wing that is often identified with the Toronto labour movement and European socialism. The two wings are very different yet contained within a single party, but this is perhaps less so since the rise of the Reform Party.

Party politics is born of political attitudes. How these political attitudes came to be is an issue that should not be removed from the larger North American movements involving political reform. Prior to 1896, American populism dominated the political landscape of reform. Populism expressed in the rural rejection of banks, Wall Street, railroad rates, and urban values contained many biases and social explanations that often turned out to be spurious.[34] Subsequently, populism was transformed into the great urban progressive movement in the United States. Women's suffrage, anti-trust legislation, and the progressive income tax, for example, also resulted, in part, from these movements.

In Canada it is this same sense of being left out, of being dominated, that has catalysed Western alienation in Canada. At the same time, a similar readiness to propose and accept political reform underlies the Western Canadian sense of grievance. Western alienation has a rich North American tradition of reaction and reform to back it up.

History and the Present

In the past, Westerners had grievances related to railroad rates, tariffs, financing of enterprise, and a perception of exploitation by Central Canada.[35] For commodity producers in areas where distances were great, transportation was paramount. Sir John A. Macdonald built the cross-continental railroad and, abetted by the patronage, the Conservative Party. He also introduced the National Policy, the core of which was a tariff initially called a revenue tariff.

Westerners joined Confederation and were linked to the rest of Canada through the nation's umbilical cord, the railroad. Not surprisingly, the rates charged for the hauling of wheat became a highly politicized matter. On the one hand, the railroad had a monopoly and could charge what it liked, thus embittering the Western farmer in the nineteenth century. The railroad also imposed certain rules such as the requirement that a farmer had to purchase space in an entire boxcar.[36] Elevators, the local storage area for wheat, became controversial middlemen in the struggle to market wheat and transport it.

On the other hand, not only did the farmer demand regulation of fees through government controls, but he also demanded subsidies from the government. Hence the battle over the railroad rates raged for decades, even into the era of the modern highway when alternative transportation would relieve, through economic competition, some of the pressure to intervene in the marketplace. For the farmer, however, the railroad became the symbol of assumed deprivation, not of salvation.

Similarly, the West felt inflamed over the imposition of the Canadian external tariff, which was supposed to be a nation-building device (in addition, it raised necessary revenue in the era prior to the income tax).[37] Nation-building was to occur in two ways. First, the tariff would force foreign investors to set up shop in Canada if they wanted to sell in the domestic Canadian market. American-based firms were obligated to start up manufacturing operations in Canada to service that market directly instead of supplying it with consumer goods produced in the United States. Hence the emergence of the 'branch plant' Canadian economy.[38]

Second, the tariff intended to build Canada through encouraging the establishment of indigenous industry. In the 'infant industry' theory, young industries were to be protected until they became mature enough to stand on their own two feet.[39] Then the protection was to be removed. Economists, however, rightly suspected that the protection would not be removed, either because the protection actually prevented the industry from maturing or because the industry was powerful enough politically to claim protection beyond the time that it was needed. The external tariff succeeded in strengthening the industrial base in Toronto and Montreal, although industrialization anywhere in Canada was to receive the same protection. However, Canadian industry seldom became efficient enough to compete successfully in world markets. Later dubbed the theory of import-substitution, the external tariff led to results that were often derided for the inefficiency of the indigenous Canadian industry and for the high level of foreign ownership.

Clearly not all of Canada benefited equally. The agricultural areas, for example, did not benefit since they were forced to 'buy dear.' 'Tariff policy – as it was specifically designed to do – diverted to the provinces of Ontario and Quebec much of the demand for the machinery, tools, hardware, articles of leather, clothing, and home furnishings which would otherwise have been supplied by American manufacturers.'[40]

For example, the Canadian farmer was expected to buy a Massey-Ferguson tractor manufactured in Central Canada instead of buying a John Deere or an International Harvester of equivalent quality manufactured abroad at a lower price. The foreign tractor carried a hefty import tariff on top of the lower price tag. Since the West was mostly agricultural, the residents quickly developed a conspiracy theory that alleged the neglect of their own interests in the overall national scheme of economic priorities.

Third, the major Canadian banks, which were headquartered in Montreal and Toronto, enforced strict financial terms that hampered the western agricultural base. The banks, for example, insisted on payment of loans at the time of harvesting, thus forcing farmers to sell their crops immediately rather than waiting for a higher price in the future.[41] Westerners were convinced, as were the American populists, that the banks did not understand agriculture, charged excessive interest rates, and favoured manufacturing industry in Central Canada over industrial enterprise in Calgary or Regina.

Fourth, Westerners came to think of Central Canada as manager and ultimate decision maker in all matters. News reporting came from Central Canada. Most services were provided out of offices in Toronto. Even decisions in the scheduling of a professional musician's performances, it was said, were made in Toronto rather than in Edmonton or Vancouver. Western Canada felt about Central Canada as Central Canada felt about the United States, or as most of the United States felt about New York City. Yet in the case of the Canadian West, these passions were much stronger than anywhere else.

Two developments clinched the attitude of the West towards Central Canada before the proposed separation of Quebec from the rest of Canada reached its apex. One was the National Energy Program that attempted to tell Westerners how and where to drill for oil and at what price (what 'the Oil Patch' termed 'political drilling'). The NEP epitomized Eastern arrogance and manipulation in the minds of citizens living in Alberta, Saskatchewan, and British Columbia.[42] The second was the development of federal government procurement and investment policies that seemed to favour Quebec over the West, regardless of cost efficiency or productivity. These policies symbolized the frustration the West felt with Confederation.

Lamentably, neither Quebec nor Ontario nor Ottawa paid heed to this growing distrust and frustration. For example, during the sixteen years of the Trudeau era, political representation was such that the protests of the West could be ignored. Most federal governments could be elected on the votes of those living in the populous provinces of Ontario and Quebec. That was the political reality which provoked a certain amount of Eastern diffidence.

Fantasy or Reality?

What troubles the rational analyst of politics is how to understand that, although the grounds for many of these grievances have for the most part since disappeared, the bitterness and imagined hurt continues to fester in the West.[43] The tariffs died with NAFTA. The railroads occupy a very small place in the prosperity of the Western economy today and the cooperatives, Wheat Boards, and government institutions have eliminated bias. Capital markets have been open for many years. Still the mythology of neglect and political abuse lives on in the popular mind of the West.

Indeed, fantasy generally seems a more important motivational device than reality in the mobilization of public opinion. Fantasy is subject to any schema and will fill any mould the politician wishes to use. Conversely, opposition to fantasy is very difficult to craft and disseminate. Thus Ottawa faces a situation in which the more it pleads reality, the less the Westerner is pledged to listen. In the view of many hardcore Canadian Alliance voters, for instance, the more Ottawa attempts to correct the record, the more it does not 'get the message.'[44]

As long as public policy continues to provide grounds for irritation, the West's suspicions of the East's treachery is reinforced. As long as the West remains disenfranchised through restricted political representation in cabinets – which is much the result of the West's own doing in terms of how it votes at the federal level – fantasy expands and rational political discussion, as seen from the perspective of Ottawa, recedes.

The very fact that the Canadian Alliance Party had had such difficulty becoming a national party reveals the paralysis that both Westerners and the federal government found themselves in. Becoming the Official Opposition should have assuaged much of this anxiety. But the gap between opposing and governing only seemed to be the wider. Perhaps, as was often discussed, a union between the Canadian Alliance and Conservative Parties would change all of this.

In contemporary terms, the plights that the Westerner describes is a legacy of the past rather than a reality. In that sense, the federal government must cope with how myth-making and fantasy affect present policy.[45] The fact that reality does not correspond to asserted political claims does not make the task of the federal government any easier. Ottawa is fighting history while trying to make contemporary policy that is fair to all Canadians and in the interest of the polity as a whole. But the West, regardless of which political party is in power at the federal level, is in no mood to give Ottawa the benefit of the doubt.

BC and Alberta, or BC without Alberta?

From the perspective of national unity, the issue of whether Westerners see themselves as united or apart is an interesting speculation. From the vantage point of the East, the West sometimes looks as though it is speaking the same political language of protest and reform. The success of the early Reform Party and the Canadian Alliance electorally only serves to confirm this Eastern impression. According to this view, Alberta and British Columbia might act in tandem to determine whatever fate English Canada may face if Quebec secedes.

In practice, this tandem interpretation means that BC and Alberta could form their own country, featuring a Pacific focus and a strong commodity-oriented economy. Wedged between parts of the United States, this BC-Alberta fragment would enjoy an opening on the Pacific Ocean, a first-class port, easy access to western U.S. markets, and a very rich foundation in per capita income. It would continue to attract immigrants, Asians perhaps first of all. To describe this region as the 'Biafra' (i.e., the rich, separatist province of Nigeria) of Canada is for many reasons disingenuous, although the petroleum-based economy is a genuine feature of Western politics. Together, British Columbia and Alberta could prosper economically, just as the Quebec economy could do so, given the right political leadership. But the real question is whether Alberta and British Columbia have much more in common than their resentment of Ottawa.

The closer these two significant Western provinces are examined, the clearer the differences in attributes and orientations become.[46] British Columbia has a political constituency that, like Alberta, is strongly affected by populism. But the BC constituency is also very split in left-right terms and regularly elects governments that by the standards of the rest of Canada, are a bizarre blend of reform and welfare proponents. Alberta is more uniformly conservative in the American rather than the Canadian sense of favouring small government and private sector leadership. While both provinces are commodity-oriented, the respective commodities produced and hence the character of each economy is quite different. British Columbia is the centre of the mining and timber industries. Alberta is a petroleum-based and ranch economy. Both provinces are making large strides towards a manufacturing and service orientation.

In sum, Alberta and British Columbia retain a unique ethos, politically, economically, and socially. Although this ethos increasingly distinguishes itself from the rest of Canada, it is not becoming any more homogeneous in Western terms. If anything, the ethos of each province is becoming more self-contained and more expressive of its own outlook on things Canadian. Thus British Columbia and Alberta are as likely to make independent decisions about the future of Canadian unity as they are to make in-tandem decisions. They could each remain in union after Quebec secession. Or, they could each decide their own fate in some other way. The myth of a common Western house is not well-formulated.[47] The mountains continue to be a factor in the social and political evolution of each province. Historical unfolding affects them in different ways. Alberta and British Columbia are rapidly shaping a political-cultural vision that corresponds to the determinants of their own individual population and territorial space.

The West Digs in Its Heels

Western political alienation has left one enduring result for contemporary Canadian politics. The West is obdurate in its attitude towards Quebec.[48] It suspects Quebec of concealing independence under its demands for greater political autonomy. It refuses to yield on the question of Quebec 'distinctness' except in a symbolic way for at least two reasons: (1) because Quebec is alleged to be no more unique in its French culture than the First Nations, for example, are in theirs, and (2) because the separatists are accused of planning to use the distinctness clause to widen their powers legally at the expense of the West and of the rest of English Canada. The West has supported First Minister decisions concerning the label 'unique society,' but the Calgary Declaration is signed by neither Quebec nor the federal government. Westerners are proud of a Canada that includes Quebec, but they are wary of granting any more political concessions – they want no further unilateral benefits given to Quebec. All of this makes negotiations by the federal government extremely awkward.

The 'Ontario Problem'

Former *Globe and Mail* columnist Jeffrey Simpson coined the phrase the 'Ontario problem' to describe the political situation that would occur in the aftermath of Quebec secession. Ontario, already the most populous and largest province economically, would tower over the remainder of English Canada, leaving the rest of the English-speaking provinces in subordination.[49] There are at least two scenarios that could emerge from this lopsided dominance by Ontario.

Passive Acceptance of Hegemony Might Result

Since the hegemony (i.e., domination) by Ontario would occur peacefully and involuntarily, the argument could be made that the other provinces, already shocked by the departure of Quebec, would accept the outcome as the price of harmony within the ROC. The logic here is that it would be safer to patch up differences rather than aggravate them and risk further unravelling. Many tasks would preoccupy the provincial governments to maintain their relationships not only among themselves but with Quebec and the United States. Preoccupation with the exigent but unromantic problems of continued governance, and with an external world that understandably would be regarded as challenging, might discourage disgraceful behaviour and facilitate productive internal communication. Fear of the ultimate upset might mellow dissatisfaction and promote necessary compromise.

Second, hegemony of Ontario within the ROC could be politically advantageous to the other provinces. If they saw fit to continue transfer payments and to retain the prior elements of the social contract, Ontario could act as the principle dispenser of economic benefit. Ontario would also possess the political weight to mediate disputes among the remaining units, both in terms of the benefits and the penalties that it might extend. Ontario hegemony might also benefit the ROC in its dealings with outside parties. Ontario alone ranks as one of the largest trading partners of the United States worldwide. It would continue to be Quebec's second largest trading partner and source of investment. The solidity and visibility of Ontario could strengthen the ROC in its internal and external political dealings.

Third, a confident and dominant Ontario should be in a frame of mind to compromise on matters that are central to the unity of the emerging federation. Benign hegemons have historically been more willing than other powers to 'take a long view' and provide unilateral concessions.[50] This farsightedness could lend stability to the new federation. Among Ontario and the other English-speaking provinces, familiar pathways of negotiation ought to be helpful in working out compromise. Even when the remaining members see themselves in a position of dependence, a confident centre possesses a very great institutional advantage in a world that is uncertain.

Or, Trouble over a New Constitution

On the other hand, demands for a political reconstitution of Canada after Quebec secession could overwhelm the common-sense business-as-usual preference. Not only would it be reeling from the departure of Quebec, the ROC would also be forced to face difficult matters of constitution-making. Much as it might like to avoid these continuing disputes, the ROC may find itself a prisoner of its history and the reality of state-building.

First, we need to understand the present-day situation. The dominance of Ontario is currently offset by the existence of Quebec. Ontario needs the other provinces in all matters involving Quebec. Central Canada is not unified, except perhaps at election time and then not always. This makes decision making within Ottawa's highly centralized institutions bearable for the other provinces. There is always some balancing of power that goes on inside Central Canada. Depending upon the issue, the balance shifts. To some extent the other members of the federation can play Ontario off against Quebec, and vice versa. Ottawa does not represent a single cohesive block of votes against which the other premiers at First Ministers' Conferences and elsewhere have negligible impact. Undoubtedly the other provincial governments would like even more power vis-à-vis Ottawa, and its assumed surrogate Central Canada, but at present they exercise at least occasional power.

In general, the provinces in Canada act as a counterweight to federal power. Lacking a Parliament that is an effective check on the power of the prime minister (except under the unusual circumstance of a loss of confidence vote, rarely exercised where party discipline is so high), the provinces, and more explicitly, the premiers, act as power brokers. But with Quebec gone, all of this would change.

Power would then be centralized in a single place, Ontario.[51] The other English-speaking provinces could not find room to manoeuvre between Ottawa and Ontario. Nor would the provinces as a group be as able to balance federal power. Unless Parliament itself devised a check on the power of the prime minister, unlikely during the turmoil of Quebec's departure, he or she would become even more dominant. Thus after Quebec secession, the Maritimes and Western Canada would face a polity with a single controlling economic and political centre, Ontario, and a federal government in which few if any offsets to the institutional predominance of the prime minister existed. This is not an institutional situation which Western Canada and the Maritimes would accept without a level of acrimony not yet witnessed in Canada.

Second, given this institutional situation of core dominance, the outlying provinces are likely to demand a reconstitution of political powers. But would Ontario be prepared to reform federal political institutions? Ontario would be required to give power up. To yield power is not a natural institutional response for any government. Political realism declares such power transfer impossible.[52] Idealist theory suggests that the acceding of power is possible but not easy.

The difficulty is not that a gap would exist between power and role and that this gap must be closed. The difficulty is not that Ontario's role would somehow exceed its power, so that its role must be cut down to size. The difficulty is much more profound: Ontario would be obligated to give up power itself. Then its role could be altered while retaining congruence between its reduced power and its commensurately diminished role. It would become less visible. This more circumscribed role would be more compatible with the interests of the other members of the ROC. But this exercise in the reduction of unilateral power in order not to offend other federation members is not an exercise with many historical precedents.

Even if members of the Ontario government were prepared to contemplate such unilateral concessions, the voting public might find this option threatening and unacceptable. They might instead hold the government of Ontario and Ottawa itself accountable to the typical historical standard. To those who want Ontario to voluntarily and unilaterally give up power so as to make its political role in the ROC less dominant, a shaken Ontario electorate might indicate that they would have to force Ontario to do so, and that they instead should look inward to increase their own positions of relative power.

Third, an adjustment of functions and capabilities would not just involve Ontario. Alberta and British Columbia would need to be prepared to forsake some of their long-standing goals as well if Ontario proved adamant about retaining its position in federation. These two provinces might have to contemplate giving up their cherished goal of an elected and co-equal senate. Such a model works in the United States, for example, because there is no state that dominates all others in terms of size and power. California may control some 25 per cent of the electoral votes, but it is effectively counterbalanced by other large states such as New York, Texas, Pennsylvania, Florida, and Ohio that are widely distributed geographically. Tiny population states such as Rhode Island and North Dakota are tolerable in a federation of fifty states where their disproportionately small size is not so noticeable or bothersome.

Alternatively, English Canada might have to contemplate not aggregation of power such as has been casually discussed for the Maritimes, but the further disaggregation of power into units smaller than the present size of most provinces. But surely if Ontario were expected to undergo this form of downsizing, then Alberta and British Columbia would be required to do some of the same. Yet the thought of this option probably holds few attractions for regions that are not envisioning a reduction or diffusion in their power but an appreciable increase in their prestige and authority within Confederation.

Fourth, throughout these negotiations and strategic undertakings, the ROC would need to discourage defections. It could not tolerate attempts to make side deals, to create separate polities, or to partition city-states. It most certainly would want to discourage overtures to the United States for statehood, however protracted such a process of application for any candidate would be. The ROC could not allow itself, or any of its members, to become distracted by rival schemes for satisfying citizen demands outside the framework of agreed federation.

In short, resolution of the 'Ontario problem' could lead in either of two directions. The shock of Quebec secession could induce governments and their public to be more reasonable. It could encourage them to compromise and postpone demands for fundamental constitutional change until a later date when the polity would be stronger and better able to cope with the tension and bargaining necessary to forge a new and lasting agreement. Hegemony of Ontario could be regarded as positive and helpful in the internal dealings of the ROC and the external dealings with other polities. Ontario itself could rise to this occasion for leadership and yield on matters that other provinces found important. A homogeneous polity could also benefit from the greater centralization of economic and political authority within the ROC to the advantage of all of the members.

On the other hand, the event of Quebec secession could begin the unravelling. English Canada could become aware of the increased dominance of Ontario, the loss of Quebec as a political counter-weight, the inability of the provinces together to act as an adequate balancer to the authority of the prime minister, and the reality of their own relative weakness and dependence upon what was left of Central Canada. Some of the provinces might make demands on Ontario to devolve some of its power. But this request would be for a unilateral devolution. Whether Ontario would accede to such demands or, given its internal political situation, could accede is a question not easily answered. Such yielding to the demands of others would involve not just the concession of political role, it would also involve the giving up of power. Governments find the voluntary abdication of power very difficult. But perhaps, given the gravity of the situation, history will not be a deterrent or a precedent.

British Columbia and Alberta would need great poise and self-restraint. They would need to compromise on primary values, including the demand for a freely elected and co-equal senate. They would face the possibility that Ontario would not or could not yield power unilaterally. They ought to consider other alternatives, too. Broad-based division of the provinces including their own into smaller political units might facilitate the move towards a senate that was a viable offset to the parliamentary lower house. Sharing of federal authority with the provinces would not take place quickly. In the end, power might be dispersed from a very strong centre, but it is not likely to be downgraded or appreciably diminished.

Meanwhile all of the provinces would need to agree to disagree without bolting federation. They must obligate themselves to forego visions of independence. They would undermine union if they began to make side deals among themselves for regional arrangements separate from the ROC. Exploratory initiatives with Washington by individual provinces would be unhelpful at a time when Ottawa was trying to strengthen the ROC and attempting to reconstitute itself. Such distractions would only serve to undermine the confidence of the other provinces in Ottawa's ability to forge a new, more durable union.

Contending with the 'Ontario problem,' however, is essential to the sustained unity of English-speaking Canada. Denial will not lead to success. Recognition that there are ways to resolve the problem in such a fashion as to reinforce federation is the first step to political reconstitution inside a new and quite different set of institutional arrangements.

The North American Crucible

Unravelling of English Canada, in the opinion of some analysts, began with the creation of the U.S–Canada Free Trade Agreement.[53] This trade agreement severed the East–West ties that had held Canada together since the advent of Sir John A. Macdonald's National Policy. According to these analysts, the beginning of free trade with the United States was the beginning of Canada's collapse. This interpretation, however, is wrong on two counts. First, free trade does not exist between any of the North American trading partners in any complete way. Inside the North American Free Trade Agreement, for example in the automobile and textiles sectors, substantial non-tariff barriers still remain in place. The best that can be said for trade liberalization is that it has moved these countries towards freer trade.

Second, if Canada collapses, and that is at this point in history far from a likely contention, the cause will not be the lowering of tariffs between Canada and the United States. Surely after more than a century and quarter of existence, Canada is held together with more than the bonds of tariff construction, especially since the lifting of tariffs has spurred economic growth everywhere in Canada and has eliminated a crucial grievance that Western Canadians had associated with union.

But how strong is the North–South pull? What are the effects of external relations on the capacity of a polity to cohere?[54] To what extent is the integration within a polity the result of forces that are unique to a specific historical interval, and the result of the impact of *external* relations upon a polity, regardless of interval? These questions, which are discussed in the next chapter, are directly related to the theme of this chapter and to the overall book.

North America is the crucible in which the Canadian identity melds. It is changing rapidly, not so much because of NAFTA but because of multinational firms whose push towards economic rationalization and globalization impinged strongly on the North American economic base and made NAFTA a necessity. But Canada, the United States, and Mexico had a choice. They could try to ignore these economic trends while the rest of the world made the necessary trade, financial, and commercial adjustments and thus reaped the bulk of the benefits. Or,

they could stay abreast of worldwide changes in technological application and in production and benefit from a higher growth rate in job-
creation and revenue-generation. Most Canadians and Americans
thought this was not a choice at all but a previously determined economic conclusion.

There is an easy way to minimize any conceivable damage should
the unravelling of Canada have anything to do with the North–South
pull. That would be to implement the recommendations of another
Macdonald, Donald Macdonald of the Commission that carries his
name. The Commission's recommendations were that all tariff and
non-tariff barriers among the provinces should be reduced to zero so
that the East–West flow of goods and services would occur unimpeded.[55] Despite the glacial pace of closure on the Agreement on Internal Trade (AIT), the economic vitality of Canada would thus be
bolstered even in the face of increased North–South trade and financial
movement. This notion, so obvious in its policy purpose, is not so simple to implement in practice. But the proper antidote to the alleged disease of 'North Americanness' that affects Canada is to apply the
medicine recommended by the Macdonald Commission. Perhaps
because this medicine has not yet been applied in full dose, the patient
is not sure that he or she is really ill. In the age of preventive medicine,
the Commission's recommendations sound prudent and discerning.

For various reasons, the possibility that English Canada could unravel
should Quebec secede is not publicly discussed. American government officials are reluctant to treat political hypotheticals, certainly for
the record. Rather than encounter an unpleasant scenario in advance,
English Canada prefers to postpone tough questions in hopes that they
will go away or never be visited. Separatist advocates in Quebec realize that one of the three 'alarm bells' for them, as far as the Quebec
public is concerned, is the admission that Quebec secession would
break up the rest of Canada. The Quebec public does not want to feel
responsible for that catastrophe. Parenthetically, the other two unmen-
tionables in the separatist movement are loss of Quebec territory due
to partition, and the lack of Quebec's automatic entry into NAFTA,
regarded as essential to the economic survival of an independent Quebec.

So the possible unravelling of English Canada in the aftermath of
Quebec separation is the topic not discussed in polite diplomatic conversation. And yet this collective repression of a potential reality does
no service to a calm and harmonious resolution of a problem that may

eventually confront North America. Better to get that potential reality out before the publics in each of the impacted domains, so that rational discussion can properly weigh outcomes and options.

It is well to call to mind the situation in the former Czechoslovakia.[56] Elites in the Slovak region pressed hard for separation and were finally given it by the Czechs, only to discover in opinion polls subsequent to independence that the Slovak public would have preferred to stay inside the Czechoslovak union! Not thinking through all of the repercussions of a political action can have unpleasant, and unsuspected, consequences for each of the affected actors.

Likewise, thinking through options in advance eliminates simplistic arguments about not having to deal with Quebec or of pushing Quebec out of Confederation because English Canada could 'go it alone' in any case. Such anti-Quebec arguments are not helpful, as this analysis is meant to demonstrate.

The argument made here is that, if Quebec leaves, English Canada will face tough difficulties regarding continued union. At a minimum, there are four key difficulties: (1) overcoming the sense of geopolitical and psychological isolation of the Atlantic provinces stemming from their abrupt severance from and loss of proximity to the rest of Canada; (2) coping with the discarding of transfer payments by governments no longer confident in the therapeutic value of these payments for union and far more aware of the financial costs; (3) managing the sense of Western alienation that continues to shape attitudes towards Central Canada and the federal government; and (4) dealing forthrightly with the 'Ontario problem,' created by its economic and political dominance at a time when other regions of Canada are demanding an end to dependence and to hierarchical decision making within Confederation. Responding effectively to these challenges is a tall order.

The respective provinces must be willing to countenance a political reconstitution of English Canada on a scale and with a flexibility that will encompass many political concerns postponed during the long interregnum of debate concerning the role of Quebec. Yet political exhaustion, combined with understandable testiness, will make the resurrection of many of these issues painful to the point of rejection. Still, the issues will not go away by themselves. English Canada will need to summon the intellectual and social-psychological strength to bargain in good faith and to persevere.

At risk will be the very idea of a union of English-speaking provinces. Individual provinces must forego the temptation to consider 'going it alone,' to separate themselves from counterparts with which they have significant political disagreements. They will be obliged to abandon notions of application for statehood with the United States. Nor will the partitioning of city-states be helpful to the goal of a united English Canada.

Language and culture make a difference to Quebec. Perhaps these same commonalities will work to keep English-speaking Canada together. Yet Canada has long been tolerant of linguistic and cultural difference.[57] None of this ought to be jeopardized in the search for a political formula that ensures continued unity. Canada in all of its aspects must retain the qualities and the governance that, in many UN polls on the subject, have ranked it as one of the most attractive countries in the contemporary world to live.

CHAPTER FIVE

Is Separatism Home-Grown or the Result of Contagion?

In world terms, is cultural nationalism on the increase or on the decrease, and why? This chapter examines this question in the context of another question. Is secession, which is often the product of cultural nationalism, largely a home-grown phenomenon? Or is secession a product of ideas, influences, interactions, and information that are imported from abroad, the international system itself becoming the catalyst for secession? Perhaps the international system acts as a constraint in certain periods of history in the context of a given structure, and as a catalyst in other periods of history in the context of a different configuration. As the number of leading states, their identity, and their capacity for coordination within the central system changes, perhaps the propensity for secession ebbs and flows as well.

Some writers such as Jean-Marie Guehenno, Kenichi Ohmae, Richard Rosecrance, and Stanley Hoffmann contend that nationalism is dead. They see the nation-state dissolving under pressure from the solvents of regionalism, the movement of global capital, the decline of political ideology, and the changing nature of the firm as it erodes the sovereignty of government. Yet others, like Martin van Creveld and historian William McNeill, see nationalism as alive and even virulent. They describe this nationalism as demotic, that is, a nationalism emerging from below, from inside the subunits of society. They see immigration and labour mobility charging this demotic nationalism with new energy.[1]

In some ways these two interpretations are not opposites. They seem to suggest the same end. Old established nation-states have become enfeebled. New and vibrant national movements are emerging from below to further weaken and perhaps replace the older polities.

But whether nationalism is disappearing or flourishing is to be determined to some extent by how the process of societal change is occurring and by the relationship between the nation-state and the internal national movements or the regional subunits. Complicating this assessment is the structural change that is taking place at the international level as well as at the nation-state level and below.[2] To what extent is change at the international level responsible for generating or at least transmitting the ideas and forces that are chipping away at the foundations of the modern nation-state?

Originating from tensions within society, secession is the attempt by a subunit to breakup or to break away from the nation-state. Are the forces of secession transmitted downward to government from the level of global politics, or are the forces of secession principally internal to the individual polity?[3] Moreover, are certain types of international systems such as the balance of power system more or less conducive to secession from established states than is the present unipolar system? Or is type of international system less important than the change that is occurring within that system, in particular during the interval of transformation from one type of international system to another?[4] Finally, is the whole matter of the type of international system structure less important than the historical interval itself in explaining the origins of state breakup? Secession may be time-dependent. The twenty-first century may be more of a catalyst for secession than was the twentieth century.

If the objective is to explain why states break up, perhaps the best approach is to begin by looking at how they form, bearing in mind that one causal process is not simply the obverse of the other. By examining how states form, the analyst is prepared for certain realities, such as whether force is associated with state creation and whether states in the formative stages have been able to survive actual political fragmentation or attempts at fragmentation. Perhaps fragmentation is just a normal aspect of the political evolution of the state, shaping and remoulding it until the optimal mix of populations and territories emerges? State formation, in any case, is critical to the understanding of both cause and consequence of state breakup.

Throughout, the principal question is whether the fragmentation of states is increasing or decreasing worldwide and why. Contagion of the secessionist idea, initially minimal, may be on the increase today (e.g., in Catalonia, the Basque country, Scotland, and now in Wales).

State Formation as Historically Determined Evolution

Nationalism in both its positive and negative connotations, as state-building and as messianic excess, is a historical phenomenon. Aspects of its presence are unique to certain intervals of time. Prosaic though the standard international legal definition of the state may be – namely a territory, a population, and a government capable of maintaining sovereignty – when combined with the concept of a nation as a self-conscious people, it is a useful definition. The evolution of the nation-state is perhaps most readily apparent when indexed in terms of the fraction of the world's population and territory that has gradually been engrossed by formal state boundaries. If Britain was the first formal nation-state, dated from about the time of the Glorious Revolution and the emergence of parliamentary sovereignty, France, Holland, Sweden, and even Poland and Russia were not far behind in terms of ethnic though perhaps not civic nationalism.[5] At the signing of the Peace of Westphalia (1648), the supposed origins of the modern state system, only a fraction of Europe was governed by the nation-state.

By the end of the 1700s, the idea of the nation-state had spread to North and South America. By the 1870s, the superior organization of the nation-state, largely imposed through military conquest, had spread to most of Western Europe. By the mid-1900s, nationalism, abetted by the wars that convulsed Europe, replaced colonialism in Africa and Asia. With the collapse of the one last sizeable empire, the Soviet Union, the contest between empire and state conclusively shifted in favour of the later. Currently numbering in excess of 180 polities, the world system has effectively been engrossed by the nation-state. Although its power is increasingly shared with international organizations, both governmental and non-governmental, and with the corporate firm, and although the personal loyalties of citizens are perhaps increasingly multiple and diffuse, the culminating achievement of the nation-state is that it provides most individuals with a conspicuous identity.

But the historical process of state-making is subtler and deeper.

Legitimization of Authority

One might argue that throughout its entire history, political theory has-struggled to define the locus and moral justification for political authority within the state, and that the history of political revolution is the struggle to alter, by force, the locus and legitimacy of that authority through the overthrow of either a class or an elite. Even more remarkable than the Cold War ending without a hot war is the fact that few of the post-communist states allowed the use of violent revolution to rid themselves of the ruling elite, even where that elite continued to govern in opposition to popular preference. Albeit sometimes primitive, some of the substance as well as the form of democracy took root in the so-called transition states.

Theorists have placed much confidence in Max Weber's assertion that the state is the institution in which resides a 'monopoly of legitimate violence.' The proposition that such a monopoly exists cannot be denied. However, the question for the contemporary analyst is, What happens to legitimation of authority within the state when the monopoly of legitimate violence is by implication made irrelevant, when the state voluntarily gives up its authority on the basis of a plebiscite in the face of sufficient will by members of a subunit? Of what relevance is Weber's rule when that government is not in a position to invoke legitimate violence, or force use? Moreover, what happens to the concept of 'legitimate authority' when the monopoly of legitimate violence is circumvented by a higher commitment to self-determination? Woodrow Wilson mortgaged the moral authority of the central government within the multi-ethnic state to an allegedly higher principle, that of self-determination. That means all regionally diverse and multi-ethnic democracies have ticking within them the political time bomb of self-destruction, whether or not they possess a hypothetical monopoly of legitimate violence.

It's as though history has seen the state mature, finding an eventual balance between authority, representation, and obedience, but in the late twentieth century, the state has handed over to subunits the provisional authority to secede. To protect their survival, states may have to institute the equivalent of the corporate 'silver bullet' designed to prevent hostile takeovers. States in advance may have to design amendments to constitutions that regularize the process of secession, while increasing the procedural cost of executing secession (as Canada appears to have done). The problem for the state is that the response to secession is just that, a passive response rather than an active strategic deterrent. If a subunit wants to secede and can do so electorally, short of applying the implications of Weber's rule, the state has very little political leverage against disunity.

'Nationalities,' according to Karl Deutsch, 'turn into nations when they acquire power to back up their aspirations.'[6] Weber's monopoly of legitimate violence (that is, force use) by implicit prior agreement has apparently been set aside within the democratic state in matters of secession. Indeed, the events of 1991 in the Soviet Union are not only monumental for international relations but are equally monumental for state behaviour towards demands for independence regarding all states, democratic or not. With respect to secession, these events seem to have rendered the practical implications of Weber's rule null and void. Yet even here secession was voluntarily acceded to by Moscow and was not imposed by the seceding fragments.

Apprehension of Purpose

Elites rather than public citizens normally apprehend nationalism first. Making the citizens aware of the nationalist purpose is an intricate part of state-building. Liah Greenfeld is correct that emergent nationalism is partially semantic, and that semantics change with the progress of nationalism.[7] Inhabitants of Quebec thought of themselves as French Canadian, indeed the *original* Canadians until the advent of the 'Quiet Revolution' in the 1960s, whereupon they became Quebecers. Then at the will of Lucien Bouchard, in the run-up to the second referendum campaign, separatism, a formerly pejorative word, became a positive descriptor. She is also correct that *ressentiment*, the suppressed feeling of 'envy and hatred,' is an important part of nationalist apprehension. Directed against another people or governing entity, it can also become the driving force for secession.

Over time, public citizens have become more receptive to the elites' nationalist stimuli. Elites have always justified their nationalism through attitudes they attributed to the masses, but increasingly they are finding that the preferences and behaviour of the masses in actuality are leading them. Karl Deutsch noted that improved communication and better 'social mobilization' can be used to hasten the arrival of the nation-state, or, conversely, tear it apart through secession, each on the basis of accelerated transactions.[8]

Thus in Quebec the apprehension of nationalism is now complete, with all sectors of society fully aware of the nationalist purpose. But more recently, the cost of separation is being understood – at first there was denial, but now there is grudging admission. A tension now exists between these two types of apprehension – the nationalist impulse to secede and the anti-nationalist impulse to push for advantage within the Canadian context.

Consolidation of Territory

Extension of sovereign control over a territory, often by conquest, is the classical notion and method of state-building. Today even sections of the Arctic, sparsely populated by the Inuit, vie for increased political consolidation of territory. In one sense, the evolutionary dominance of the nation-state is indexed by the disappearance of empty territory or *terra nullius*.[9] There are no empty spaces left, and very few 'political vacuums' over which to fight. The cost to an aggressor of challenging another nation-state, weak though it may be, for a disputed territory is high when a government and a population with some allegiance to it are present to defend that territory.

Territorial consolidation of the nation-state is in part responsible for the relative decline in 'war per unit of the state system.' While it is true that the absolute number of wars does not seem to have changed much over the last century and a half,[10] and while it is also true that foreign war is extremely stochastic (subject to variable probabilities) and therefore very difficult to generalize about across time, the number of wars *per unit of the state system* has clearly fallen off. In fact, the number of wars per state must have more than halved since the mid-twentieth century, since the number of states has more than doubled. This is a trend with political significance.

Underlying this decline in 'war per unit of the state system' are two obverse tendencies. On the one hand, the number of states has increased from a handful in the seventeenth century to nearly 200 at the end of the twentieth century. On the other hand, warfare itself, which began as a seasonal thing[11] – halted by winter ice, spring planting, and the fall harvest, but practised at every other time – gradually receded as governments raised the cost of such warfare (and certainly the risks of defeat) while lowering the potential benefits.[12] Fighting at home, populations effectively defended their territories. As the strength and certainty of state consolidation has increased in several areas of the globe, North America and Europe primarily, foreign war in some regions is becoming obsolete.

Analysed from this causal perspective, warfare per unit of the state system declined *because* the cohesion and durability of the state increased. Instead of arguing that state sovereignty increased because warfare fell off per unit of territory, territorial consolidation becomes the independent variable and the relative decline in warfare becomes the dependent variable. Mature states do not fight as much as immature ones did. A mature state is like a well-formed atom, very difficult to subject to fusion or fission, and thus not as likely a target for aggression as a former 'power vacuum' composed of weak, ill-defined entities.

In the past, nationalism was most successful when wedded to force use. But in the modern world in which Canadians (and others in democracy) live, force use is forsaken by all governments and elements of the population. Today, the limits for political change are much narrower than they were in the past. Referenda on secession cannot go on perpetually. Strategic choice becomes paramount. That is why Premier Bouchard opts for another referendum 'only if it can be won.'

Differentiation of Function

The final process involved in state-making is that of the differentiation of function. Over time, states have evolved very specialized functions of government. This specialization has in turn led to complexity, greater cost, and more services. A more adequate tax base than the 'revenue tariff' has made these services possible. Progressive taxation is the embodiment of redistributive justice, practised to one degree or another by all modern states and many developing polities. Legal requirements to protect citizens has led to a further specialization of responsibilities not envisioned prior to the existence of present-day technologies in communications and law enforcement. Differentiation of function has led to three paradoxical consequences in the modern state.

Specialization of regulatory responsibilities in the marketplace has, in the case of foreign investment, invited reassessment. Efforts to attract companies has replaced screening to keep them out. Injustice can occur not because of a lack of regulation but, when measured in terms of inefficiency, because of too much regulation. It has been recognized that a trade-off exists between equity and efficiency.[13]

Specialization of services sometimes must be revamped on a large scale. Reform of medical care services, welfare distribution, and social security require more than cancellation or minor fine-tuning. Reform requires a major restructuring of how these services are organized and delivered. It is significant that this large-scale reform is occurring in the advanced-industrial states at the same time in history. These programmatic reforms are conspicuously time-specific processes.

Especially at the federal level, specialization of government has been rolled back by shifting responsibilities to another level of government, usually to the state, provincial or metropolitan level. With responsibility must come the right to tax, or the right to reliably obtain tax proceeds. And with the right to expect tax proceeds comes a kind of regional entitlement, evident in the system of transfer payments used in Italy, Germany, Canada, and many other polities. Specialization of function through regional diffusion adds a new layer of complexity to administration and politics.

In practice, this fourth process of state-creation, differentiation of function, is the most radical of all. Its application takes the form of *regional autonomy.* In order to offset the desire for independence, central governments are offering the concession of political autonomy to dissident regions in hopes that this concession will satisfy the demand for outright independence. Scotland seems intent upon increasing its political autonomy from England, encouraged by discussions about the proper distribution of North Sea oil revenues. Coming at the end of the twentieth century in a number of advanced-industrial as well as developing countries, these offers of autonomy may add to the burden of governance and even to bureaucratic complexity, thus generating natural political limits of their own. So far Portugal has rejected offers to decentralize powers on just these grounds.

The outcome for each of these processes of state-building is time-specific, yet progress cannot be made without some backsliding. It is true that territorial consolidation has largely improved for most states – until today the boundaries of these states have been considered sacrosanct. But the comprehension of the state's purpose, so important in its formation, is in tatters in a number of multi-ethnic societies. Likewise, differentiation of function through decades of state development amounted to a comparatively simple increase in the specialization of central government, abetted by technology and greater access to revenue. But insofar as differentiation of function has begun to roll back services, programs, and benefits, and insofar as central administrations have resolutely devolved functions to lower levels of government, specialization is far from a process that is moving in a single direction. Similarly, the legitimization of authority, articulated from Hobbes through Locke, Rousseau, and the American Founding Fathers, has taken a different direction; it has turned away from individual rights to the right of collective self-determination and, in some instances, eventual secession.

Instead of moving towards some kind of teleological goal of ever-increasing justice, efficiency, complexity, unity, and cohesion, the modern multi-ethnic, multi-lingual states finds themselves in something of a political crisis. The 'end of history' for these states could mean fragmentation, or at the least a radical devolution of political authority along regional lines. State-making may, in some instances, terminate in state-breaking.

The Influence of the International System on Secession

Type of System

The theory of bipolarity is perhaps better understood now in the aftermath of the collapse of the Soviet Union than during its existence.[14] In his explanations of his theory of bipolarity, Kenneth Waltz acknowledged the essentially conservative character of the superpower system. Locked in a polarized stance vis-à-vis each other and encircled by allies that were also subject to a polarizing tendency, the superpowers extended their reach to all corners of the global system. Any radical change in the international balance among states or in the internal constitution of any of their members was suspect. That brake on radical change provided the system with its essential stability; it also provided the domestic societal cohesion and political strength of many of the individual governments. It is only now being understood just how much of the internal political steadiness manifested by some of the polities was the result of the general international political atmosphere of conservatism and how much was the result of top-down sanction stemming from superpower initiative.

When it is tolerated at all, secession in this context may occur in spite of top-down opposition. It is not too much to conclude that this form of stability must go beyond mere order *between* governments and must include as well minimum public order that stems from stability *within* governments and societies. This does not mean that such stability is coercive (although stability in the Eastern Bloc surely was). It may just mean that the kind of world order that is generated is conducive to or supportive of internal political order within states. These unipolar international systems are not inimical to harmony within polities. But it is yet to be determined whether the stability that results inside the state under the circumstances described by the bipolar and unipolar theories is causal, catalytic, or merely incidental.

Both bipolarity and unipolarity may be conducive to fraternity inside the society of the polity, which would correspond to the assumptions of an earlier system initiated at the Congress of Vienna in 1815. The assembled diplomats believed they were establishing an end to the horrors of the French Revolution and of Bonapartism and restoring the *ancien régime*. This restoration had clear implications for top-down order, just as justice and order within states had 'bottom-up' implications for the kind of international balance that might be expected of the European system. That this international Congress system was the most peaceful of any experienced since the origins of the modern state system was due in no small part to the firmness with which the nation-state itself was being established. Still flexible enough to allow the entry of new states and the new political ideology of democracy, the Congress system prevailed until the Revolutions of 1848 swept away Metternich and the classical mechanism of balance he was chiefly responsible for having established.

International Structural Change

Break-up of empire leads quite naturally to a proliferation of nation-states or proto-states.[15] When the Austro-Hungarian Empire (subsequently the state of Austria-Hungary) and the Ottoman Empire disintegrated, a number of smaller political entities emerged in the Balkans and Central Europe. When the Soviet Union collapsed, Central Europe was released from Soviet control, and the former Soviet Republics outside the Russian core sought independence.

But the modern notion of secession is deeper than these outcomes and much more strongly affiliated with massive structural change inside the central international system of states – referred to as systems transformation, it is the impulse of state fragmentation. Systems transformation is most visible in the central system, that is, among the big powers. Abrupt and sweeping, systems transformation involves change in the number of actors at the top of the system, in the trend of relative distribution of power among all of the leading actors, and potentially in the nature of the equilibrium among these actors. Systems transformation signals the death of one type of system and the birth of another.

Historically, each of the first five systems transformations led to major war.[16] The apparent causal relationship with major war is neither deterministic as in some kind of social scientific law nor inevitable in terms of statistical correlation. Yet the *direction of causal inference* is clear.[17] The massive alteration of international political structure (systems transformation) that precedes war is capable of precipitating major war and all too often has done so. Vice versa, major war is not the cause of systems transformation.[18]

It is instructive to examine the impact that each of the systems transformations had on nationalism at the state level within society. Disintegration of the Hapsburg Family Complex at the end of the sixteenth century led to the Thirty Years War. From this systems transformation emerged the territorial outlines of France, Britain, and Holland. With the final defeat of the armies of Louis XIV's France and the Treaties of Utrecht (1713) came an exchange of territories and a rationalization of the colonial empire outside Europe, especially in North and South America. Following the defeat of Napoleon and the rise of the five-power European balance of power system after 1815, nationalism spread across Europe, ultimately leading to the centralization of the Germanies under Prussia (Bismarck) and of the Italian principalities under Piedmont-Savoy (Cavour). Systems transformation associated with the First World War precipitated the formation of many small states in the Balkans and Central Europe, appealing to Woodrow Wilson's 'threshold formula' for self-determination of peoples (nations). The systems transformation of the European balance of power and the colonial system of the interwar period into the post-1945 bipolar system produced one very specific result in terms of nationalism: A surprisingly stable nation-state system spread throughout Africa and Asia.

Contrasting each of these systems transformations with that of the end of bipolarity leads to two conclusions. First, unlike all of the others, the contemporary transformation has so far been peaceful. This is partly because of the strength of the West, which makes war by a decaying Soviet Union unthinkable, and partly because of the prudence of Soviet foreign policy and the internal erosion of the Soviet economy in the looming presence of the west's ICBMs and second-strike nuclear capability. Second, this systems transformation to unipolarity has made a new type of nationalism commonplace.

Building States by Breaking States: Divisive Nationalism

Seen from the perspective of the subnational units, those prophesying the end of nationalism are surely wrong, for inside the nation-state a new, sometimes virulent, nationalism is burning. On the other hand, the nationalism of the mature nation-state itself is increasingly vulnerable to challenges by these subnational movements. There are several reasons why this vulnerability exists.

Ethnic regionalism does not dissipate easily. Nationalism is often imagined or created.[19] Subunit or ethnic nationalism can smoulder for decades or even centuries, and the fires, though frequently contained, seldom appear to burn themselves out. Assimilation is not a realistic strategy in many cases of ethnic regionalism and will only serve to fan the nationalist flames. Neither education in a dominant language, nor the effects of the market economy, nor common technology appear to cool the embers of subunit nationalism, especially where a sense of group grievance prevails. Thus the idea that unity is guaranteed in the mature multi-ethnic polity is itself something of a myth.

At the end of the twentieth century – and here historical change seems to be responsible for explanation – the apparent viability of small size appears to act as an incentive to secession (see chapter 6). In areas where security is not threatened, a small-sized polity can survive militarily. Even in turbulent Central Europe, the Czechs decided that militarily they were no worse off without the Slovak sector because of their imminent memership in NATO.[20] Likewise, in areas with access to large markets such as the European Union and North America, a small polity, regardless of the actual economic opportunity costs it may have to assume, can always hope to prosper economically. Together the effects of security and economy serve to mitigate some of the worries that in the past might have deterred nationalist movements from demanding outright sovereignty.

William McNeill may be right that immigration and labour mobility will catalyse the forces of disintegration within the multi-ethnic state in the future. But so far most of the secessionist movements are based on historical nationalisms. Much also depends upon how immigration takes place. For it to be a new radical source of nationalist fervour within polities, the immigrants would need to concentrate in a geographic region where they feel socially or economically inferior and where the language difference becomes an issue. These criteria could exist in Mexican immigration to the American Southwest, for example, or in Palestinian immigration to Jordan. But there are not many examples, since most immigration is diffuse and controlled, and since the effects of such immigration are often offset by social policies that counter the negative effects for the newcomers.

Perhaps central government itself is more tolerant of divisive nationalism than in the past. The Soviet Union broke up without significant force use. Although the United States fought a bloody civil war to save the union, both Canada and the United States seem prepared under certain electoral circumstances to accept a decisive outcome in favour of Quebec separation. The Czech Republic quietly accepted the Slovak departure. Slovenia left the Yugoslav federation with the support of Germany and the European Union. The only comparable secessions earlier in the century were that of Norway and of Singapore, each rather special cases. Hong Kong of course has gone the other way.

Governments seem more tolerant of secessionist movements abroad than at home. Mexico expresses little concern about illegal immigration into the United States and the nationalist feeling that it may generate, but it cracks down against the peasant nationalists in Chiapas. India and Pakistan each encourage subunit nationalism in the other country but constrain it in their own country. Iran supports Kurdish nationalism in Iraq but suppresses it at home. Something of an international double standard, common to much of international relations, does appear to exist when it comes to divisive nationalism.

Moreover, there are many current examples of violent challenges followed by repression: Azarbaijan, Turkmenistan, Kampuchea, Sri Lanka, Georgia, Chechnya, the Basque region of Spain, Angola, Kurdistan, Northern Ireland, Lebanon, even the fitful terrorism of a few Welsh nationalists. Elsewhere in Scotland, Flemish Belgium, and in Northern Italy (Lombardia), for example, the respective central government is no more supportive of the nationalist movements than where the opposition is more violent. It would be difficult to argue that a groundswell of tolerance for secession exists in the countries today in which such movements flourish.

How then can the upsurge of divisive nationalism be explained in the context of the most recent systems transformation? What part do developments at the state level play in the developments that occur below the state level?

Divisive Nationalism and Systems Transformation

Secessionist movements are for the most part not linked by international terrorist operations, or by state actions, certainly not from the upper reaches of international power. This is not to say, however, that diffusion of the idea of secession does not occur.[21] 'There must be,' conclude Michael Hechter and Margaret Levi, 'an international dimension to the problem.'[22] But, notwithstanding some contagion effect, secession is for the most part home-grown. Culture determines its intensity.[23]

Systems transformation explains the clustering of secession in historical periods, as observed by Hechter and Levi. Rousseauian explanation once again accounts for conflict; it occurs during systems transformation because in these historical periods there is less to stop divisive nationalism. Systems transformation is permissive. If war accompanies systems transformation, war also will be upsetting to state and society.

With the onset of systems transformation comes the disappearance of the verities of ideological motivation. Under bipolarity, this motivation had been two-pronged. It drove the two superpowers to take the prospect of the breakup of states seriously. With whom would the resultant parts ally, and what would the impact be on the overall systemic balance of power? Bipolar ideological motivation also encouraged secessionist movements to remain quiescent for fear of a negative response, not so much by the United States directly (although the same could not be said of the Soviet Union in Central Europe), but by the respective central government acting out its own perceptions of the Cold War. Systems transformation swept away each of these motivations and in their place created a yearning on the part of many citizens for a new ideological verity. That new verity became in some cases cultural nationalism.

The permissiveness of systems transformation is a result of the structural turbulence that can distract the systemic leadership. So much change is going on and so much political attention is demanded of the decision maker – conducting foreign policy among the big powers during the adjustment period, for example – that there is little time, diplomatic attention, or resources to devote to the management of more finite problems such as divisive nationalism within smaller states. During rapid structural change, leading governments are not very accustomed to giving, taking, and reading political signals by their partners and potential rivals. This is the obverse of the situation articulated by Waltz concerning bipolarity at its most seasoned. Secessionist actors can attempt to 'read' all of this ambiguity and make it work for themselves.

As the system shifts towards unipolarity, the limits to intervention are increasingly relevant. Gone is the impetus to intervene from the other side of the bipolar matrix. This hesitance operates to the advantage of secessionist movements. Unless the effort becomes externalized and violent, the public within other states is inured to secessionist efforts. Since secession is a process more than an event, the governing elite within the leading state or states becomes tired of false calls for help from central governments that claim to be threatened by divisive nationalism. Other central governments are extremely protective of their sovereignty and make any assistance from the top of the system difficult to implement. Repeated interventions use up a lot of 'political capital' at home.[24] The government of a leading state, especially if it is a democracy, rapidly becomes discouraged with further actions that political intervention requires in order to shore up central governments that appear to be in trouble.

Supranationality implicitly weakens the resolve of central governments to take action to halt secession, even secession that is violent. The European Union's initial hesitant response to Bosnia is an example. But even in the absence of war or a warlike situation, it is not clear how central governments of the leading states will act during systems transformation. U.S. policy towards secession in Belgium, or Germany's policy towards divisive nationalism in Northern Italy, are cases in point. The blurring of foreign policy responsibility under supranationalism is only magnified by the manifold uncertainties associated with systems transformation. It is not so much a problem of figuring out how to 'pass the buck' as determining where the buck ought to stop in decision-making settings and in periods where there seems to be a premium on taking no action.

In short, systems transformation, the interval that occurs between the demise of one type of mature international system and the emergence of an alternative system, is filled with political uncertainty caused by rapid structural change at the top. Systems transformation is responsible for the creation of new nation-states and for the war that has followed these transformations, shaking up old empires and dynastic alliances. Nationalism spreads from all of these causes.

A New Variety of Systems Transformation?

With the end of the Cold War, a new, peaceful systems transformation from bipolarity to unipolarity is in the making. This systems transformation is unique not only because it has not caused a major war, but because it has also created a new type of nationalism. Unlike other nationalisms of the past, this nationalism is as relevant for the mature nation-state as it is for dying empires or fledgling governments.

Secession of regional units is the hallmark of this new nationalism. It results from the confluence of two developments. Some nation-states seem more vulnerable, as though they have reached the apogee of their political cohesiveness. Although central governments are scarcely more tolerant of secession than in the past, and although the impact of immigration and labour mobility on the multi-ethnic state has yet to be felt in any regionally evident way, contemporary government has fostered a setting that is kind to secession. A recrudescence of secessionist movements has occurred in the wake of the disappearance of communism and fascism as mass ideologies. People have sought identity in cultural collectivities to replace the loss of faith in political ideology. At the same time, comparative peace and security have given the secessionist state hope of survival. Access to giant trade areas or common markets has also given divisive nationalism a new faith in its vitality. Success of the nation-state has in some sense contributed to the strains upon it.

From the top of the system has come a permissiveness that complements the nurturance of divisive nationalism coming from below the nation-state. Systems transformation in the aftermath of the Cold War has been accompanied by many structural uncertainties that have distracted the systemic leadership, hindering concentration and the effort to combat national divisiveness. The United States has understandably acknowledged limits to the extent that it is willing to intervene on behalf of nation-state unity and stability. Who is to share what responsibility and what cost, even if strategies are agreed upon and clear, is a matter that has not yet been worked out in terms of a coherent security regime. Finally, supranationalism adds ambiguities about foreign policy action at a time when ambiguities already abound in the midst of massive alteration of the distribution of world power.

Secessionist movements have responded to this confluence of forces within and above the nation-state during the rigours of systems transformation. Once thought immutable, the nation-state of the twenty-first century looks neither cohesive nor self-confident, especially in situations where long-standing regional cultural-linguistic movements have managed to find real or imagined adversaries and a new rationality for resistance.

Can Democratic Pluralism Survive? Divisive Nationalism and the Future

Much of the argument in this chapter has explored the origins of secession and has, in consequence, given the impression that state fragmentation is on the rise. But indeed, as this chapter has also tried to show, the late twentieth century has been a celebration in statehood. Every corner of the international system is occupied by the state.[25] For the present, empire has conceded defeat to the nation-state. Fourteen thousand bureaucrats administer the European Union, but in most matters of high policy involving foreign affairs and defence, decisions still reside with the nation-state. NATO may be the most powerful military alliance in the world, but the NATO Charter still allows national parliaments the last say in the decision to go to war. NAFTA and ASEAN may signify breakthroughs in cooperative economic policy, and surely in the commitment to regional (and partial) trade liberalization, but the concessions in terms of autonomy are still quite compatible with national sovereignty.[26]

As observers who are both participants and analysts, we do not always see the triumph of the nation-state clearly. Our vision is obscured by the incremental nature of the historical process and the temptation to take the existence of the territorial state for granted as though it has always existed with its present-day solidity. This assumption of permanence and security is in reality only a late-twentieth-century phenomenon.

Although not teleological in the sense that it is moving towards a predestined outcome, the process of nation-building is certainly evolutionary in nature.[27] An index of the historical nature of the state enterprise is the gradual filling of the system by states as they replace other forms of social and political organization. Another index is in the nature of state institutions themselves over time as they incorporate with greater sophistication the four mechanisms underlying state-making: legitimization of authority, apprehension of purpose, consolidation of territory, and differentiation of function. Each of these mechanisms is continuous and ongoing and achieves positive results. Chirac's France, notwithstanding its problems of social adjustment and reform, is an instrument that provides benefits for far more people, at a much higher level of safety and prosperity, than Louis XIV's France in all of its cultural grandeur could possibly have imagined.

To engage the question posed at the beginning of this chapter – Is the rise of secession placing the durability of the nation-state in doubt? – requires quite a different answer. Most of the fragmentation of nation-states at the end of the twentieth century outside Africa has been associated with the collapse of the Soviet empire, in the Balkans and inside Russia itself. The collapse of the Soviet empire in turn has resulted in the systems transformation from bipolarity to unipolarity. Like two other systems transformations earlier in the twentieth century, the legacy of unfulfilled promise from the peace treaties at the end of each major war has been further political instability.

Each of the three major trouble spots in the post-1945 system was a result of the treaty compromises following the Second World War: a divided Korea, a divided Vietnam, and a divided Germany. Two ended in reunification – one on Western terms (Germany), one on communist terms now slowly being modified (Vietnam) – and one remains unresolved (Korea). Yet what is most striking about these huge post–War preoccupations is the propensity of these societies and states to cohere and endure even when torn by ideological difference and, to some extent (Korea and Vietnam), cultural difference between North and South.

Each of the problems in southeastern Europe in turn is a legacy of the systems transformation following the First World War, where Wilson tried to unite small polities, rearrange populations, and 'rationalize' the 'crazy zig-saw puzzle of the Balkans.'[28] Yugoslavia, Czechoslovakia, Hungary, and Romania were state solutions to problems that came to the fore during the systems transformation that preceded and was associated with the Great War. Hence systems transformation is to some extent the cause of state fragmentation, but it is also used in attempting state-building.

With the systems transformation at the end of the Cold War, it is not surprising that state fragmentation should once again become a problem. Nor is it surprising that the type of international system prevailing today is perhaps more tolerant of devolution and increased regional autonomy within states than was the bipolarity system, especially in the Soviet realm, during the latter half of the twentieth century.

But there is a fundamental difference between the effects of systems transformation on secessionist impulse, and even the effect of type of international system on that impulse, and the overall fate of the nation-state in the twenty-first century. Once outside these geographic areas of massive structural strain most often associated with the collapse of a past empire, the nation-state is thriving. Not only in numbers but also in terms of the efficacy of governance, the state is a success story.

What is remarkable in terms of secessionist impulse among the advanced industrial countries is not so much how widespread the sentiment is, but how halting the movements are and how politically pragmatic the adherents are. Secessionist claims find so many possible state responses. Proponents of secession are themselves cross-pressured and given to multiple affinities. Expressions of interest in secession, moreover, are different than examples of successful secession. At the turn of the twenty-first century, what is striking is the state's political capacity through a mixture of democratic compromise and resilience to cohere and prosper.

That the nation-state has become more difficult to administer as it becomes larger is undoubtedly true. But there is little evidence of 'systems overload' within decision circles, in part because information and communication have advanced so fast and so far. Devolution of tax and other responsibilities is not the same as making good on a claim to secession. 'Downsizing' of the state is more often a substitute for state fragmentation than a prelude. Reform of state bureaucracy is less an indicator of crisis of state purpose than an appropriate response to such crisis.

Tolerance, indeed celebration, for communities with cultural and linguistic preference that is at odds with that of the majority in the polity is now the rule for the liberal democratic multi-ethnic state. Culturally and linguistically homogeneous states are less common than in the past. Almost every state of consequence as a target for immigration has been changed by the very populations that it has sought to attract and integrate within its institutions and values.

Democratic pluralism is slowly becoming not the exception but the norm for the advanced industrial polity. Slowly even monolithic societies like Germany and Japan are coming to grips with the presence of long-standing minorities within their populations who are demanding citizenship and full rights. It was after all not so long ago that segregation paralysed the American South, that apartheid sickened politics in South Africa and Zimbabwe (Rhodesia), and that double social standards denied women everywhere equal opportunity. Democratic pluralism walks hand in hand with legal equality and cultural toleration.

For the most part, as the international system confronts the twenty-first century, the modern nation-state, whether binational or multinational is, because of democratic pluralism, not weaker but stronger. All the more reason why, when there is backsliding away from democratic pluralism, or when secession occurs along ethno-linguistic lines such that democratic pluralism is negated, these events damage all of liberal democracy.

Centralization, Globalization, and North America

Evolution and devolution have accelerated worldwide since the end of the Cold War. Centralization and decentralization are coterminus processes, and in North America, movement of governmental functions along these lines has been shifting up and down the federal ladder for even a longer time. Ever since the New Deal of Franklin Delano Roosevelt, the U.S. federal government has added functions and expanded its role to ensure that individual states follow the dictates of the welfare society. Under the Great Society programs of Lyndon Johnson, the centralization of authority in Washington over civil rights, welfare, education, and health care sharply increased. Only under the Reagan administration was a sincere bid made, with the exception of defence, not only to downsize government (or slow the increase in size) but to reallocate functions and authority to the states. In all of this decentralization of function, one large problem stood out: If 'fairness' was to be applied across the country, the problem became how to enforce equal standards throughout the nation when each state did its own enforcing of these standards.

Canada has experienced its own roller-coaster of shifting governmental decision making and functions. Quebec and the conservative Western provinces, or constituencies within those provinces, have reacted most strongly to the attempted centralization of leadership during the sixteen years of the Trudeau administration. One sees this increase in centralization in everything from policy towards the First Nations Peoples to the way decision making was carried out in the Department of External Affairs. With the advent of the Clark and the Mulroney governments, some devolution of functions took place. As far as Quebec relations are concerned, the Chrétien government seems to be caught between the desire to devolve more authority in specific areas such as manpower training and social policy to Quebec and not wanting to upset the other provinces or to deviate too far from the general liberal philosophy of a strong central government.

It is probably safe to say that Ottawa is suspicious of both too much centralization and too much decentralization. That this is so is not surprising because each trend, at least in the extreme, is a threat to nation-state sovereignty. Yet decentralization of the subsidiarity type (devolution of authority to the lowest possible level consonant with efficiency and justice) is also essential in the context of greater regional integration. Otherwise everything gets tied up in bureaucratic knots at the federal or supranation-state levels. The dilemma is much like that regarding taxation. As inflation increases the nominal income of the citizen, the tax rate also increases for that citizen, even though he or she does not earn any more money in real terms and, because of the inadvertent tax increase, is taking home less. Without subsidiarity, regional integration would lead to a bureaucratic mess at the top levels of decision making. Brussels is often accused of being mired in this quandary. Quebec is not out of bounds in its claim that Ottawa should take more seriously both the historical balance of power within the original British North American Act between province and federal government, and the contemporary situation in which the provinces can do a better (more responsive and probably more efficient) job of administration than can Ottawa. Every policy area must be treated on its own merits, but subsidiarity is a principle all the members of NAFTA ought to heed.

But all of this is very far from saying that centralization at one level 'causes' decentralization at another level or that the advance of regional integration will expedite the breakup of Canada. Evolution and devolution go hand in hand, just as do centralization and decentralization. They seem like opposites but, in fact, are complementary processes that, when allowed to proceed, will strengthen the nation-state as a whole while meeting the needs of the individual community, province, or state.

In terms of the evolution of the system towards globalization, what is the impact on the nation-state as we know it? According to Jeffrey Sachs:

> We are therefore in the midst of a startling, yet early, tug of war between polities at all levels. Where will the future of decision making, tax powers, and regulatory authorities reside: with localities, subnational regions, nation-states or multilateral institutions (both within geographic regions such as the European Union and at the international level)? To the extent that increased regulatory, tax, and even judicial powers shift to the international setting, how should and will international institutions be governed in the future? Will there be a democracy deficit, as is now charged about decision making in the European Union.[29]

In this view, globalization will remake the nation-state. The locus of taxes, regulation, and even justice is likely to move either upwards or downwards within the authority structure of the international system, but mainly upwards. Regions and systems are likely to be shuffled like cards, as governments rush to shed functions or adopt new ones. Borders are not likely to remain constant. Whether political authority will remain stable is open to question, though revolution is not among the predicted outcomes. This is not the first time such a challenge to world order as we know it has been prophesied.

In *The End of the Nation-State*, Jean-Marie Guehenno asks the question whether the world will become 'Lebanonized,' quite a bit more disturbing a prophesy than that of Sachs, given the breakdown of authority in Lebanon and the resulting civil war. He claims that a one-dimensional reality will emerge: 'The community is likely to appear as the natural framework within which everyone may recover his identity.'[30] Since communities and nation-states often do not occupy precisely the same territory in North America, such a conclusion about the supremacy of communal values fails to correspond to 'recovery of identity.' This is increasingly the norm for communities within the modern nation-state.

Similarly, Kenichi Ohmae, in his book also entitled *The End of the Nation-State*, asserts that 'regional' states will replace the nation-state because the new economic engines of growth do not conform to the territorial dimensions of the nation-state.[31] These engines are conglomerations of cities, interlocked by common transportation links and mostly educated populations producing for world markets.

However, these regional entities for the most part, as identified by Ohmae himself, fall inside the nation-state, not across national borders. Silicon Valley, Route 128 Boston, the Washington, DC/Baltimore corridor, the larger metropolitan areas of Ottawa, Montreal, and Toronto all conform to Ohmae-like engines of growth, but none spills over borders. Indeed, if they did spill over, they might solidify existing borders, since one-half of an 'engine' would operate on either side of the border, spurring growth on each side.

This empirical observation about substate regions, as opposed to extra-state regions, is borne out by Michael Porter's discussion of 'clusters' of industrial growth within nation-sates in which he highlights the enduring comparative advantage of each nation-state.[32] Porter's clusters do not often cross borders either. For reasons that must reside ultimately in the way people organize themselves, both politically and economically, these lasting industrial specializations seem to respect the borders of existing nation-states, even in highly concentrated Europe, showing no signs of overlapping borders or further subdividing the states in which the industrial clusters flourish.

But other reasons exist as well for doubting the prognostications of Sachs, Guehenno, Ohmae, and others that the nation-state is dead because of globalization.

First, the firm and the nation-state are not opposites; they are not colliding with each other for space and power. More often than not, they are complementary institutions, each performing responsibilities and functions that cannot be performed by the other. Yet they are organizations that are dependent upon each other for contributions without which the other would be poorer, both materially and institutionally.

Second, globalization, the phenomenon of the spread of financial, marketing, production, and management functions of the firm worldwide through specialization, has been going on for fifty years at least and is yet far from complete. This could of course suggest that 'we haven't seen anything yet' and that future impacts will be even more shocking. In reality, even greater effects on the national economy are occurring from within, in the absence of any similar claims regarding devastating political consequences. The far greater effects on production stem from technological innovation, often confused with globalization but having almost none of (indeed often the converse) effects such as downsizing. Technological innovation is a faster, more encompassing process that threatens few if any political structures and promises no border revisions.

Third, the most traumatic shock often associated with globalization is the movement of capital. Combined with volatile exchange rates, the massive shifts of capital instantaneously across borders does present difficult problems of monitoring and management. In time, these will be dealt with both by national initiatives such as minor restrictions on the flow of short-term investment capital (an interest-rate surcharge perhaps for capital movement under a year in duration), and by better macro-management at the global level through enhanced IMF reserves. Though they could unseat a government or two, these capital movements will not 'Lebanonize' countries. Nor will the territorial or political fragmentation of the nation-state in any way improve the management of short-term capital movements.

Fourth, only for those countries that persist in attempting to sidestep the market or intervene against its effects rather than encouraging market forces and thus extracting benefits liberally from them, only for such governments will globalization present any threat to governance. The East Asian financial crisis of 1997 was abetted by the governments' poor management practices that allowed bad loans to persist for too long and that became too dependent upon short-term foreign capital loans as a 'bridge.' Other much poorer governments in the same region, such as India, with some of the same management problems in banking but less reliance on a 'quick-fix' from abroad, were better able to weather the financial storm. Markets are unforgiving if the individual, the firm, or government tries to go against them. But globalization that is allowed to proceed in unison with good economic practice on the part of the government will not only leave the polity undamaged but will enrich its citizens beyond anything the twentieth century otherwise produced.

Despite calls of premature death, the nation-state and the firm are here to stay. Their adaptability and clear accountability make them the two most vibrant forms of institutional organization today. Some might aver that the university and the church have a greater lineage. While I would agree, I would claim that without the firm and the nation-state, the other two quasi institutions would exist in isolation and would not thrive.

In North America, neither regionalization nor globalization is a threat to the vitality of Canada. Mildred Schwartz has assessed the sociology of Canadian thought regarding international trade.[33] Protectionism, she reminds the reader, was long regarded as a bulwark of the national identity. NAFTA and freer trade represented a break with this view. While the traditional view was that trade protectionism reinforced the national identity, the advent of freer trade need not be seen as a threat to the Canadian identity. On the contrary, a stronger, more robust Canadian economy resulting from NAFTA membership may be the best guarantee that Canada can survive as a unified state.

Inside Canada, Quebec will find great opportunity and flexibility because of the contacts and access that regionalization and globalization afford. Each process tends to strengthen the other. Regionalization enables the polities of North America to proceed with structural changes in the marketplace more quickly and more sensitively in terms of local needs, cultural as well as social. Globalization ensures that the process will not become too parochial or too out of touch with the trade, financial, and commercial trends necessary to deliver optimal increases in economic welfare for each citizen.

If globalization and technological change are allowed to operate effectively, then Canada and Quebec are not likely to fall behind in terms of the self-sustaining growth necessary to preserve the physical and social environment in the twenty-first century. A self-confident and prosperous Canada will create the political space for a vibrant Quebec to share fully in all the benefits that modern Canada offers its citizens. Inside such a Canada, Quebec will attain the height of self-expression that it requires to fulfill all of the promise associated with that remarkable development of the 1960s known as the Quiet Revolution.

This chapter began by articulating a barrage of non-rhetorical, analytic questions concerning whether in general the impetus for secession is home-grown or whether it stems from influences throughout the system that can cause a contagion effect in shaping attitudes in local communities. Related to this question was the more specific question of whether a certain type of international system was a deterrent or catalyst to secession and whether certain periods of history are kinder or less solicitous of separatist intent.

Searching for a clue to these questions in the way states are formed, four processes of state-making were identified: legitimization of authority, apprehension of purpose, consolidation of territory, and differentiation of function. While some international reinforcement may have occurred in fixing boundaries and strengthening state bureaucracies, no evidence exists for a kind of teleological evolution of the state towards a final phase in which democratic pluralism can be said to have triumphed. Rather, evolution of the nation-state seems to be afflicted by backsliding and periods of deconsolidation as well as consolidation. Each of the four processes may reinforce each other either to strengthen or to weaken the state. Cyprus, for example, has gone through phases of suzerainty and colonialism, partial independence, external invasion and occupation, partition, and international supervision.[34] The European Union appears to want to incorporate it as a whole, unhealed political wounds and all, into the body politic of the grand supranational experiment.[35] But in the absence of generating a Cyprus-wide sense of statehood across both the Greek Cypriot and Turkish Cypriot communities, through an amplification of the four processes of state-making identified in this chapter, it is very difficult to see how external cooptation can overcome internal societal division.

The chapter likewise demonstrates that certain periods of history have been characterized by state-building and certain other periods like the present may witness more broadly the attempted deconstruction of states. In intervals of post-colonialism, or in intervals after the great wars, state-building may have accelerated. But little evidence suggests that divisive nationalism, to this point in history at least, has received much impetus from generalized external influence, behaviourally or attitudinally. Moreover, as far as Quebec is concerned, separatism is even more than elsewhere an indigenous phenomenon whose pace seems to be determined by internal political and socio-economic developments rather than by any external encouragement.

At the same time, as Stephen Krasner has warned, there is little possibility for any norm, including that of national unity, to become universally established. 'In the international system, norms, including those associated with Westphalian sovereignty and international legal sovereignty, have always been characterized by organized hypocrisy.' States will always be subject to the limits of 'organized hypocrisy' and therefore to the possibility of breakup.[36]

As the discussion on types of international systems as cause of secession reveals, extremely polarized systems such as that of bipolarity so emphasize security considerations that the propensity for state breakup may be veiled if not actually hindered. But the discussion also makes clear that the greatest stimulus to state breakup is the thoroughgoing structural change associated with systems transformation when the very nature of the international system itself is in question. These cataclysmic intervals of massive structural change have occurred on only six occasions since 1500, the most recent of which was the collapse of the Soviet Union and bipolarity. Some of the current impetus to state secession may be fallout from this most recent case of systems transformation.

As I also have shown, globalization is perhaps inevitable, but it is far from inevitably damaging, either to the state or to the process of democratic pluralism within the state. Foreshadowing and acting as a transition to chapter 6, the discussion on globalization shows that while the diffusion of production and distribution worldwide, assisted by the information revolution, can bring enormous benefit to heretofore isolated populations, globalization is not a panacea for those with separatist intent. It is not a vehicle for the breakup of existing states. Close integration inside existing states remains invaluable to the welfare and rapid economic growth of local communities. Hence, in the end, globalization and democratic pluralism are complementary and are not opposed processes of social and political change.

Despite the comparatively benign nature of these conclusions regarding the external effects on separatist impulse inside polities, one unanswered question remains. Suppose Canada broke up? Would this fact of secession, rather than just its prospect, not have an effect on the capacity to pursue democratic pluralism in other potentially fragile advanced-industrial democracies such as Great Britain, Spain, and Belgium? Even if states were able to ward off outright breakup after a

long political struggle, would not a contagion effect then ensue, causing a corrosive impact on democratic pluralism? Moreover, if democratic pluralism fails in the very societies in which its conditions for
success were thought to be most propitious, what kind of example
would this set for other large democratic polities in the Third World
struggling to cope with communal difference and communal conflict?
Following a quite specific discussion in the next chapter of some possible long-term economic costs of separation to the secessionist entity
itself, the discussion will return to these bedevilling questions that lie
at the very doorstep of democratic pluralism.

CHAPTER SIX

Is Small Size a Stimulus or Obstacle to Separatism?

According to the previous chapter, contagion alone does not explain the contemporary phenomenon of secession, although tumult in world politics caused by systems transformation can trigger state fragmentation. Conversely, the breakup of Canada could unleash a contagion effect on the processes of democratic pluralism by putting these processes at risk worldwide. Causation does not so much move from international system to state, according to these arguments, as from state to international system. This chapter asks a similar question about secession and the direction of causality: Is the small size of a potentially secessionist actor a stimulus or a hindrance to separatism?[1]

Economic Costs of Separation to Quebec

In an October 1997 issue of *The Boston Globe*, Lester Thurow, former dean of the graduate school of business at MIT, claims that secession from Canada would not harm Quebec economically, and might even help it, as long as Quebec becomes a full partner to NAFTA.[2] This thought that small size need not obstruct economic advancement is often put forward by separatists in Quebec as well. Thus the statement from an articulate and highly visible American economist that all Quebec needs to do to preserve its economic future is to become a full member of NAFTA is quite astounding. Visions of Singapore, however different the underlying cultural, political, and economic structures and settings may be, immediately come to mind.

This viewpoint that small size does not diminish the possibility of unlimited economic progress also receives backing from Harvard growth economist Robert J. Barro. 'There is no relation between the growth or level of per capita income,' he argues, 'and the size of a country, measured by population or area.'[3] 'No relation' implies that as the population or area of a country increases, no increase in the level or rate of growth in welfare occurs. On this evidence, size does not facilitate growth.[4] Even small countries with a population size as little as one million, Barro further asserts, can do well if they do not close their borders to trade and investment.

In fact, in an empirical study, Alberto Alesina and Enrico Spolaore see large size contributing to secession because of the greater propensity for internal conflict resulting from the heterogeneity of populations.[5] Democracy can facilitate secession, they believe.[6] Trade and investment liberalization, according to these views, is a threat to the large, multi-ethnic state because there is no economic cost to secession. In an open international trading system, a small state can do as well economically as a large state. Conversely, there may be a genuine political cost involved in maintaining unity. Thus from the perspective of such unity, unity may not appear 'cost effective' either in economic or political terms.

What is remarkable about these theoretical speculations is how they challenge traditional assumptions regarding the movement towards economic integration.

Neoclassical Notion that Size Promotes Growth

In the neoclassical Vinerian model, the prospect of trade creation as opposed to trade diversion determines whether international integration brings benefits to the overall trading system.[7] There is no way of knowing a priori, or in terms of generalization of the theory, whether preferential trade unions are good or bad for the welfare of the system as a whole.[8] Each case must be analysed individually. But as textbooks in international economics affirm, the 'argument leads back to the classical proposition that a customs union, because it moves us closer to free trade, is presumed to be welfare-improving.'[9] That certainly is the policy interpretation of the trade unions' architects.

So far the argument of the neoclassical school may seem in agreement with that of the modern economic theorists. But the crux of the difference is that the modern theorists believe that the present international economic order is open to both large and small polities, either through large regional trade areas or the global trade order more generally, and that small political size is no longer a limitation to economic growth. The neoclassicists have always held that small size is a hindrance to growth.

Neoclassicists have regarded economic integration as desirable because, through economies of scale, firms that were otherwise too small for optimum efficiency could enjoy longer production runs. This definitely was the assumption with the creation of the European Coal and Steel Community, the predecessor of the present-day European Union. Local steel companies within each European country were too small to compete with the much larger American firms.

With larger market size, international economies of scale become feasible associated with specialization regarding subordinate segments of production. Elimination of national monopolies that restrict competition would be possible as small markets are replaced by larger ones and local monopolies face new competition. Managerial efficiencies created out of the opportunities to expand and to restructure are also among the dynamic benefits of the neoclassical model of economic integration. Finally, factor market integration, that is, the movement of firms or of labour from lower productivity locations outside the customs union to higher productivity locations inside the customs union, can also be welfare-creating.

Perhaps the neoclassical argument that best illustrates the salutary benefits of larger economic size for increased welfare is a study by Kemp and Wan.[10] They argue that insofar as a larger economic entity is created out of smaller entities with excess supplies and demands, the larger entity can always theoretically organize itself in a fashion that will improve the welfare of its citizens. By eliminating distortions in the smaller markets, the larger market can always create a preferred equilibrium position. Despite the questionable assumptions about international welfare transfers and other movements of resources across prior borders inside the larger economic entity, this model's optimism about the prospects for economic integration is the cornerstone of intellectual support for the pro-integration school of international economics.

In short, the architects of the neoclassical integration model identified many efficiencies as enhancements to economic growth. This fundamental assumption, that larger economic size promotes economic growth and productivity, underlies the establishment of every preferential trade area starting with the European Union. The assumption that larger size negated war among polities, eased trade disputes, and through stability provided an additional political benefit to market integration went hand in hand with neoclassical assumptions about the economic benefits of integration.

Inverting the Neoclassical Logic

Contemporary economists now appear to be standing the neoclassical assumption on its head. Small market size is as attractive as a large market size because the open trading system allows for specialization that is as good as that found within the larger market whether that market is a state market or a preferential trading area. If there is no relationship between an increase in per capita income growth and a larger market size, then why integrate?

Equally, if the relationship between growth and larger market size does not hold, then why *remain* integrated inside the nation-state? If such is the case, balkanization of nation-states will not harm world economic welfare or the welfare of the resulting smaller state. If there is no association, notwithstanding increased heterogeneity of society, between reduced political conflict and larger market size, then why form larger political unions? Again, the assumption seems to be that external security is already provided for. Under these circumstances, it is better to have a series of small states than a single larger state in which opposed populations vie against each other internally.

Global trade and investment liberalization appear to be eroding the incentive for regional economic integration. As well, global trade and investment liberalization appear to be undermining the modern nation-state, as secession becomes more likely, because the neoclassical assumptions about economies of scale internal to the state become less valid in the face of a world market that offers the same advantages through openness.

Who is right, the neoclassical integrationists or the modern revisionists? Does small economic size no longer penalize a state in terms of foregone economic growth, a penalty that thwarted secession and strengthened the bid for regional economic integration? To put this central question into the larger context of the work on international political economy that generated it, the analysis explores four key points: (1) the per capita income growth rate cycle; (2) the economic underpinnings of the power cycle (curve); (3) logic of the security imperative and trade openness (the implications of power cycle analysis and how security policy helps shape the context for trade and investment liberalization, including regional integration); and (4) the impact of convergence (on the identification of the size/growth thresh-old). The chapter then returns to a specific theoretical and empirical treatment of the size/growth threshold and the even more specific impact on Quebec.

The Structure of World Order and Trade

International political economy to some extent marches to its own cadence, but it also responds to the underlying structure of world order. This section explores that linkage.

Sketching the Per Capita Income Growth Rate Cycle (Curve)[11]

Two intuitive models, seemingly opposite to one another, put the dis-cussion of the relationship between per capita income growth rates and size in an appropriately larger context. Their reconciliation makes possible the resolution of the problem of growth and size in this study.

WIDENING RICH/POOR GAP

The first model is commonly known as the rich/poor gap model.[12] It describes the situation in which, although both rich and poor states are increasing their wealth, the richer states have the higher growth rate. They are leaving the poorer states farther and farther behind in growth terms because the rate of their per capita income growth is higher and the level of their per capita income is already greater (they are richer). The gap results from the quickly growing Newly Developing Coun-tries leaving behind the countries that have not really started to grow, like those in the Sahel region in Africa.

CATCH-UP: GROWTH RATE ASYMPTOTE(S)

In contrast, the model commonly known as 'catch-up' describes just the opposite situation.[13] As states mature, their growth rates decline. Thus, far from lagging behind as the rich/poor gap model maintains, the growth rate of developing countries can catch up with the growth rate of advanced industrial countries. The reason this catch-up is possible is because the *rate of growth* of the advanced industrial countries declines towards an asymptote. In practice, the United States, which is the leading economy in the world as measured by level of wealth and size, is closer to this asymptote than say China or Mexico. Economists have labelled this phenomenon of declining per capita income growth rates and underlying total productivity growth rates as 'convergence.' In dynamical terms, a better description of the phenomenon is that each country as a mature economy reaches a rate-of-growth asymptote. The convergence model contends that, in the long term, the rate-of-growth asymptotes for all of the advanced industrial countries will be identical when the rates of growth for the individual countries will have converged.

TWO ENDS OF THE GROWTH EXPERIENCE

Although opposites, these two models are in fact both correct.[14] Each describes the partial situation of the state's growth at a given time in its development. Both are seen to be correct when they are combined as the opposite ends of the growth experience. The rich/poor gap model describes the situation early in that experience when the faster growing countries are leaving the slower growing countries behind. The catch-up model describes the situation in which the decline in the rate of per capita income growth of the advanced industrial countries allows the more rapidly growing developing country to 'catch up' with the advanced industrial country in per capita income.

Hence, in combination, the two perspectives are accounted for by an 'idealized' per capita income growth rate cycle (curve) through which each developing country eventually is expected to pass. Each developing country enters a rapid growth phase. This phase then dissipates, albeit at a much higher level of per capita income. Hence the actual marginal output may or may not continue to increase relative to smaller but faster growing states that are in an earlier phase of development. It is the interaction of both rate and level that will determine the extent to which a given country's overall per capita wealth will actually catch up with the advanced industrial country.

Causation accounting for the catch-up of countries in terms of economic growth must be explained first by what determines the remarkable acceleration of growth in the middle phase of development and second by what explains the decline in the rate of per capita income growth to a growth asymptote thereafter.

Some of the explanation is found in the reality that technological imitation is easier than technological innovation.[15] Some is found in the relative shift from efficiency concerns to equity concerns involving welfare, pensions, education, health care, workers' rights, environmental protection, and oligopolistic behaviour of firms, in the mature economy.[16] Some of the explanation is found in the dynamic of the growth curve itself. Larger economies may grow more slowly than smaller economies because factor combination and productivity will fall off as economic size increases. This phenomenon is illustrated inside the firm as well as inside the state.[17]

In short, the per capita income growth rate cycle or curve reconciles all of these conceptual and empirical loose ends, thus creating a single unifying interpretation of how the entire growth experience accounts for very different growth patterns at different points in time. All of this is key to understanding one additional cycle central to statecraft – the power cycle.

Economic Underpinnings of the Power Cycle (Curve)

Composed of a number of indicators of national capability such as GDP, population size, per capita income, and military spending, the power cycle is a *relative* concept.[18] It indexes the national capability of one state relative to that of others across time. It traces the state's rise in relative size and importance, the period of its participation as a major player in the system, and its relative decline as other states increase their economic and military capabilities at a faster rate. Reduced to its simplest structure, state power has a size and a wealth dimension (substantive aspects of capability to which we will return after a brief review of the dynamic of change itself).[19] The relative capability of a state is a ratio – the state's capability is the numerator, and the competitors' capability is the denominator. Hence relative power can be regarded as the percentage of power that a state possesses at each point in its evolution within the international system.

Importantly, the cycle of relative power has properties of the logistic (less formally referred to as an S curve): acceleration to a point of inflection followed by deceleration to an asymptotic level. In reality, the cycle conforms to two logistic curves, one on the upside and one on the downside of the cycle; it thus has a minimum, a maximum, and another minimum asymptotic level.[20] The relevant logistic for each is the asymmetric logistic, that is, the time required to reach the inflection point does not necessarily correspond to the time from inflection point to upper (or lower) asymptotic peak (or trough). Properties of power in international relations correspond to the conditions for such asymmetric logistic growth in a limited environment (100 per cent shares of power in the system). The dynamism of other states (and eventually, if it becomes big enough, its own size) places limits on how far and fast an individual state's power will grow.

Underlying the dynamic of the power cycle is the dynamic of the per capita income growth rate cycle. More precisely, underlying the power cycle for each state are the per capita income growth rate cycles for all of the states encompassed in the relative power ratio. Therefore what happens to the per capita income growth rate cycles across the system very much affects the periodicity and amplitude of each state power cycle.

On the other hand, since power is composed of a size as well as a wealth dimension, what happens to per capita wealth over time is only a partial determinant of change on the overall power cycle. It is uncertain whether the wealth dimension is a more important determinant of power than the size dimension. But when movement on the wealth cycle is upwards, everything else being equal, an increase in position on the power cycle also generally occurs.

How does the power cycle affect the secessionist impulse in wealthy states? Mature states or states on the declining side of their power cycle may be particularly vulnerable to secession. States that are in relative decline may be more subject to political challenge by communal groups dissatisfied with their cultural or socio-political position inside the state and no longer attached to the unified state by an earlier, more ardent nationalism within the society as a whole. With security provided, and with the promise of access to a larger preferential trade area in the offing, secessionist groups feel the loosening of ties internal to the state and at the same time assume that they may be able to do better by striking out on their own in the world of high finance and statecraft.

Thus, as momentum changes on the power cycle, secessionist entities feel the altered nature of the political-economic equilibrium within the state and are encouraged to search for a new grand bargain. In this sense, locus on the power cycle of the state is causally related to the impulse for revisionist nationalism by communal groups inside the state, perhaps epitomized by the situation in which the United Kingdom finds itself. The same might be said for Belgium, Spain, and Italy. But is the unity of Germany, with its growing decentralization of the Laender from Bavaria to Baden-Wuertemberg, any less vulnerable to these secessionist urges?

The power cycle has another important impact upon the theoretical and empirical relationship between size and per capita income. This effect follows because the state power cycles map the changing structure of the international system.

Logic of the Security Imperative and Trade Openness

Presence of structural stability among countries creates a rather certain and confident political environment that is conducive to trade and to increasing trade openness.[21] Conversely, presence of structural instability causes a more uncertain and insecure political setting in which protectionism and a closure of the trading system become more likely. The claim is that structural stability generates a propensity for trade liberalization, whereas structural instability causes a breakdown of confidence in security, a political inwardness, a commercial defensiveness, and an inclination towards protectionism. Linking the realms of commerce and security, the argument advanced here explains important constraints and stimuli to trade liberalization.

HOW STRUCTURAL STABILITY FOSTERS TRADE LIBERALIZATION

Structural stability describes a situation in which the *expectations* of governments about their future roles in foreign policy and their power are congruent with the *actual change* in their power and role.[22] Since in practice the only time this congruence occurs between the change in state power and role on the one hand, and the change in foreign policy expectations on the other, is when growth is linear, major periods of structural stability are indexed by linear change.

In long periods of comparatively linear change on the power cycle of a state, there are no surprises in terms of future foreign policy expectations. Future foreign policy expectations are expressed as a line drawn in tangent to the power curve. Indeed, when a state increases its share of relative power at an accelerating rate prior to the first inflection point, each forecast of future foreign policy expectations is too conservative (slopes of the consecutive expectations lines trend ever upwards) rather than too alarmist. (Similarly, the continuation of prior trends reinforces predictions for states on other segments of the cycle, whether it is experiencing diminishing rates of increase, accelerating decline, or deceleration towards a lower threshold.) The confidence in past forecasts therefore reinforces the confidence in future forecasts.

Linear change thus means that states are able to forecast their futures with some consistency and a minimum of surprise. A sense of confidence emerges during such periods of linear change in the state experience. This confidence is amplified when it is shared across states (i.e., when a number of states experience linear change in the growth of their power during the same interval of history) and encompasses the most powerful states in the system. This ambiance of certainty and confidence associated with a stable structural situation in the international system is a pre-condition for security.

In such a stable structural situation, extending over a period of decades, the sense of assuredness about the direction of power trends becomes irresistible to the policymaker. This confidence spreads to the private sector as well. The argument made here is that in this 'secure' kind of decision environment, trade liberalization becomes easier.

Business thrives under these circumstances of certainty, calm, and predictability. Firms are able to make decisions about investment and production in an atmosphere of comparative trust and confidence. When the international conditions of structural stability prevail, some of the risk associated with international business is removed.[23] Firms are better able to forecast their own futures, their profitability, and their potential for expansion.

In these commercial circumstances of greater predictability, firms and governments are much more prone to support trade liberalization. They enjoy growth and profitability. Trade liberalization is looked upon not as a threat to their output but rather as a vehicle to even greater prosperity. Confidence associated with a more certain and predictable political environment is transmitted to the commercial and trade setting, resulting in willingness to open markets. Firm and government together facilitate a liberalization of trade that is systems-wide and reinforcing. Structural stability becomes the key international catalyst to a more open trading world.

HOW STRUCTURAL INSTABILITY UNDERMINES TRADE LIBERALIZATION

Structural instability generates effects that are the opposite of those associated with structural stability. That is, structural instability creates a propensity for protectionism. How this occurs is seen more easily when structural instability is examined more fully.

As argued above, most periods of history involve structural change that continues prior trends and hence is fairly predictable. But there are also periods when a number of leading states in the system experience an abrupt and monumental *shift in the trend* of their respective trajectories of relative power (that is, of their future expectations). These shifting trends map the changing structure of the system. The argument here is that these so-called 'shifting tides of history' force states to abandon long-held projections of future foreign policy role, creating great political uncertainty, and even bellicosity. Such a setting of massive structural change and uncertainty, called systems transformation, is likely to generate protectionism as states look inward, viewing the external environment as essentially competitive if not also hostile, and become extremely averse to economic risk.

Structural instability results from such abrupt and monumental shifts in the trend of expectations as states move either up or down their respective power cycles. These times of abrupt change are indexed more specifically as passage through a 'critical point' on the state power cycle. These critical points are the places on the curve where long-experienced linear change abruptly becomes non-linear change, an inversion from the prior trend. There are four critical points of non-linearity on the power cycle: first inflection, upper turning point, second inflection, and lower turning point. When these critical points will occur is not predictable. This is the exact obverse of linear change, where predictions (expectations) are more or less certain. Unpredictability is a characteristic of non-linear change, which is the most abrupt and total alteration of past behaviour possible. Non-linearity is the denouement of the forecaster, since all linear forecasts will fail by definition in the face of non-linear change.[24]

Hence major structural change involves abrupt, unpredictable, and massive change on the state power cycle. At a critical point, everything changes: the slope of the expectations line moves in the opposite direction, away from the trend of the previous period of history. A complete discontinuity has occurred. Such change is totally upsetting to the foreign policymaker, and, as it happens, also to the commercial firm attempting to operate in such a political environment. This is what is meant by structural instability. The effects of structural instability find a focus in the foreign policy expectations of government. Change that is abrupt and monumental unsettles the international system, and it unsettles the commercial and trading environment as well.

When governments are unable to project policy trends reliably, they function poorly, sometimes overreact, and become defensive. When firms experience the same type of inability to plan and to anticipate the future because of a sudden discontinuity in governmental (and their own) expectations, they become wary, defensive, and prone to risk-aversion. In such a context, both government and firm become vulnerable to easy solutions. The answers to what were normal problems of competition now commonly become requests for government assistance. A familiar type of government assistance requested is the imposition of some form of trade impediment. Protectionism takes root.

Hence, during periods of structural instability, the firm must contend with an ambiance beset with governmental uncertainty, overreaction, and foreign policy strain. This is not an environment in which commerce thrives. Rather, in such an environment, government is vulnerable to the pleas from business for a halt to imports that seem to erode the market share of the import-competing industries. Export industries at the same time may experience growing interference with trade abroad and thus may seek to enlarge their domestic market share through the imposition of tariffs, quotas, or other non-tariff barriers. The reaction of foreign firms to recently erected trade barriers, in an atmosphere of increasing uncertainty and distrust between governments, tends to reinforce the protectionist tendencies of domestic firms as they assess what for them seems to be an increasingly hostile foreign trade environment as well.

The essence of the problem of increasing protectionism, as seen from this perspective, is the discontinuity in foreign policy expectations that eventually affects the power trajectory of each government.[25] When a number of major governments all go through critical points on their power curves at about the same time, the problem of uncertainty and foreign policy tension is magnified considerably. Indeed, this is the interval of systems transformation that takes place when structural change is at a maximum within the international system (chapter 5). Such intervals of systems transformation are especially problematic for the trading, financial, and commercial arena as well as for the arena of world order. Structural instability undermines the prerequisites within the political order for the kind of commercial and trade openness and farsightedness that is essential to the furtherance of the liberal trade regime.

In sum, intervals of history with low to moderate structural change are periods when increased trade and investment liberalization become possible. Abrupt non-linear change in the system unsettles this confidence, causes governments to think increasingly in relative gains and zero sum terms, and undermines willingness to open borders to trade. The possible relationship between this structural variable and per capita income growth (past and future) is a theoretical question we return to later in this chapter.

Impact of Convergence

Convergence is the decline of total factor productivities and hence of per capita income growth in the later stages of economic development towards an asymptotic level.[26] By dint of its wealth and size, the United States is closest to this asymptotic level. According to Paul

Krugman and others, 2.5 per cent is the maximum growth rate for the United States in the long run given its structural and industrial composition.[27] It cannot achieve a higher rate of growth without inflation.

All states converge in their per capita income growth rates. Newly Developing Countries such as China, Brazil, India, or Mexico enjoy very high rates of growth in per capita wealth. But for various reasons associated with the age of the economy, switches from efficiency to equality concerns, changes in the age composition of the workforce, and an inability to innovate technologically as easily as to imitate, the productivity of the more advanced economies tends to decline. Per capita income growth rates follow, although only to an asymptotic level since the decline in rate is somewhat offset by the increasing size of the economies in terms of the generation of jobs and revenue.

Convergence would reinforce the strength of a size/growth threshold. Convergence would generate a tighter statistical fit for the non-linear threshold, since as economies mature, their per capita income growth rates tend to converge towards that of the present-day United States. Japan, for example, in the 1983–93 interval enjoyed a per capita income growth rate measured in PPP (Purchasing Power Parity) of about 4.3 per cent. But in the next ten year interval its growth was in the range of 2.5 per cent (perhaps below this figure because of the financial crisis and banking reform), much like that of the United States. While in the earlier period its relatively high growth rate makes Japan look like something of an outsider, which will somewhat distort the regression fit of the size/growth threshold, in the subsequent period its per capita income growth rate looks much more like that of a 'normal' advanced industrial country.

The likely effect of economic growth and of convergence will be to reinforce the limiting characteristics of a growth threshold imposed by size on per capita incomes of the advanced industrial states.

Relationship between the Size of a Polity and Its Economic Growth

Analytically, the problem of whether size is a brake on economic growth can be posed by calling attention to the following empirical observations and theoretical assumptions.

Controlling for Development

Since patterns of per capita income growth exist for countries across the developmental experience of a polity, these patterns must be controlled for. Otherwise a pattern of conflicting per capita income growth rates associated with level of development will distort or obscure the relationship between state size and growth. Countries at each phase of the developmental experience ought to be treated relative to each other rather than relative to countries in earlier or later phases. Inasmuch as the set of countries of greatest interest to studies of regional economic integration as articulated here are the advanced industrial countries, the easiest way to control for stage of economic development is to isolate this set of advanced industrial countries for analysis.

Movement to a Larger Trade System Diminishes Integration

The secessionist entity is smaller, usually much smaller, than the original state of which it was a member. The modern theorists see this entry of the secessionist fragment into the world trading system as painless since size and the increase in growth rate are said to be uncorrelated. Neoclassical theorists only went so far as to say that the level of economic growth could improve if a state as a unified entity entered a larger trade area or union. Following neoclassical theory on economic integration, the size of a polity and the degree of its integration are associated with (a) economies of scale, (b) international scale considerations, (c) management efficiencies, (d) monopoly effects, (e) factor integration efficiencies, and (f) reductions of border risk. Increased productivity benefits from the concatenation of these influences. With secession, an entity moves from a larger, highly integrated state economy to an even larger entity (a regional trade area or union, or the liberalized global trading system itself) at a lower degree of integration.[28]

Levels of Integration

The process of separation evolves over the three stages of statehood, secession, and entry into the larger trade system. Under the further pressures of globalization and technological change, the degree of integration may be increasing everywhere. But the greatest economic and political cohesion still exists within the nation-state. From the perspective of economic efficiency, 'separation of nations is never desirable.'[29] Unified countries possess advantages in terms of avoidance of duplication costs for administration, local security, and defence.

The next highest level of integration occurs within the regional preferential trade area or community such as the European Union or

NAFTA. Investment figures, for example, show that the concentration of investment by a state's own investors is of course highest within the state itself, next highest within a regional trading bloc of which the state is a member, and finally least high or most diffuse within the international trading system as a whole. Concentration of investment is at the heart of integration.

While increasingly interdependent, the polities within the trade order at large are the least economically cohesive in both trade and investment terms. Hence the secessionist state, facing loss of the benefits of integration even as the advantages of scale may increase, within the preferential regional trade area but even more so among the states of the larger global trading system, must decide how to establish a better bargain.[30]

The problem for the secessionist entity is that no one at the regional, much less the global, level is going to replace the benefits of integration that the entity has foregone through separation. No one is going to provide the support for education, technological innovation, greater financial stability, international security, absence of border risk, and bargaining leverage that the entity had enjoyed when it was part of the larger, more integrated, unified state. There is no economic or other reason to suppose otherwise.

Placed in the Quebec context, for example, the advantages to Quebec from consistent and beneficial regulations[31] across Canada (as opposed to across North America or across the larger global trading system) are quite apparent in the single crucial sector of transportation. In the absence of such intra-Canada regulation favouring Montreal in terms of choice airline routes, Quebec may discover that the natural geographic and economic advantages of Toronto will cause a shift of airline activity to that city away from Montreal after 'deregulation' or 'reregulation' on a North American if not world scale.

Integration within states is higher regarding regulation not because the fact of regulation is less prevalent within the global trading system (it is not), but because regulation within the nation-state is often more homogeneous and more plausibly administered than within the international trading system of very dissimilar governments. Of course, when the *level* of regulation is reduced, whether inside the state alone or within the larger trading area, then trade will normally benefit overall. But the matter of the *coherence* of regulation and the *effectiveness* of regulation is as important as the level and is exactly what is involved in the notion of integration within Canada as a whole now favouring

Quebec and other provinces, but what is not present to the same degree externally across the global trading system.

Non-linearity

Standard linear models do not fit the relation between market size and growing per capita income. A simple thought experiment indicates why. If a direct relationship existed between size and the rate of per capita income growth, then the larger the market became, either treated cross-sectionally or across time, the higher would be the rate of per capita income growth. Since size is open-ended (limitless) in terms of magnitude, i.e., ever-expanding, the *rate of growth* in per capita income would be ever-expanding. This is logically and empirically an impossibility.

Hence the relation between market size and rate of per capita income growth must be non-linear. Suppose population size is the independent variable indexing market size, and growth rate of per capita income – or of Purchasing Power Parity (PPP) per capita – growth is the dependent variable indexing the rate of increase in wealth. If percent change in (PPP) per capita is plotted on the Y-axis and population size is plotted on the X-axis, then the form that the non-linear curve must take is concave downwards. Specific shape of the curve and the actual quantitative values of the functional relationship are an empirical matter.

It is a mistake simply to dub any curve that is concave downwards as 'diminishing marginal returns.' In this case, the relation for small states between increasing size and rate of increasing per capita wealth is direct and strong. But the relation suddenly hits an upper limit and disappears. What happens here mathematically is quite different from the traditional diminishing marginal returns curve found elsewhere in economics.

Size/Growth Threshold

On theoretical grounds we thus posit a *threshold effect*. At some point the increase in size of the polity and of its market no longer possesses a positive impact upon the increase in the rate of per capita income (or PPP per capita) growth. This threshold is likely to be sharp and quite impermeable as the need for specialization is satisfied across industries at a given level of technology by a market of adequate size. The thresh-

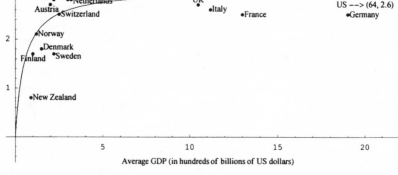

Figure 1   Percentage Growth of Per Capita Purchasing Power Parity As a Function of Economic Size for Eighteen Advanced Industrial Nations (1983–93)

old effect causes the previously strong relationship suddenly to disappear. For the larger states the relation between increased size and increased per capita wealth is non-existent.

But for very small states of the size equated with most secessionist entities, the relation between size and the rate of growth in welfare is quite different. For these very small polities, especially in the advanced industrial world where growth rates have already stabilized, the association between size and the rate of per capita income or PPP growth will be strong and direct. For these small polities, the lack of size is a damper on growth rate.

Empirical Analysis on the Size/Growth Threshold

When we carry out the empirical analysis, the results are striking, as evidenced by Figure 1. The relationship is indeed close and positive for the smaller economies. As the economies increase in size past a certain threshold, the rate of increase in per capita income (PPP) does fall off precipitously. Thus the relationship between size and the rate of growth of per capita wealth is decidedly non-linear as is captured in Figure 1.

The nonlinear function rises rapidly for the small state, then level-ling out at a per capita growth rate of about 3 per cent.[32] When aver-aged over the 1983–93 period, and indexed separately either by population size or by GDP, each indicator of market size revealed approximately the same result. Similar results occurred for the interval 1988–98. For a single indicator to explain so much of the variance in the dependent variable is welcome. Regarding this set of advanced indus-trial countries at least, such strong and parsimonious statistical results suggest that the relation between size and rate of growth is quite robust.

An objection may be raised to this research design, however. The objection is that Quebec is assumed for the purposes of the argument to accede directly to membership in a regional trade agreement. This membership is supposed to offer all of the benefits of scale and secu-rity that a state in isolation does not have. Therefore, it might be argued, the research design is spurious because it pits countries in the international system, some of which are not members of a regional eco-nomic entity, against a situation in which Quebec might find itself a full member of a preferential trade area. Thus, results from the empiri-cal test, so the argument might go, would not apply to an independent Quebec that immediately becomes a full member of NAFTA.

The problem with this criticism is that it ignores the composition of the sample of countries employed in the empirical test. These countries are either members of the former European Economic Community (EEC) or of the European Free Trade Association (EFTA). Many have become members of the European Community or of the subsequent European Union. Thus the empirical relationship that is observed in this analysis is fully compatible with any situation that a future Que-bec might experience. The key observation is that the threshold effect regarding the relation between size and growth holds in spite of the reality that many of the states in the sample are members of preferen-tial trade areas or unions.

But this conclusion prompts a further question. How can the pres-ence of a direct relation between size and the rate of growth be explained for the very small state when the relation appears to hold even inside a larger regional trade area or union? If the explanation is pursued in the context of the Vinerian model, the extension by Max Corden may be helpful in terms of scale economies.[33] First, part of the reason that the small state still experiences a drag on its rate of growth inside a regional trade area may be that trade diversion occurs from the state of which the secessionist entity was originally a member to the regional trade grouping of which it subsequently becomes a member.[34] The regional trade area benefits from the membership of the secessionist entity but the entity itself does not. Hence small size continues to be penalized even though the secessionist entity continues to enjoy access to the larger trade grouping, albeit as an independent political actor.

Second, following Corden, there may be important scale effects that also account for the direct relation between size and growth for the very small state. Corden posits cost-reduction as well as trade creation effects on the one hand, and trade-suppression as well as trade diversion effects on the other. Trade-suppression could result if 'imports' from the state of which the secessionist entity was originally a member are replaced by domestic production after secession. Scale effects would make this new production possible for firms within the secessionist state after secession. Perhaps non-tariff barriers ought to be substituted for formal tariffs to make this use of trade diversion and of trade-suppression plausible since tariffs themselves are presumably being phased out throughout the regional trade area. Together trade diversion and trade-suppression help explain the perpetuation of the size / growth relation for the very small state.

Translating Abstract Costs into Social Meaning

As far as Canada is concerned, the results are particularly interesting. According to the expected results for a country of the size of Canada, Canada ought to have a growth rate of wealth of 2.75 per cent. In reality, for the period 1983–93, Canada averaged a growth rate of about 3 per cent. Thus Canada has been growing faster than the systemic norm for a country of its size.

Now let us further address the question we started out to measure, that is, the relationship between economic size and the rate of growth in per capita wealth for Quebec.

Notwithstanding the fact that Quebec has been in recession (a high level of unemployment, for example) because of the hovering threat of secession (a problem that was reversed considerably by 2000), let us assume that Quebec in Confederation can do at least as well as any other province in terms of the generation of personal wealth. This means that in the decade of 1983–93, the growth rate of per capita PPP ought to be about 3 per cent, the same as for the growth rate of Canada for the decade 1983–93. However, if Quebec were plotted on the graph (Figure 1) depicting the relationship between economic size and the rate of per capita PPP growth, the corresponding growth rate expected of Quebec would be only about 2 per cent.

This means that if Quebec were to separate, its generation of per capita wealth would occur at a rate that yields over the decade perhaps one-half of what Quebec could generate inside Confederation. That is a profoundly significant result!

According to these findings based on the experience of some eighteen advanced-industrial nations, if Quebec goes independent it sacrifices a large percentage of its aggregate economic growth and increase in per capita wealth. This is the trade-off that the Quebec voter must contemplate on referendum night. This is the hard empirical evidence necessary to back up the speculation that 'heart' and 'head' were different after the 1998 Quebec government election on the matter of secession, and that emotional appeals to sovereignty had to take into account the sacrifice expected of the voter in personal economic terms.

Since the empirical analysis was done on countries that were for the most part members of some type of preferential trade area or union, NAFTA membership for Quebec would not change the disparity in the figures between a Canada growth rate for Quebec and a much lower independence growth rate for Quebec even if it were eventually a member of NAFTA. Membership in NAFTA for an independent Quebec is not likely to erase the threshold effect on the relation between size and growth. The myth is that NAFTA can substitute for Canada as an integrated market in strengthening the Quebec per capita income growth rate. But this myth is wrong. Quebec as an independent entity, inside or outside NAFTA, will always pay a growth premium to a Quebec that remains inside Canadian Confederation. If Quebec had become independent in 1983, the average Quebec citizen today would be poorer by about 50 per cent of his or her increase in per capita income. This means the following in terms of income for an average Quebecer over the last decade.

In 1997, a per capita unit of Purchasing Power Parity (PPP) for an average Canadian was about $20,970 U.S. If PPP per capita were the same in Quebec as on average in the rest of Canada, then the amount gained in Confederation in terms of growth over the prior year by that same average Quebecer was about $210 U.S. That figure is calculated by recognizing that the growth rate of per capita PPP was about 50 per cent more (i.e., 3 per cent) for Quebec as a province than for Quebec as an independent country (i.e., about 2 per cent). In 1993, for a Quebec family of four, this growth premium resulting from participation in Confederation amounts to about $850 U.S.

If Quebec had seceded in 1983, that same family of four would have relinquished more than $8,000 U.S. by 1997, not counting interest, relative to the amount of per capita PPP the family actually enjoyed because Quebec was a full member of Confederation.

This figure may not seem like much to those at the top of the income pyramid. But to those at the bottom of the income pyramid, and to many of those in the middle, this is a very high economic price to pay for slightly greater political sovereignty after secession relative to the extensive sovereignty (sovereignty-association according to the late Robert Bourassa) Quebec already possesses. Aggregated over the life of a child and properly invested, this is an amount that could pay for the higher education of a couple of children at public universities. Or if such an amount were aggregated over the lifetime of an individual and again properly invested, this amount could yield quite a retirement nest egg. In an era experiencing uncertainty over pension funds, such an amount could reasonably be considered a kind of insurance policy to augment the possible inadequacy of public pension proceeds.

All of the costs identified in this study that would accompany secession add up to something very real and represent a considerable loss of wealth for the average Quebecer. Whether the average Quebecer is willing to assume these costs is not for others to decide. But the Quebec voter should at least have the requisite information available to him or her upon which to make an acute and balanced judgment about the opportunity costs associated with small economic size of the secessionist state.

A further caution is also in order. Based on our earlier discussion of the relation between structural stability and trade liberalization, the question arises whether the future international system will support the same rates of growth of the past half century. It is well to remember that all of the growth in per capita income occurred amidst monumental trade and investment liberalization, through some eight major rounds of global tariff reduction, during a very propitious interval of structural change from 1945 to 1990. Notwithstanding the Cold War, the underlying structural situation was quite stable and free of abrupt or massive surprises. With the advent of systems transformation in the 1990s, the effect on the trading regime in the first decades of the twenty-first century could be less helpful to existing liberalization impulses.

Causal Assumptions Underlying Costs of Secession

A paper by Maurice Obstfeld and Kenneth Rogoff reinforces the assertion of different levels of integration for state, preferential trading area, and global trading system in that an increase in trading costs increases the preference for domestic goods at a rate much faster than linear.[35] According to their analysis, where trading costs are near zero, home bias is near zero, but when trading costs are moderately high, home bias 'is exponentially sensitive to trading costs.'[36]

A thought experiment suggests that the ability to offset high trading costs by such home-country bias is likely to be more pronounced within the large rather than the small state. Specialization, which is at the heart of the trading costs non-linear pattern, is more feasible in the large state than in the small state. The small state must depend to a greater extent for specialization of production and consumption on the international trading system.

As in the Obstfeld–Rogoff study, the language used in the McCallum and the Helliwell studies[37] is that of 'home bias' in the trade of goods or the 'segmentation' of goods markets across countries. While that language is accurate and well-grounded in the literature, the notion of home 'bias' suggests an implication of something 'distorted' or 'unusual' about home markets as opposed to international markets. I prefer to examine the matter of transport costs and other impediments to the perfect movement of traded goods (and regarding 'other impediments,' in terms of services as well) from the analytic side that stresses how incompletely integrated the global trading system truly is. From this side, the problem is a bias in the lesser degree of integration in the international trading system than within the regional preferential trade markets, which in turn are less integrated than the individual home-country markets. If there is a bias, the distortion lies in the larger trading system, not in the home-country market.

Second, the focused work on the role of transport costs in traded goods has helped explain various important puzzles, primarily in international economics and finance. Regarding the difference in level of integration between the state market and the global market, many other rigidities surely will be discovered, such as the changeability, unevenness, and imperfect implementation of regulation and deregulation that interfere with the perfection of global markets, thus rendering certain domestic markets both more comprehensible and accessible to the investor and businessperson.

It is the effect of transport costs and all other rigidities and encumbrances between state markets that will mean a loss in the PPP growth rate and economic welfare for the average citizen inside the secessionist state.

Resolving the Paradigmatic Controversy

The findings of this chapter resolve much of the controversy between the neoclassical and contemporary theorists on economic integration. Both appear to be wrong. Both are right. Relation between economic size and the rate of per capita income (or PPP) growth is more complex than originally thought.

Each group of theorists appears to have been wrong in some measure. The neoclassical theorists did not foresee how sharply the economic benefits of a larger market size tends to fall off. They may also have underestimated the propensity for secession among multi-ethnic states that also are democracies once regional economic integration among polities of a certain size proceeds. Likewise the contemporary theorists of size and integration appear to be wrong about their assumption that there is no relation between market size and per capita income (or PPP) growth.

On the other hand, and more significantly, when the size/growth threshold effect is introduced, each group of theorists appears to be right in their respective assumptions about how integration impacts economic growth. The per capita income growth rate cycle (curve) explains the accelerative and subsequent decelerative growth rates for countries at either end of the growth experience.

The neoclassical analysts were correct that there is a substantial impact of market size on the increase in per capita income (per capita income growth rate) for the very small polities. Economic integration offers the possibility of reduced border risk for the firm and various efficiencies that the very small market cannot supply. In these matters, the neoclassical theorists were on solid conceptual ground.

But the modern theorists of growth and economic integration are also correct in that these benefits of economic specialization seem to fall off quickly. Big countries, especially in the context of globalization, can supply most of the needs of exchange and specialization as well as security for the firm. The modern theorists may well be right too in their seeming conclusion that moderate-to-large sized polities in conjunction with liberalized world markets may have little need for the preferential, regional trade order.

Key to a resolution of this difference of interpretation between the neoclassical and the modern theorist is the existence of the threshold effect. Suitably reinforced by empirical evidence, the existence of the threshold effect helps sort out conceptual contradiction and makes possible a reconciliation of the two sets of theoretical argument.

Assessing the Policy Implications

Existence of the threshold effect now clarifies several long-standing policy ambiguities. First, when in December 1958 the Common Market was formed, the Benelux countries and the larger Italy surely joined to obtain the economic benefits of scale economies and related efficiencies that are so evident prior to reaching the integration threshold of 25 million or so citizens. These considerations probably meant less to the bigger German and French populations (and economies). Germany and France entered the Common Market largely for political reasons – to overcome centuries of animosity, a problem that the smaller polities in turn did not pose towards one another. Thus different governments sought membership in the regional collective for different yet complementary economic and political reasons in a fashion that the threshold effect now makes explicit.

Second, it is now beginning to be clearer why the propensity for secession has not gone very far in Spain, Great Britain, France, Italy, Belgium, and other advanced industrial countries. Even though the World Trade Organization has advanced the cause of global free trade from which all may have the chance to benefit, and even though the EU and NAFTA respectively offer potentially secessionist fragments the prospect of enhanced specialization of markets, the degree of integration within each of these realms is still less than that afforded by the individual nation-state of which each secessionist fragment remains a member. Similarly, trade diversion and trade-depression may hold back the very small state from experiencing the scale effects and freedom from border risk that states beyond the size/growth threshold seem to enjoy.

For instance, for the Basques to rely (after secession) on the European Union instead of the Spanish economy for primary commercial and trade interchange means that the Basques will be assuming significant opportunity costs. The degree of integration within the European Union, all things considered, is still considerably less than the degree of integration presently enjoyed by the Basque community and by Basque enterprises within the Spanish economy. For the Basque business community to make the abrupt adjustment to the lower level of integration afforded by the European Union, and to be shorn of many of their prior cultural associations, institutional contacts, subsidies, and commercial preferences, despite wealth that exceeds that of some other Spanish provinces, is a step many of them may not be prepared to take.

Third, is the size/growth threshold applicable to internal polities as well, to the agglomeration of cities? Evidence indicates that, although the largest cities grew fastest in terms of productivity gains in the 1980s, the group of cities in the second largest category of employment grew fastest in productivity terms in the 1990s.[38] Explanation is that innovations in communications technology have allowed large companies to relocate operations to smaller cities where labour costs are lower. Overall, size remains important because the larger cities are the urban areas that offer the most skilled workers and specialized services needed by corporations. But, as the advantage of urban size suddenly changes under the influence of the information revolution, the size/growth threshold may be operating internal to states too.

Fourth, to advocate for example that Quebec – if it should secede, and even if it becomes a full member of NAFTA (not without making many changes perhaps for the better in its own government to economy interaction) – can do so without loss of economic advantage is simply not borne out by this theoretical argument and set of empirical findings. Given its population of 7.5 million people, Quebec will continue to enjoy the advantages of association with the more highly integrated Canadian economy relative to NAFTA at a lower level of integration. According to these findings, not until Quebec obtains a population perhaps three or four times as large will it entirely be able to dispense with the benefits of Canadian economic union. Secession, according to the threshold effect, will come at a high economic price for Quebec and other similarly small separatist-minded communities.

Fifth, small size is undoubtedly not the only effect on per capita income growth worth studying and hence worth contemplating by Quebec and by other fragmenting movements. Analysis showing an association between the use of English language by a polity and higher volumes of trade surely is relevant to per capita income growth rates and hence to the increase in economic welfare for a polity as well.[39] But the lesson of the language-growth rate argument, just as with the economic size-growth rate argument, can be read two ways.

Some will conclude that small size, like use of French rather than

English, is a stern warning not to secede. A better way to look at the empirical evidence is that small size and use of a primary language other than English is a positive reason to stay united with another diverse society, e.g., with the rest of Canada. Quebec can enjoy all of the advantages of disproportionate trade with France and Francophonie for reasons of language, while enjoying intense trade with English Canada and the United States as well by reason of high degree of integration and proximity respectively. A united Canada including Quebec can indeed enjoy enhanced economic growth and welfare based on the strength of both its principal cultures and sets of resulting economic ties.

Language and trade ought to be explored more fully in an expanded model that looks beyond the relationship of GDP/trade and the association with English speaking countries. This relationship ought to be looked at against the following four variables: (1) hegemony – the effect of British economic dominance in the nineteenth century and of U.S. economic dominance in the twentieth century; (2) ideology – the degree to which elites accept and institutionalize free trade as a cultural ideal; (3) geopolitical maritime status – the extent to which large naval-maritime fleets and access to good port facilities are key to trading volume; and (4) English as a second language – the extent to which English as a second language supports the earlier findings that English as a primary language assists communication and therefore trading activity. In this last context, Quebec presumably flourishes according to this model of economic performance.

In conclusion, notwithstanding arguments to the contrary that do, or appear to, alter neoclassical theorist's interpretation of the value of size, a small state that secedes from a larger polity pays a price in terms of a reduced rate of growth. Of course, in an era of trade liberalization and assured territorial security, the small state can survive. Some like Singapore may 'beat the odds' and even grow at disproportionately high rates, especially if they enjoy the benefits of early development long known to be correlated with faster rates of growth than advanced industrialism. But, on average, until it reaches a population size of perhaps 25 million, the rate of growth of the small, advanced industrial state is constrained.

At that point, a threshold effect occurs in which the association between size and rate of growth changes. For the large state, size no longer has much impact on rate of growth since scale, degree of integration, factor efficiencies, and reduction of border risk all become much less important to the large state as rates of per capita income (PPP) growth approach an asymptotic limit.

Postulated theoretically, and tested empirically, a threshold effect exists in the relation between increasing state size and increasing rate of growth in Purchasing Power Parity. Secession carries a burden for the small independent actor, regardless of whether it enters a regional trade bloc – secession will affect the rapidity with which it is likely to grow.

Does the small size of a separatist entity stimulate the propensity to secede, does it hinder secession, or is size an irrelevant variable in the equation that accounts for secessionist behaviour? In the judgment of many of the proponents of secession, minus supporting evidence, small size is a stimulus to secede because these proponents have convinced themselves that a small state can do better by itself in the context of the liberalized trading system than inside a larger polity. Most growth and trade economists will not go this far. All they will contend is that a small state recently carved out of a larger polity is likely to be able to do as well economically as it did prior to secession, but with the proviso that the entity participate fully in some sort of preferential trade area or union where it has access to a larger market. According to these economists, the small secessionist fragment will not be penalized economically by secession. Size for them is an irrelevant variable, at least as it is expressed in terms of economic considerations.

This chapter comes to quite different conclusions. It contends that the international trading system, however liberalized it may be in terms of tariff reduction and the elimination of many restrictions on the movement of the factors of production, is still far less liberalized (integrated) than the market of one of the leading trading states. The cut-off point where size no longer counts, according to the empirical findings in this study, is a market about that of the UK in 1990. Above this threshold the economies of scale and other benefits to regional integration tend to fall off very rapidly. But below this threshold the benefits to regional integration increase very rapidly as an inverse proportion of size. Measured in terms of per capita income growth rate foregone, the economic cost of separation to a state the size of Quebec will over time be quite appreciable.

Hence based on the findings presented in this study, small economic size *should* act as a deterrent to separation. But *whether* small economic size actually *does* hinder separation is a question that depends upon perception, politics, and how seriously individual members of a separatist entity value economic costs. If, however, they give serious consideration to their long-term economic well-being, then small economic size will indeed act as a deterrent to separation.

CHAPTER SEVEN

What Kind of Canada in the Twenty-First Century?

At a minimum, there are five interpretations describing the unity implications of the 1997 and 2000 federal elections and the 1998 Quebec election. Options for governance flow more or less readily from each of these.

Some of the interpretations complement the others. It is therefore likely that more than one of the options could be practised simultaneously. For example, one or more modes of decentralization could accompany the effort to establish a relationship of 'asymmetrical federalism' with Quebec. Ideally, the analyst would like to rank the interpretations as to likelihood, yet the degree of political uncertainty is so great that such a ranking would be overly bold. Assessing possible responses to each of the scenarios is perhaps a safer course.

In Arend Lijphart's assessment, Canada is located somewhere between the 'consociational' category of polities in which elite accommodation prevails and the 'centrifugal' category in which the relationship between Quebec and the Rest of Canada is more politically distant.[1] The richness of typologies and scenarios for Canada in the twenty-first century goes beyond these two possibilities.

The history of Canada has been a brilliant effort to balance the forces of concentration and expansion. For instance, as Thomas Axworthy observes, 'Trudeau is best known for his elegant defense of classical federalism, opposing federal centralization in the 1950s when the provinces were weak and just as stoutly opposing federal decentralization in the 1960s when the provinces were strong.'[2] Guy Laforest argues similarly, in a piquant passage on political theorist Charles Taylor's thought, that a democracy centered more around citizen participation, a political system open to national pluralism, and a liberalism able to balance the rights of citizens with those of communities – all of this will become possible in Canada only if we succeed in renewing our federal system from top to bottom.[3]

The room for federal reform in any polity is substantial. So are the potential benefits.

Aboriginal Peoples, Cultural Survival, and Democratic Pluralism

For Aboriginal peoples, the problems of cultural survival are greater than for other cultural-linguistic communities. Traditional Aboriginal culture was established on a framework of the hunter-gatherer activity that is difficult to sustain because of the decline of habitat, competition for the same activity by other groups including sportsmen, and internal population pressure. In some cases, there is a committed rejection of materialism, the desire to provide one's children with health, education, and opportunity that creates inevitable stress vis-à-vis traditional values and ways of life. Wives and mothers feel this tension profoundly. Cultural survival is also difficult because of the small size of some bands, diffusion over huge territories, and diffusion within larger populations of diverse backgrounds.

Autonomy for the individual and for the collective is at the heart of cultural survival. But what type of autonomy is necessary, and how much autonomy? For some, contemplation, practice of ritual, and observance of custom is highly personal but is compatible with a modern existence and the practices of other cultures. For others, the collective life of the community is key and isolation from other cultures is thought to promote such collective values. Currently, maximum political independence (self-government) is held to be beneficial. But even if the idealized goals are clear, many inevitable trade-offs exist in reality.

According to Peter Russell, Canada and New Zealand have approached the matter of Aboriginal self-government in a similar way, while Australia and the United States seem to reject many of these proposals. Perhaps different philosophies whether the rights of special groups transgress the liberal values of 'the common good' and regarding the individual are in part responsible for these different approaches. Likewise, the provision of services, attitudes towards basic human needs, and attitudes towards the idea of universal human rights also account for the differences in governmental policies. Actual governmental policy differs far less across these countries however than professed policy doctrine.

An irony of Aboriginal policy in each country is that peoples so different are in fact treated so similarly. Likewise, the contradictions in Aboriginal policy remain striking. For instance, Will Kymlicka claims that there are not enough Aboriginal peoples in Canada to justify political secession (the 'viability as justification' argument). This may be true for the majority of bands and communities. Yet from time to time, the Cree seem to advocate quite a different position. There is also a clash between financial dependency on the federal government and asserted self-government. Likewise, a policy that denies full mineral rights and the advocacy of self-government may be at odds, especially where financial dependency exists. Nunavut may become the test case. Access to full mineral rights could feed the desire for full political independence.

Democratic pluralism is a large enough concept to encompass a number of different notions of political autonomy. Some of these notions are adequate to ensure cultural survival where the commitment to that survival is pronounced. As long as 'self-government' is not equated with secession, democratic pluralism can assist in preserving the culture of Aboriginal peoples.

Responding to Quebec If Secession Fails

Quebec secession is by no means a guaranteed outcome of current political developments in the province. The federal government may eventually broker a deal between English Canada and Quebec that meets with the approval of both constituencies.[4] A new bargain may knit together the regions and cultures of Canada under a leadership that is broadly represented and that can cajole both cultures to reach terms on an optimal level of political centralization within the polity as a whole.

Politics within Quebec itself is, after all, multi-party. There will always be a political party (as is currently the Quebec Liberal Party) that is more pro-federalist and more able to work with Ottawa. There will also be a 'nationalist' party (as any political party in Quebec must be) in the sense that it defends the francophone nation inside Confederation. A nationalist party will also seek to extract as many benefits as possible from Ottawa, much as any provincial government seeks to do. Because of its favoured position as a cultural pole within Canada, a nationalist party may be more successful than most governing provincial parties in servicing the needs of its own constituency. But this party will not seek to take Quebec out of Confederation, even though its tactics may at times look a little ambiguous on this point.

If the pro-secessionist party (currently the Parti Québécois) loses office, the Rest of Canada (ROC) will obtain a reprieve from Quebec's quest for greater political autonomy. This will not necessarily mean that such a quest has permanently ended, although the start-up costs for a secessionist movement pursuing its cause seriously are very high in terms of emotion, leadership, and stamina.[5]

There are many reasons why the pro-secessionist party (or parties) in Quebec may fail. It may fail because it divides. Division could occur because leadership is either too authoritarian or not authoritarian enough. The independence wing of the party could become totally disenchanted with the party's commitment to pursue separation vigorously and to govern in a way that insists on the dominance of the French language, education in French schools only, and immigration that supports French culture and politics. The question of slow versus fast could divide the party more in terms of strategy and means than in terms of the general goal of secession. Incompetence or inattentiveness of leadership could undermine the pro-secessionist party. Dissatisfaction with the party's governing agenda, for reasons that have little to do with the larger goal of secession itself, combined with the loss of a favoured and effective leader might limit the chances of a pro-secessionist party at election time.

A shift in political support for the secessionist party, despite a general agreement on the goal of separation within the Quebec constituency, would pose an interesting problem of governance. A prominent reason for a shift in support would be a decline in the economic fortunes of the province – a decline tied to a more general downturn of the business cycle throughout North America or to home-grown problems from within the Quebec industrial base itself. If there were already very high levels of unemployment – caused by structural difficulties within the economy and by loss of investors' confidence (indigenous and foreign) in the vitality of the economy – any further economic downturn would be disastrous and would turn the Quebec constituency away from the provincial governing party, whatever the convictions of that electorate might be about independence.

The Action Démocratique, the party of Mario Dumot, could benefit from appearing to be more nationalist than the Quebec Liberal Party. But it also claims some of the same commitment to a greater (though still qualified) willingness to allow the private sector to solve Quebec's economic problems. In the past, the lack of organization, money, and viable candidates (other than its leader) to the National Assembly have hindered the party's success.

Conversely, a political party like the Parti Québécois could solve economic problems such as deficit reduction, welfare reform, tax moderation, and labour relations in a convincing way, and at the same time invigorate its other programs, including secession, even among a somewhat reticent electorate. Governing well will be the key to everything for the secessionist leadership.

Most of the momentum for secession is likely to be internally generated within Quebec. What the Rest of Canada does, however, will have some consequence. What comes to mind, albeit in a different era and on a very different matter, are the attitudes towards French-language schools in Manitoba and Ontario between 1890 and 1916 and the attitudes within Quebec towards Conscription during the First World War.[6] Overt acts of rudeness on the part of Western provinces or constituencies, as opposed to mere discussion and grumbling, could tilt events in Quebec towards secession. Unfortunately for the federal government, the influence of events external to Quebec is asymmetric. External events can damage support for federalism, but only rarely and under very special circumstances do they damage support for secession.[7] The volatility of Quebec public opinion is probably exaggerated by Quebec-watchers elsewhere in Canada, but that is good because it keeps English Canadians on guard and on good behaviour towards Quebecers and things Quebec more generally. Outsiders can observe how much change has taken place for the better in English Canada towards francophones in a mere twenty-year period. Although foreign analogies are not often useful, the pattern of tolerance and openness on such social and cultural matters is actually a much broader North American phenomenon.

In such an environment, support for secession will always be fragile because it cannot easily find a catalysing event either internal to or external to Quebec. The electoral battle will always be for the middle 20 per cent of political opinion that can be swayed either for or against the notion of secession. As the Quebec electorate becomes richer and older, it also is likely to become more conservative regarding a host of political and social matters. Despite the retention of increasing support for independence by each successive age cohort of opinion in Quebec, there is the counter-phenomenon that as the overall population ages, it becomes more cautious. Like other constituencies throughout Europe and North America, aging Quebecers are worried by such overriding matters as retirement policies, medical insurance, and social security benefits. Should any of the related programs seem threatened by plans for Quebec independence, the support for independence among the crucial 20 per cent of voters may drop suddenly and without obvious explanation.

The question that follows from this awareness of Quebec's delicate political preferences is, What role should the United States play in Canada's problems? An argument sometimes heard in Canada is that the United States has intervened politically everywhere in the world, so why would such interference not be expected in Canadian affairs when, after all, U.S. interests and foreign policy preferences seem to fall so decidedly on the side of the preservation of a strong and united Canada? Under these circumstances of clear choice, combined with the fact of proximity, the United States certainly has a stake in the outcome of the Canadian debate.

Notwithstanding the truth of these contentions, the United States would be well-advised to let Canadians decide this debate. Anything the United States might say or do officially in the way of assertive partiality will only confuse politics in Canada and create a backlash there against the United States, even perhaps among those who would stand to benefit from the interference.

A crude but telling analogy occurs in domestic affairs when one or other spouse is threatened physically in a marital dispute. The neutral (or possibly not neutral) police officer attempts to intervene to preserve domestic peace and prevent bodily harm. At the point of intervention, both husband and wife – the spouse that was threatened with severe harm and the threatener – turn on the police officer and start criticizing him and his effort to help. This situation is known to police officers both in the United States and in Canada.

The United States might naively offer its 'good offices' to act as mediator. But it has no superior insight to offer, no formula for reconciliation that would be unknown to either side, or to Ottawa and Quebec City. American motives throughout will be suspect. In fact, the United States is not a disinterested party. Any kind of political intervention would only transfer the animus of the dispute from the two contestants to the foreign, 'imperial' power, leaving no opportunity for a lasting resolution of the dispute on Canadian terms, which are the only terms that will count in the end.[8]

In contrast, what the United States ought to do is to make its preferences absolutely clear, not only to the governments involved but also to the constituents. Inasmuch as the majority of those who support Quebec independence work in French, this task of communication is more difficult than it may seem, necessitating thoughtful means of conveying fact and idea. Otherwise, statements from Washington will totally miss the intended audience in small-town and rural Quebec.

Such advice is counterintuitive for Americans since, in its politics, the United States has always acted somewhat like a poker player. The U.S. proclivity is to keep both tactics and strategy 'close to one's chest,' revealing nothing in advance, and making up 'moves' as the situation demands. In the context of Canada–U.S. affairs, this is a remarkably unproductive approach.

First, it forgoes the opportunity of educating both the Quebec government and its electorate to the conditions and costs likely to attend separation. The strategy of finesse is likely to mislead Quebecers into believing that the United States really has no interests or preferences at stake. It is apt to encourage Quebecers to make all the wrong assumptions about what the international political and economic climate would be like after separation. Quiet diplomacy of this sort is not diplomacy if a clear and firm expression of position is not given in advance.[9] Otherwise, Quebec quite rightly might expect that the United States really does not care what happens to Canada. Under these circumstances of 'poker diplomacy,' Quebec would have every justification in protesting U.S. consternation after the fact of possible separation.

Second, poker diplomacy is a bad idea for the United States in U.S–Canada matters, because it is likely to mislead Ottawa and the whole of English Canada. By not making clear both its preferences and the limits of its involvement, the United States is likely to delude English Canada into thinking that the United States actually will come to the aid of Ottawa politically and will in the end 'save Canada' (assuming, of course, that if this were the U.S. intention, it had the required skill and wherewithal). Americans may find this presumption preposterous. However, Canadians quite naturally, in the absence of clarification, may believe that the United States will not allow its economic or security interests to be damaged by Quebec secession.

As a result, English Canada may do much less than it should on its own behalf, especially in terms of imaginative bargaining, because of a conviction that long-silent Washington will eventually reveal its hand and come to the assistance of the ailing Confederation. This conviction is just as counterproductive to working out a political resolution with Quebec as is Quebec's view that the U.S. has no interest in the outcome. When Quebecers hear a prominent American jokingly say, 'One embassy or two embassies, what's the difference,' they can be forgiven for believing that Americans are nonchalant on this issue.

Now suppose that the United States shows restraint but forthrightness, that Ottawa acts with skill and magnanimity, that economic and other political events inside Quebec signal to the constituency that secession is very risky, and, as a consequence, Quebec independence falters. How should the United States respond to a Quebec whose independence initiative has once again been defeated?

Some analysts may consider this situation free of complications. But handled poorly, the outcome could be problematic. In a referendum defeat on separation, perhaps more than half of the francophone population of Quebec will have failed in its aspirations. This is not a political and social predicament to take lightly, because there will be repercussions.

First, relationships between the anglophones and allophone in the province are likely to be testy.[10] Francophone *indépendantistes* will be reminded everyday of their inability to escape Ottawa's alleged reach. In this context, the government of Quebec will need the understanding of all sectors of Quebec society – from volunteer organizations to urban and communal groups to churches and synagogues to the media and schools – if awkwardness is to be avoided.

Second, the relationship with Ottawa will not automatically improve. Indeed, the opposite could be true. Ottawa could enter one of its most difficult periods with a Quebec whose majority population is largely disappointed in its secessionist ambitions. Ottawa will not be pictured favourably in the local French press – it will be seen as having acted in a dishonourable way. But communication between English and French Canada must somehow continue and improve after another referendum defeat to reduce the gap between the two solitudes. Ottawa cannot just ignore the relationship between French and English Canada after another failed referendum attempt. This would be tantamount to calamity for Canada as a whole, unless it can, with outside empathy on the part of the United States, make a good faith effort to better integrate all parts of Canada politically.

Third, within francophone Quebec itself, another referendum defeat is likely to generate a good deal of 'political blood-letting' within and between the Parti Québécois and the Liberal Party. It is very possibly that a defeat could lead to the emergence of more radically committed political parties.[11] Such internal political restructuring could be the most important challenge to Quebecers.

Does the difficulty of reconciliation after the collapse of another independence bid imply that political instability could arise? Much depends upon what is meant by 'political instability.' If it means an interval of political restructuring, then stability would be close to normal. If political instability means, however, an upsurgence of violence, on an individual or quasi-organized basis, that is quite another matter. Although some of the propensity for political violence could exist under these conditions, its actual manifestation is improbable. According to Kent Weaver:

> the most obvious indicator of successful cleavage management is the absence of symptoms of deep alienation from the system – political violence (such as riots, assassinations, and bombings) and political parties or movements that seek drastic changes in the countries' institutions or boundaries. Canada has largely avoided political violence.[12]

There are enough safety-valves for venting dissatisfaction to prevent violence from breaking out within Quebec society. Through a long historical tradition, Quebec has learned to live with frustration. There are layers of authority in a tightly patterned communal society, starting at the local and urban levels, to monitor and offset violent proclivities. If local authority cannot cope, provincial authority will. If provincial authority does not, federal authority will.

'Peace, order, and good government' is not a euphemism.[13] Canada's record is remarkable by North American standards. Americans should not use their own experience to impute behaviour to another society where the conditions and traditions are quite different. Whatever the political outcome, dealing with significant political violence in Canada is not a policy priority that one must spend a lot of time worrying about.

In the past, francophone Quebec has shown great patience and respect for democratic procedures, more than one might expect to find among other cultural groupings in similar circumstances in other societies. This record of civility and respect for the law ought to be formally conceded. It is a standard invariably emphasized by Quebec political leadership as diverse as that of René Lévesque and Robert Bourassa.

Is a Unilateral Declaration of Independence Possible?

In a potentially crucial decision, Canada's Supreme Court declared that no province could secede unilaterally from Confederation. Given the stakes, and the Court's definitive conclusion, why was the reaction from the government of Quebec so muted? Moreover, suppose a province did attempt to secede unilaterally? How would the United States respond to a province's attempt to secede without consultation or negotiation? Although these questions may have a rather clear direction of argument, their explanations are inevitably clothed in politics.

There are many and obvious reasons why a Quebec separatist party would contest denial of unilateral secession by the Canadian Supreme Court. The more interesting question is why it did not. One reason Quebec reacted so benignly to the Supreme Court's decision was the cold political reality that support for secession was down in the polls. A second reason was that the Bouchard government had no intention at the time of broaching an immediate campaign against unity; the creation of a great fuss over the decision would only have stirred separatists into demanding a kind of action that the PQ leadership regarded as untimely and tactically counterproductive. The political decision, therefore, was not to oppose the Supreme Court's decision and not to mount a noisy Canada-wide challenge. But there was a deeper reason the Bouchard government acted as it did.

Regardless of what it said in public about the Supreme Court's decision, the PQ government was in fact pleased with it. First, the separatist movement, beginning with René Lévesque himself, had always argued that it would negotiate with the federal government. The very notion of a 'sovereignty association' implied such negotiation. In a formal sense, each Quebec referendum was about the right to negotiate with Ottawa on matters of Quebec–Ottawa relations, not unilateral separation. A critic might argue that such an offer was merely an indirect route to the true goal of full and complete separation, because if the proposed negotiations ended in failure, as was likely, the Quebec government then would be in a stronger position to declare immediate secession. The same critic might point out that this commitment to negotiate, because of the inherent ambiguity of purpose involved, likewise had the dual objective of gaining internal support for separation from an electorate still sceptical (indeed often confused) about breaking up Canada, on the one hand, while on the other, putting off opposition elsewhere in Canada by convincing people that the PQ was less than serious about a complete schism since it appeared so willing to negotiate rather than to act precipitately. In either case, however, the Supreme Court's decision to deny unilateral secession took nothing away from the actual PQ strategy of the moment. Therefore, it is not surprising that the vocal opposition to the decision from the separatist camp was muted.

Second, the PQ government was pleased with the decision (indeed the decision was, from the point of view of jurisprudence, admirably balanced to meet the needs of many sectors of Canadian society) because, for the first time, Ottawa was committed to accepting secession as a fact. Of course such secession would be required to leap certain legal and political hurdles. But the reality remained that the Canadian government, through this Supreme Court decision, had publically and legally committed itself to the acceptance of a breakup of Canada. For the PQ, this was a considerable victory in public relations.

But as everyone knows, not all the members of the PQ, in particular Jacques Parizeau, were supportive of a gradualist strategy for separation. At the time of the 1995 referendum, as the then Premier Jacques Parizeau indicated later, the PQ government was prepared for immediate withdrawal from Canada. Although without much visible success, the Parizeau government had sent letters to Canadian francophone military officers who might have been persuaded to join an independent Quebec government. He also had made some preparations on the financial and economic side to reassure financial markets and investors that separation would not mean doomsday for them. Thus if the separatist forces had won a majority, even by a small margin, the PQ government was ready to act immediately. Negotiations might have occurred, but these would have taken place after independence had been declared, not before. This is no small difference.

Suppose such a scenario had actually occurred. What would the U.S. response have been? U.S. decision making would not have shifted because of recognition by any other actors in the international system of a titularly independent Quebec government on its borders. Indeed, the U.S. government would more likely have taken the lead to prevent

other governments from making hasty decisions. Democratic procedure would be meticulously examined. For the purposes here, political
stability is assumed. Moreover, the wording of such a referendum (was
it unmistakably clear as to assumptions and intent?) and the size of the
majority (was the margin large enough to avoid any doubt regarding
voter fraud or manipulation?) would be key issues in the minds of
Washington bureaucrats. That neither the Supreme Court nor the Parliament of Canada has determined an acceptable majority would certainly affect these U.S. judgments.

In the end, the United States would stand by its assertion that any
decision regarding national unity would remain a Canadian decision.
The Canadian Supreme Court's decision on denial of unilateral secession would not change this predisposition. An independent Quebec
under any circumstances would be required to negotiate not only with
Ottawa and with individual provinces but also with the United States
and many other countries. The fact of negotiations is not the issue.
What is at issue is when these negotiations would start (either before
or after the assertion of independence) and around which issues. Even
more important is whether such negotiations are undertaken in good
faith or as the prelude to a fait accompli. Since the Supreme Court's
decision did not have much to say on these crucial aspects of the hypothetical decision to separate, Canada's neighbours would not have a
lot to go on as to how they might deny unilateralism.

In the unlikely eventuality that both Ottawa and Quebec City sought
U.S. assistance as mediator, the United States of course would oblige.
But the United States would much prefer that Canada settle its own
problems by itself. This preference is founded not on altruism but on
the conviction that however the United States would act in such a crisis, it would likely be accused of heavy-handedness and intervention,
not just by one side, but probably by both sides.

In short, has the Supreme Court's decision affected the potential
decisions of any of the actors who themselves are materially affected
by such a decision? Probably not. But what the decision has done is to
make it clearer to Quebec citizens that any vote in favour of a referendum to separate is scarcely instrumental. A 'Oui' vote in a decisive
majority is likely to be a vote that is irrevocable, not a down payment
on further concessions from the federal government inside Confederation. This explicit change in awareness indicates that the Supreme
Court's decision did clarify the outcomes.

Probing Plan B

If Plan A involves all those strategies and initiatives that the federal government could offer Quebec in the form of concessions, Plan B supposedly involves all of those strategies and initiatives Ottawa could confront Quebec City with prior to, during, or after secession. Plan A leans towards conciliation; Plan B towards toughness. Proponents have dismissed the fact that no coherent strategy is encompassed by either plan – a fact emphasized by as knowledgeable an observer as Prime Minister Chrétien. However, it is generally recognized that a number of provinces and the federal government have devoted considerably more thought to these issues since the October 1995 referendum on Quebec sovereignty. Let us examine some of the more prominent issues raised by the Plan B discussions.

Unilateral Declaration of Independence

The unilateral declaration of independence (UDI) has been one of the most contentious issues raised. But, from the tactical perspective, it is one of the least troubling to dissect. Should secession occur, UDI will inevitably be present, and yet at the same time it will not be acknowledged. How could UDI be both things at the same time, and yet neither?

Immediately following a majority vote in favour of separation, the Rest of Canada should realistically be prepared for a Quebec take-over of all government functions inside the province. But at the same time, a sovereigntist government in Quebec will surely claim that it is open to negotiation with Ottawa on a host of issues, and it will of course enter discussions on those issues. If the negotiation is not to the liking of Quebec City, however, it will merely walk out and officially declare independence; following such a majority vote, nothing can legally prevent Quebec City from asserting that the negotiations have broken down and that it has been left with no choice but to officially secede. Other discussions may start or continue on other issues such as distribution of debt or commercial interactions. But a determined Quebec will become an independent actor even if the decision to declare early independence leaves it in a less favourable bargaining position on many issues yet unresolved. This reveals the poverty of studies designed to prevent a UDI from happening. There is no advance guarantee that the negotiations will be open, balanced, and mutually productive. It is a mistake to assume that following a majority vote by Quebecers for independence, Quebec will remain in Confederation until the negotiations have turned out to Ottawa's liking.

Clarity of Referendum Wording

Plan B discussions have raised public consciousness about the wording of the referendum. Even if Quebec is able to convince world opinion that it and it alone is the proper government to decide the wording of a referendum on separation, the old days of purposeful ambiguity are over. Neither Canadian opinion nor world opinion will accept purposeful ambiguity as grounds for breaking up Canada.

This means that either the referendum will be about separation, and separation alone, or the referendum outcome will not be definitive. In other words, a referendum to negotiate sovereignty will not provide a sufficient basis upon which a Quebec government is able to declare sovereignty. At a minimum, another referendum would then be required in which the wording describing the decision to separate or not to separate was impeccable.

If a Quebec separatist government believes the votes exist to win a referendum on separation, then it has the right to call such a referendum. But it cannot expect support from any government in Canada or abroad for a back-door separation in which Quebec obtains the 'right to negotiate' separation and on the basis of such a vote eventually declares that negotiations have broken down and separation has become inevitable. Such a tactic will, given current public awareness, lead to unending political trouble for an independence-minded Quebec government. This is a tactical road no Quebec government should contemplate, much less take.

Size of Majority

Neither the Supreme Court of Canada nor Parliament has declared how large a majority vote must be to allow a province to declare independence. This is the more ironic since polls throughout Canada, including those in Quebec, reveal that the public believes a majority larger than '50 per cent plus one' is necessary to countenance a breakup of the country. Not only is there no clear threshold for an acceptable majority, but the grounds for so deciding such a threshold are very uncertain.

Given that the federal government has never clearly contradicted the claim that a 50-percent-plus-one vote would represent a mandate to achieve secession, it would now have difficulty arguing that a higher threshold must be met. Moreover, if it did so argue, what principled way could it use to select which of the various possible thresholds was to be achieved? The choice of any number larger than 50 percent would appear to be entirely arbitrary. The Canadian government would seem to be raising the bar after having implicitly accepted the legitimacy of a 50-percent-plus-one vote because it now realized that it was possible that it would lose the next campaign.[14]

This sums up the entire problem of dealing with the secession question retroactively. By acting too early, the federal government fears it might precipitate a problem it would not otherwise need to face; conversely, by waiting too long to establish a strategy for dealing with secession, its actions may appear post hoc in character and therefore have less political legitimacy.

Additional Partitions

As the proponents of Plan B, particularly the members of the Reform Party, like to remind the Parti Québécois or the Bloc Québécois, if Canada is divisible then Quebec is divisible. According to the old rules for political self-determination – rules that do not, in fact, apply in the Quebec case since Quebec cannot claim that it is rebelling against tyranny or oppression (any more than any cultural community in Quebec can claim such grounds for rebellion against the Government of Quebec which after all has been a generally fair and competent government) – any government seeking independence from a larger polity must be large enough territorially to be politically and economically viable. For Quebec itself to meet these criteria is obviously not difficult, although it will pay a price in terms of per capita growth rate after independence because of its smaller economic size. An entity with an even smaller population or territory might not be able to make this claim. Even a Cree community with a large enough territory might fail to meet the economic criterion. Yet for quite a different reason, speculating on whether or not the viability criteria for self-determination are met is probably moot.

Communities fleeing an independent Quebec would probably seek to remain attached to what was left of Canada. This could create a new type of legal problem for the international community to adjudicate. In this case, the viability criteria would not matter. The international community would need to decide whether such transfers of sovereignty were possible. These communities could argue that they were *always* a part of Canada and that they merely wanted to remain a part of Canada. In this sense, the francophone Quebec community would be the community actually making the decision to secede, not individual francophones. What could transpire is a very messy international legal problem over which jurisdiction took priority, the Canadian jurisdiction or the Quebec jurisdiction. What would make the controversy even more interesting from the international legal and perhaps the international political perspective is a situation in which the local communities announced their plans for remaining part of the remnant of Canada on the same day that Quebec declared its independence.

But the proponents of Plan B are undoubtedly correct that, just as Quebec under certain circumstances could obtain its independence from Canada, so under certain circumstances could other cultural communities in Quebec obtain their independence from Quebec. What makes these fragmentations even more feasible is that Quebec is stuck with two very awkward political and legal realities: (1) Quebec chose to abandon other francophone members along the Ottawa valley, for example, and in Acadia (largely because they lived in other provincial jurisdictions which Quebec did not want to contest and because a majority living in these areas were probably content with the status quo) even though some of the members of these French-speaking populations would feel cut off from their compatriots in an independent Quebec after separation; and (2) Quebec contains significant populations that consider themselves culturally and linguistically distinct who vote overwhelmingly and enthusiastically for remaining part of Canada (even though they want as enthusiastically to remain a part of Quebec as long as Quebec stays in Canada).

The reason these two realities are problematic for Quebec is that a significant number of people who perhaps would like to be part of an independent French-speaking polity would be left outside Quebec and a significant number of people who would not want to be part of such a polity would be trapped inside Quebec. If Quebec really encompassed all of the French-speaking population in Canada, and only such a population, its chances for independence would be far greater. By attempting to sell independence on the basis that it is the French-speaking alternative to English Canada while leaving more than three-quarter of a million French-speaking citizens outside its borders, and conversely by advertising itself as culturally diverse and pluralist even though the culturally diverse elements by an enormous margin reject independence, the separatist agenda fails to overcome huge contradictions in its mission and cohesiveness.

Border Revision

That the upper part of Quebec only became part of the province by treaty in the twentieth century is sometimes used as an excuse for arguing that an independent Quebec would leave Confederation in a shrunken condition. Notwithstanding the ongoing political and economic dispute between Newfoundland and Quebec, these border arguments do not seem very compelling to the citizen of a country that was created out of land grants and purchases from foreign governments. In any case, any international claims would need to be handled through mediation or submission to the World Court. Submission of disputes to the World Court is not mandatory. If a plausible argument has been made why the Quebec borders, ought to be revised, that argument has received no serious scholarly public attention inside Canada or abroad. The plain truth is that further discussion of border revision based on such weak claims is invidious to Quebec and unhelpful to the spirit of Canadian unity.

FROM PLAN B TO PLAN C

Alan Cairns has made the important argument that what Canada needs is a Plan C that goes beyond the arguments of Plan B and prepares Canadians for life without Quebec.[15] No one should deny Canadians outside Quebec the right to prepare themselves for a bad fate. Lack of preparation sometimes earns its own reward. On the other hand, there is the argument made by Jean Charest, which is analogous to a husband and wife who keep talking about divorce. Eventually this talk itself may become deleterious to the strength of the marriage. But there must be some middle ground here between the Cairns and the Charest positions. Perhaps the answer for Canadians outside Quebec is to make some of the necessary preparations for the worst while not unduly talking about the prospect of breakup. Knowing where the tax documents are and how to access the bank accounts is surely not imperilling the marriage nor should such awareness imply pessimism.

Responding to the ROC If Quebec Secedes

Suppose now that despite application of the principles of diplomacy earlier described; despite the best efforts at bargaining by a government in Ottawa that has solid support in the country and great skill and imagination in its bargaining strategy; despite bold leadership inside Quebec by the pro-federalist forces, a referendum passes in favour of Quebec independence. Such a referendum would need a solid and unquestioned majority. If the outcome was challenged for reasons of corruption, or if the majority vote was so narrow as to be uncertain (since the margin of error exceeds the margin of victory), then the Quebec 'Oui' forces would have to expect a summons by the provincial and federal electoral commissions for a recount, and even a possible reversal of the vote. Provincial electoral authorities could not be expected to prevail on a matter that so involves federal authority. If there was a close vote, the federal agencies, including the court system, would be legitimately involved. Only a clear-cut majority vote would confirm a decisive victory in favour of separation. Following the November 2000 presidential elections in the United States, Americans have become embarrassed experts on matters of vote recounting.

But suppose that such a clear-cut vote was achieved and was not subject to debate. At that point Quebec would leave the country. Much discussion has revolved around whether international law would have the authority to overturn a judgment of the people of Quebec. Likewise there are questions of whether foreign governments would recognize an independent Quebec, and if so which governments they would be, and in what order, and whether the United States would be among them. These questions have been examined in detail in Ottawa and in Quebec. Yet neither has heard a unanimous opinion to its own liking, although each has assembled evidence and opinion for its own side of the argument.

Notwithstanding the disputed character of most of these judgments, and the deep legal history behind all interpretation regarding the supremacy of the jurisdiction of international law or of the law of national recognition, the conclusions ironically are made simpler, not more difficult, when politics is mixed with the question of the purely legal interpretation.[16] For example, if Quebec refused to submit its claim of independence to the World Court, and if before the matter of secession arises there are no clear prior rules for secession worked out in the Canadian constitution beyond that declared by the Supreme

Court of Canada, the legal basis for determining the priority of international law over national law in this application is not well-defined. If Quebec does not budge legally on these matters, Ottawa will find the legal basis upon which to buttress its political resolve.

Whether or not Quebec has received a majority vote in favour of secession and is legally allowed to do so, some foreign governments are likely to recognize Quebec's independence. France has virtually assured the Quebec government that it would be the first to offer recognition. The United States will not base its judgment on whether to recognize an independent Quebec upon what others do. But if there is a decisive vote, and if there are no other issues that are outstanding (such as gross human rights violations) which could not be settled after independence, the United States is not likely to deny Quebec its democratically determined preference for national autonomy.

The real point here, however, is that all of these matters of recognition are moot. Unless a government is willing to use force to stop a sovereign Quebec from achieving independence, once it has met all the criteria of democratic procedure established by the Supreme Court of Canada, nothing can derail that event. While lack of recognition might be used to try to prevent an independent Quebec from obtaining full access to international banking, for example, those doing business in Quebec would be no more interested in seeing this outcome than the Quebec government itself.

Recognition is a nicety that comes to virtually all governments in time because of its value for international comity and discourse. Quebec might be obliged to wait for an interval, and undoubtedly would prefer not to have to face such an obstacle as temporary denial. But if Quebec independence were determined by democratic majority decision, independence would prevail. Recognition cannot make Quebec politically independent. The lack of recognition by itself cannot stop Quebec from becoming independent. Insofar as Ottawa and other governments waive the right to use force to halt independence, these other legal matters become of decidedly secondary relevance.

Whatever the status of international law on the matter of Quebec secession, and assuming an uncontested majority in favour of a clearly worded referendum on secession, Quebec would become an independent polity. Independence would not end its political problems, especially in terms of placating its anglophone and allophone constituents. But the reality that Quebec had become a separate country would quickly settle into the consciousness of all North Americans. Steps to normalize relations would take place. The task of dividing debt and of securing treaties would go on with Ottawa. But many of these discussions could not take place without U.S. participation. If called upon by both parties, and this is conjectural, the United States or another third party could become involved at that point as mediator or conciliator.

After the shock of Quebec's scession has been absorbed, the Rest of Canada would need to adjust to its new political circumstances. As chapter 3 argues, this task of adjustment for the ROC would not be easy. Without reviewing these arguments in detail, the principal problems would involve (1) coping with the sense of geographic and psychological isolation felt by the Atlantic provinces, (2) resolving the matter of disappearing equalization payments and the negative impact this will have on the poorer provinces, (3) overcoming the legacy of 'Western alienation,' especially in Alberta and British Columbia, and (4) solving the 'Ontario problem' of highly unequal size and representation within the ROC. All of these problems are manageable. But governments must be able to hold discussions and present proposals for settlement in an atmosphere of trust and confidence. Major changes in the way Canada would henceforth be governed would be essential. These changes are not likely to be easy to formulate, far less to implement.

Whether the Rest of Canada could make the necessary changes before further unravelling occurs is the unanswered question. During this time of uncertainty, after the reality of Quebec secession had entered the political consciousness of the ROC, bold initiatives would become necessary. The United States would not be in a position to prepare new constitutional formulae or to advise on strategy. But as a general principle, the United States would have to offer strong, public support for a united Canada without Quebec. More than ever, the Rest of Canada would need this visible political support from Washington as it worked to reconstitute itself politically. This would be the time for the United States to reiterate the imperative nature of unity in the North American region and within English Canada in particular.

Not Necessarily 'Affiliation,' but 'Affiliation' If Necessary

What happens if the Rest of Canada is unable to reach a modus vivendi over the terms necessary for continued operation as a single unit? What happens if some of the provinces declare their independence of the unity process? What happens if sections of Quebec begin to splinter, declaring their existence as independent city-states, for example? Should Quebec secede, these are not impossible scenarios.

If Canada begins to unravel to this extent, the United States could no longer remain on the sidelines as a spectator or at best a cheerleader; it would have to become a coach. In this context of political uncertainty, structural fragmentation, and dissolving good feeling, the United States must take the necessary steps to reverse the unravelling.[17] 'The Canadian economic union,' according to Murray Smith, 'could unravel to the much lower level of integration of the NAFTA.'[18] He claims that even the Canadian currency union and customs union could be in jeopardy. This is a degree of backsliding in trade and finances that would send reverberations throughout the NAFTA region.[19]

Experts polled across Canada in the Fraser Institute's Canada Clock project indicated that at best there is a 50-50 chance that the Rest of Canada could remain unified after the departure of Quebec. This is the same conclusion that Canadian journalist Gordon Gibson had come to earlier.[20] Poll results vary somewhat over time, as events and responses to those events change and as governments take actions. Ironically, when the news is not the main focus of the media, even though nothing else has changed politically, public optimism increases concerning unity. But such a high average level of anxiety suggests that knowledgeable observers fear that unless countered with alternative initiatives, political unravelling could occur, possibly starting in the West. Social scientist Seymour Martin Lipset maintains that highly integrated political subunits along lines of language and ethnicity are in general likely to separate from a larger political entity with different societal composition.[21] What could also happen is that the shock of the initial secession may set in process an unravelling that undermines the entire nation-state as a centrally governing unit.

At the point of incipient unravelling, the United States would unavoidably become involved. It could not tolerate a fragmentation of the North American security space, tantamount to sacrificing its strategy for the maintenance of world order. It could not give up the hard-fought multilateral gains associated with NAFTA that each member has in terms of economic adjustments now 'bought and paid for.' It could not risk the importation of political ideas that could threaten its own sense of mission and unity, regardless of how impervious to externally induced fragmentation and cultural divisiveness it had always thought it was. Events, or the prospect of unfolding events, would now force the United States to act.

The first thing the United States should offer is a proposal for *regional affiliation*. Regional affiliation is a unilateral extension of political association with the United States. It is designed to overcome fissiparousness among entities that have broken away from either the ROC or from Quebec and to prevent the political chaos and uncertainty that would result from the emergence of a number of competing political units, each small, weak, and isolated.

Regional affiliation for Canada would have three primary elements. First, it would allow each of the fragments to pursue its own domestic policy. Presumably that is why the entity decided to break away in the first place. If there could have been agreement on the conduct of domestic policy, the union would never have collapsed. Thus the effort to seek independence is premised on the desire for autonomy in the making of domestic policy, including such matters as education, roads, health care, retirement, cultural policy, language, and resource management. When the inventory is examined fully, the provinces including Quebec will discover that they have long exercised most of these powers anyway. But regional affiliation would not reduce this authority over domestic policy and is compatible with a reasonable expansion of this authority.

Second, regional affiliation would be designed to retain the same or a greater level of regional economic integration than that currently experienced under federation. The same level of economic openness and benefit would be extended to the fragmented entities as is now enjoyed by the American states. In other words, there would be no reduction in economic integration resulting from this otherwise damaging process of political fragmentation.

Previously possessing a common currency and a common set of rules affecting trade, commerce, taxes, and finance under the law of Canada (though with many provincial variations), these entities would now enjoy the same level of economic integration experienced in the United States and would be required to subject themselves to the terms. This arrangement would prevent the extensive backsliding of economic integration as experienced under NAFTA. Indeed, the participation of these entities in the economic conditions and benefits already observed in the U.S. polity would not be a gift. All of the economic rules, regulations, and conditions that apply to American citizens and to American institutions would automatically be expected of the counterparts in the affiliated entities. Conceivably this extension of economic privilege to the affiliated entity would increase the overall level of economic integration. But in no circumstance would affiliated status decrease the level of economic integration.

Third, the United States would provide international security for the affiliated polity. This means that the affiliated polity would have no need for an army or militia of its own. It could save the expenditure on such costly items, which must possess a critical mass to have much value, and which exhibit economies of scale in financing. The net effect of this arrangement would be two-fold.

Since all affiliated polities would be treated equally, none would face the cost of staffing an army. In the absence of multiple armies and other armed forces, there would be no competition among the units for security. None would reduce the security of any other and each would be provided security equally and effectively by the United States. They would, however, retain their own constabulary. Mutual sharing of security information among the internal units would be highly desirable. But the matter of external security would be handled in such a way as to eliminate redundancy, inefficacy, and competition. Moreover, the troubling external problem of multiple and overlapping alliances with extra-regional powers would be eliminated.

Likewise, the vexing matter of who controls what airspace and underseaspace would disappear. With more than a couple of jurisdictions involved, the political complexity and frustration of this problem could become mind-boggling. In an affiliated regionalism everybody controls all of the respective spaces, and with control comes responsibility for monitoring, law enforcement, defence, and, importantly in the age of oil spills and other perils, protection of the environment. That responsibility would be fused in a collective body in which the individual entities would have representation and decision-making capability.

Responsibilities would accompany the privilege of secure territorial boundaries and coastlines. The affiliated entity would be obligated to provide a mutually agreed-upon fee to share in the cost of this security. Citizens in the affiliated regions would be given an official opportunity to serve in the defence forces of the United States. A significant number of young people might well seek a career in the armed forces.

Affiliated regionalism currently has no parallels. It is a new concept shaped to fit the needs of North America at a time when political fragmentation threatens the efficiency and serenity of the collective space. Some critics may argue that North America might just as well opt for the creation of a common market or a monetary union. While attitudes could change, just as attitudes towards the creation of a North American trade area changed very abruptly in the mid-1980s, at present the notion of tighter economic integration between the United States and Canada is scarcely propitious. Part of the problem is that neither country wants to create the kind of large, overriding political institutions that would be necessary to manage more elaborate international economic integration.[22] In the absence of such a willingness, regional affiliation is a substitute that could enable North America to avoid the worst consequences of political fragmentation of English Canada. If that fragmentation is obviated, the option of regional affiliation will not be needed.

Even More Unlikely Options

If fragmentation threatens and Ottawa is not able to fend off the attacks on unity, however, then the burden of salvaging the political situation could fall on regional affiliation. But some citizens and some provincial governments may at that point decide that regional affiliation is insufficient. They may request outright statehood. This would present Washington with a difficult decision. Perhaps it is useful to explain why such a decision would generate political complications.

There is an old and historically accurate fear in Canada of U.S. Manifest Destiny, of the race to the Pacific Ocean. That Canada too has its own Manifest Destiny, which led to the building of the continental railroad and the peopling of the West, is no solace. Canadian ambitions merely fuel the anxiety that U.S. ambitions are real and even larger. The trepidation that the United States is about to 'take over' Canada has been a part of the Canadian psyche at least since the exodus of the United Empire Loyalists after the American Revolution.[23] The problem is that this interpretation does not conform with the facts on either side of the border today.

On the Canadian side, there are many Canadians, Quebecers, Westerners, and 'new' Canadians who do not believe in the American annexationist myth and who are indifferent to it because they have more immediate and practical things in their daily lives to worry about. On the American side, there is satisfaction with the borders as they are and a deep sense that the United States has enough problems of its own to manage without 'importing' any others.[24] Translated, this means that most Americans who think seriously about these issues understand that Canada has done quite a good job of administration and governance.[25] The United States could not improve upon this record. Canadians who anticipated better would probably be disappointed.

The annexationist myth argues that the United States seeks two things that Canada, appended to the United States, could provide: (1) Canada is rich in natural resources, and manufacturing in the U.S. is allegedly hungry for these resources and would like to obtain greater access to and control over them; (2) security-conscious as the United States rightly has been, annexation of Canada would substantially increase U.S. security, especially along the east and west coastlines. These two components of the annexationist myth are so strongly believed that they require careful examination.

The reality of the twenty-first century ought to illuminate the flaws in the first argument, as it has for most Americans. Today, even the resource business is global. There are no 'shortages' of natural resources, renewable or non-renewable, and never will be. Water, for example, can be reprocessed and used again and again for a price lower than that which any sensible Canadian would demand for this scarce resource. A price exists for a given quality and quantity of a resource.[26] If the resource becomes relatively scarce, such as was true for rubber during the Second World War, often a synthetic substitute is found. Canadian resources are presently available to any bidder at the world price. If a section of Canada were a part of the United States, the price of the resource for American companies would not change. Appending Canada to the United States would not make corporate America richer, nor would the average American live better or earn more. They can invest in Canada now if they wish. The commercial border is open and has been for a very long time.

As far as security is concerned, the United States can readily defend itself today and will likely be able to do so in the future. Moreover, the coordination with Canada of the defence of the continent through NORAD has been an unprecedented example of trust, efficiency, and excellent organization.[27] How annexation would enhance this level of coordination is not apparent. While from time-to-time Ottawa and Washington have jostled politically over rights to the Northwest Passage, for example, there is much more 'medium' here than 'message.' The United States formally admits that the Northwest Passage is contiguous to Canadian territory, not American, but does not want to acknowledge that this strait or any other internationally used strait is subject to American or any other nation's control, for such control would be to potentially inhibit the movement of the navy worldwide.

The issue is moot because the only movement in the Northwest Passage of consequence is that of submarines. As long as this movement is not held to be an international legal precedent, Canada does not dispute such movement.

Likewise, both the Pacific and Atlantic coastlines are patrolled by the coast guards, naval fleets, and air forces of each country with the best of good will and a sharing of information. Military security is not a problem for either country. If coastal provinces joined the United States, the United States would not be safer or more secure from international threats, which for the most part are either non-existent or are managed (i.e., the international drug problem) as effectively between countries as within countries (which is to say quite far from perfectly).

So the myth of annexation is exactly that, a myth. Myths can of course be manipulated for political purpose, and they are, but that is a different issue. If Manifest Destiny for all practical intent is dead, then what does this mean if a Canadian province wants to become a state? The immediate answer is that statehood would be more difficult because there is no natural constituency in the United States, such as the business lobby or the national security lobby, to ease the application over the political hurdles.

One problem is that statehood would have a serious effect on the electoral balance in the United States. With the one exception of Alberta, every other province of Canada is, in terms of its voting patterns, left of the political median in the United States.[28] This means that a majority of the voters in any province other than that of Alberta would be likely to vote for the Democratic Party rather than for the Republican. If all of Canada were to become part of the United States, in some extremely unlikely scenario, the Democratic Party would build up an insuperable hegemony at every level of the U.S. government. Despite this electoral impact, the Democrats are probably even less likely than the Republicans to entertain visions of territorial expansion for reasons of internal ideology. So there is always the prospect of a party-veto on applications for statehood. More likely, party differences would simply prevent the process from starting.

Having listened to these and other obstacles to statehood, a Toronto TV anchor exclaimed off screen, 'So you don't even want us!' This may be a natural human response to the difficulties of application for statehood, indeed a natural response to the sudden dispelling of the myth of annexation so long nurtured in parts of Canada, but it is not quite justified. Every opinion poll touching on the subject shows that Canadians rank at the top of the scale of foreigners admired by Americans. Frankly, as most Canadians know, Americans do not really regard Canadians as foreigners. This shows up in the pattern of immigration to Canada and in the large presence of 'Green Card holders' from Canada in the United States. If Americans were in the mood to extend citizenship to others en masse, the United States would put Canadians at the head of the line. The reality is, however, that the most Canadians are quite content to remain Canadian, and most Americans are not prepared to establish a queue for mass immigration, territorially based or otherwise.[29]

So does this mean that for disenchanted fragments of Canadian federation the statehood option is impossible? No, it is probably not. Realistically, however, the process would be a complicated one for any political entity, on either side of the border. Canadians might find adjustment to the American lifestyle and social safety net troubling. Americans might find the disparagement of American values upsetting and the ways of doing things that could inadvertently accompany the admission of a new state uncomfortable. Americans do not possess the same capacity for humour about their own political institutions as Canadians do. What Canadians regard as legitimate criticism, Americans often regard as carping.

Canadian application for statehood is an unlikely option for reasons innate to each society and polity. While on theoretical grounds the option cannot be ruled out, in terms of practical feasibility it is an extreme option of very low probability.

Responding to Asymmetrical Federalism

Asymmetrical federalism is opposed by many in Canada because it is thought to be an abridgment of the equality of the provinces. Treating one province differently from others suggests favouritism. Likewise the United States might be sceptical of asymmetrical federalism because it looks like a recipe for slow strangulation of the federal process. A Canada that does not work politically is not an attractive prospect to its neighbours. Yet in each case, the critics may be wrong.

Asymmetrical federalism need not undermine the principle of the equality of the provinces. Because two provinces are treated differently does not mean that they necessarily will be treated unequally. One province, for example, may receive one benefit from the federal government while another province receives another, but both benefits may be equal in terms of value to the province or cost to the federal government. If provinces are given some choice, they may choose a different route but reach their destination at the same time. Indeed, allowing provinces some flexibility about the choice of direction (i.e., the choice of program) may lead to innovativeness and an overall increase in efficiency. Complementarity is often better than parallelism, and complementarity can be just as fair.

Similarly, there is little reason for the U.S. to doubt Canada's ability to make some form of asymmetrical federalism work. Louisiana, for example, because of its French heritage, has adopted a legal system that is more indebted to the Napoleon Code than to British Common Law, unlike the rest of the country, but justice is no less likely in Louisiana than in any other state. Hence to the extent that Canada can make asymmetric federalism or some variant of it work, the United States ought to be neither disappointed nor surprised.

Asymmetrical federalism may have its beginnings in the February 4, 1999 social union package, which will send perhaps two billion dollars a year to the provinces for health-care support. Each province can decide to use the federal funds on programs 'in the same or a related priority area,' which suggests that a way has been found to give Quebec the room it needs to shape its own version of a health care program. The result makes sense for everyone. Each province may have slightly different needs in health care. The federal government in what is called the Sussex Accord may have innovated more administrative flexibility than the Meech Lake Accord itself ever envisioned.[30]

Responding to a Scenario of Deep Decentralization

Of all the possible outcomes of the 'Great Canadian Dialogue,' the most likely is deep decentralization. Decentralization is likely to come about because in the attempt to placate separatist Quebec through continued bargaining, Quebec will demand more powers, and although the tactics and style will vary with each government and with the personality of the prime minister, on the whole, Ottawa will be disposed to grant those powers. Considering the alternative, the granting of more authority to Quebec will look like the lesser evil. But the problem for the country is that, although Ottawa can unilaterally and through continuing pressure from Quebec grant the province some additional powers, the federal government cannot do this selectively.

In 1998, this political proposition was legally formalized as the Cal-

gary Declaration by the First Ministers. As of June 1998, all the provinces but Quebec had accepted the terms of the Declaration. Of course
this lack of completion is central. Quebec's principal criticism is that
the Declaration fails to recognize Quebec as a people. In some ways the
battle over whether Quebec is distinct or unique is a battle for public
opinion with the real objective being the winning of elections and possibly of the next referendum.

Ottawa has discovered that what it gives to Quebec, it must now
give to the rest of the country, especially the West. Such transfer of
authority from Ottawa comes at a 'zero-sum' cost to itself, to its own
power. Since the failure of the Charlottetown Accord, that is the new
reality, and those are the new parameters in the federal-provincial bargaining equation. The days of unilateral, one-sided benefits to Quebec
are over.[31]

One of the most difficult tasks is to determine what the split of financial benefits is among the respective provinces, especially Quebec.
Some of the assessment is easy. The big givers are Alberta, British
Columbia, and Ontario, and the big receivers are Newfoundland, the
rest of the Maritimes, Manitoba, and Saskatchewan. Yet there is a lop-
sidedness into this assessment, because the economic size of the givers
is so much greater than that of the receivers (Ontario alone accounts
for about 40 per cent of Canada's GNP). But in general, this is how the
benefits flow throughout the country.

For Quebec the story is much more difficult to assess. Both the federal government and Quebec exaggerate the interpretation with selective citing of figures from their own political vantage point. Ottawa
emphasize past disproportionate benefits to Quebec (but not too
strongly for fear of a backlash in English Canada), and Quebec stresses
failure to receive its fair share.[32] There are, however, three facts and
trends that are quite clear: (1) In the 1970–90 period, Quebec did very
well in terms of the balance of inflows relative to outflows, averaging a
favourable net surplus of perhaps $2.5 billion Canadian per year. (2)
This favourable net inflow has been in decline. (3) Currently, Quebec's
inflows and outflows are in balance, with a small per capita margin in
its favour. The closer the financial inflows and outflows balance for
Quebec, the higher the rhetoric seems to rise on both sides and less
plausible the interpretations.

But the debate will shift from outcomes, where the balance is evident, to power and authority over policy, where the accounting rules
are more difficult to identify. To make sense of the debate over policy

authority, much of which is shared in highly complex ways, the distribution of power within the polity must be assessed in a concise way. A contrast with the United States may help illustrate the debate.

There are very confusing discussions as to whether, according to world standards, Canada's political organization is centralized or decentralized.[33] The prime minister's authority suggests very high concentration of power in Ottawa. This concentration is achieved through (1) the organization of the Prime Minister's Office; (2) the power of appointments, including Cabinet appointments; (3) the enormous significance of party discipline and the effect this has on reducing the relative power of Parliament; and (4) the power of budget-making and the purse. Without doubt the prime minister of Canada has greater powers than the U.S. president. In 'responsible government,' where the Cabinet is in theory responsible to Parliament (but only rarely because of the inability of members to crossover in voting without career-destroying penalty), power is not divided among the 'branches' as it is in Washington. Where then is the check on the prime minister's power?

The check on the power of the Canadian prime minister does not come from Parliament, the judiciary, the bureaucracy (though it is relatively more powerful than that of the United States) or the press, despite the reality that each of these institutions acts as something of a counterweight. The principal check on the power of the prime minister, and therefore on the power of the federal government, comes from the provinces, specifically from the actions of the premiers.[34] In brief, the role played by Congress in the U.S. government as balancer is played by the provinces in Canada. Not only are the provinces individually more powerful than the U.S. states because there are fewer of them, because some of them (Ontario and Quebec) are relatively so large, and because the Canadian constitution reserves so many powers to the provinces, but because the only truly effective offset to the centralized power within Ottawa is by the provinces who are closer to the actual voter.

Under these circumstances of principal balance, not between Parliament and the prime minister but between the federal government led by the prime minister and the provinces, it is not hard to see why the battle lines over Quebec matters have been drawn between the premier and the prime minister (or as separatists like to translate the title, between the prime minister and the prime minister). The clash is not so much between personalities as between structural authority at each level of government.

Sometimes the argument is made that since power is so concentrated in Ottawa, it must also be concentrated in the provinces, and the only natural counterweight to high concentration of power in the federal government is concentration of power at the level of the provinces. Of course the opposite could as easily be argued. Since power is concentrated in the provincial governments, it must also be concentrated in Ottawa.[35] The problem for Canada is that most of the kind of deal making and logrolling associated with politics in a democracy is done between executive officials at the federal and the provincial level, hence the term 'executive federalism,' rather than between elected representatives in Parliament at the federal level. That is the one startling contrast between governments in Canada and the United States, or Britain, or Germany, or any of the other parliamentary democracies.

If, therefore, power is to be redistributed between the prime minister and the premier of Quebec, it will also be redistributed among the other premiers. Call this Type X decentralization, which is probably how the notion of decentralization would take place. That is certainly how Quebec would like to see decentralization occur. The Bloc Québécois's presence in Ottawa is a downpayment on this type of solution.

But of course there is another kind of decentralization that would serve the polity much better. It is the kind that would probably be acceptable to the West. Whether it would be acceptable to Quebec governments of all political complexions is uncertain. Such a change would bring Canada more in line with the configuration of power among the other democracies.

This alternative form of power decentralization would occur in Ottawa itself, that is, between the prime minister and the other organs of government, principally Parliament. Call this Type Y decentralization. It would in turn leave the relationship of power and the direct reform of institutions at the provincial and federal levels untouched. Indirectly, however, a decentralization of federal power in Ottawa would have important implications for a sharing of power with the provinces since their own power concentration would remain the same while that of Ottawa's was altered. With this change, a relative shift of power would take place because the structural changes towards decentralization would occur at the federal level but not the provincial level. The provinces ought to be happy with such a shift of power since it is what they, including Quebec, have long been advocating.

Type Y decentralization of power at the federal level alone is less risky than a direct shift of power from federal to provincial levels. It could take place in a variety of ways. It could involve a strengthening of Parliament through a reduction in the penalties for crossover voting. It could involve institutional revision within Parliament as the West wants a stronger senate in which at least some of the provinces (the less populated ones) would obtain a relatively greater amount of representation. It could involve a change in the electoral rules making it easier for a political party to win representation across the entire country and conversely more difficult for a regional party to dominate elections.[36] It could change the rules for party representation in Parliament, thus encouraging coalition government among several parties, and thus assuring greater balance nationally.

But to the extent that Quebec wants greater power for itself at the cost not only of Ottawa but of all of Canada, neither Type X nor Type Y decentralization will be satisfactory. Indeed, because Quebec wants power at the expense of everybody else at whatever level of government, it is asking for a federation-breaking kind of structural change. That is the kind of change that the West is not willing to extend to Quebec.

Either Type X or Type Y decentralization of authority is operational, however. Critics have said that Canada is the most decentralized polity in the world. The above discussion indicates that such a description is not really apt. In fact, in terms of a series of crude measures of centralization, compared with Switzerland, everyone's favourite example of a 'successful' decentralized country, Canada is about equally decentralized.[37] For example, Switzerland allows its local governments and Canada allows its provinces a larger share of spending power. The same share of power is retained at the federal level in each case.

In its foreign relations with Canada, the United States could endure either Type X or Type Y decentralization. However Type Y would be preferable to the United States because it would still be dealing, for the most part, with a single federal government, albeit with some diluted executive power. With Type X decentralization, the United States would face many more examples of situations in which the provinces themselves would want to deal directly with Washington. This would mean more of the kind of bargaining that occurred during the East Coast Fisheries talks where Ottawa was accompanied by 'a provincial representative' in many of the discussions. At best, a multilateralization of bargaining between Canada and the United States and a diffusion of the chain of command would take place. Many more provinces would probably want full diplomatic access to Washington in a direct way. In the end, such proliferation of diplomatic links would not be in the interest of either Canada or Washington. If the end result is a unified Canada, the cost is bearable.

Either Type X or Type Y decentralization, but particularly the former, will have one other very likely impact on the Canada–U.S. relationship. Decentralization that shifts power directly to the provinces (or to local governments) and away from Ottawa will tend to undermine the interest in foreign affairs by Canadians and the capacity to prosecute that interest through effective foreign policy.[38] Canada could become less internationally oriented and more focused on domestic political issues, making it more like Switzerland in one other respect.

In international affairs, Switzerland does not try to retain a high profile as a 'maker and shaker' among nations. It is content to run its domestic economy well and to defend its borders. It is not much of a joiner even though it is a great host to international organizations (whose delegates spend a lot in foreign exchange). It has become influential through its private international financial operations (banks) but not directly through public international financial organizations, even when they tend to meet in the beautiful environs of its cities, mountains, and lakes.

Canada would become more like Switzerland under Type X decentralization – it would lose its incentive and capacity to pursue an active foreign policy. Since its governing authority is very balanced, divided, and closer to the people, the concentration of power at the federal level to carry out an active foreign policy simply would not exist. Loss of representation for Canada in the Group of Seven might be the first casualty. Many Canadians might find this a very high cost of decentralization. Surely the United States would miss the vigour and effectiveness of its northern partner on the world stage. But as the Swiss have shown, in a world where order is elsewhere preserved and effectively preserved, citizens can live very well under such a decentralized political authority inside the nation-state. In any case, the decision will not be made abroad but will be made by individual Canadians.

Summing Up the Options and the Consequences

There will always be a Canada.[39] The question is, what kind of Canada will it be? This chapter has explored some possibilities.

It could be a Canada in which Quebec separatists try once again and fail to win independence, leaving a rump of quite dispirited advocates to decide their next step.

It could be a Canada in which Quebec separates, leaving the ROC to fend for itself, stay united, and reformulate its structure and institutions. This could lead to the unravelling of English Canada (and possibly of Quebec).

In an effort to placate Quebec, Canada could also decentralize. It could decentralize through reform at the federal level, shifting power from the prime minister to Parliament and thereby easing the relative burden of authority from the perspective of Quebec and the other provinces. While Ottawa could acknowledge the reality that Quebec is a distinct or unique society, it could not transfer large amounts of sovereignty in a one-sided, selective way to Quebec alone.

Canada could also decentralize by shifting authority to the provincial or local levels of government, although Canada is already not very far from the degree of decentralization (when the provincial and local levels are considered together) of a Switzerland. The next degrees of decentralization hold large implications for Canada's international role as a principal power.[40] Finally, varieties of 'asymmetrical federalism' could be developed to allow each of the provinces, including Quebec, greater flexibility in the establishment of its own programs even though the financing or broad policy guidelines remain in the federal dossier.

From the U.S. perspective, each of these alternatives holds different consequences for policy. If Quebec separatists fail once again to achieve independence through the ballot box, this may embitter as many ardent proponents as it discourages. This could hold some implications for Canada's relations abroad. Of course, if Quebec secedes, the possible bitterness would be on the other side, the side of the anglophone and allophone minority inside Quebec, an equally uncertain situation that could sputter for a long time or boil over into fragmentation. All of this means that U.S. policy towards Canada and its internal relations with Quebec will become more complicated in the years ahead, not less so, in contrast to what many in Washington might like to believe.

If Quebec secedes, the United States would face an ROC under much internal stress as it attempts to reconstitute itself. If the ROC is unable to do so, the United States would then face the prospect, not to its liking, of an unravelling along its northern border. To forestall this prospect, the United States might consider invoking a new concept, the notion of 'regional affiliation.' This concept attempts to balance the objectives of the individual fragments and the goals of North American regionalism.

If a dissident province decides that regional affiliation is not enough and applies for membership in the American union, despite the difficulties that this imposes on both sides, the United States would be forced to take that application seriously. The unravelling of Canada is an unacceptable prospect that must be taken seriously.

Lastly, if Canada adopts decentralization of either the Type X variety (devolution of powers from federal government to province), or the Type Y variety (shift of power from prime minister to Parliament), the United States will also be affected. Done carefully, Type Y decentralization could ease some of the bickering inside Canada and might appeal to some kinds of government in Quebec City. Done precipitously and wrongly, Type X decentralization could radically amend governance in Canada, undermine its foreign policy, and significantly alter the way Canada and the United States do their political business.

There will always be a Canada. Many who believe Canada to be a wonderful country[41] – noble in its dreams, generous in its hospitality, and caring – would like to think that Canada as it now exists, in its social totality, will be the Canada that will always exist. In many respects that will remain true. This analysis suggests, however, that in terms of institutions and distributions of governmental functions, the more certain wager is that Canada is in the midst of acute, consequential political change.

CHAPTER EIGHT

Self-Determination and Democratic Pluralism

In the new millennium, when liberal democracy is celebrating its proudest successes, the democratic polity finds itself confronting a challenge from within that is so fundamental and so persistent that the very core of democracy's achievement is put at risk. Let us begin by very clearly stating the arguments leading to this stark conclusion.

The Threat to Democratic Pluralism

(1) Democratic pluralism argues that diverse communities in a liberal democracy can live in harmony with each other inside a single state, and, what is more, that in this condition of social and political interdependence the members of these communities can thrive spiritually, economically, linguistically, and intellectually.[1]

(2) Separation along ethno-linguistic lines is a statement that democratic pluralism has failed, that the only way each communal group can obtain its goals is through isolation. Ethno-linguistic separation is also a statement that when, on cultural grounds, one community decides it wants to distance itself politically from another cultural community, notwithstanding the intense and total opposition of other cultural minorities within that entity who reject secession, then breakup of the nation-state is permissible on the basis of a majority vote within the secessionist entity. For a majority of the members of an ethno-linguistic community to opt for secession means that cultural difference has been accepted as the overwhelming and sufficient justification.

(3) After the act of separation, such a justification for separation will have two further consequences, each deleterious to democracy: (i) Ethno-linguistic difference becomes the legitimate and accepted moti-

vation for the breakup of the nation-state, thus further weakening the principles of state unity and sovereignty and, at the same time, *undermining the trust that conflicting interests can be accommodated by the democratic process.*[2] (ii) Other decisions within the democratic polity, some of them invidious, are now also likely to be made on the basis of ethnic and cultural difference. Unless a polity is completely homogeneous, discrimination against a community within that polity for religious, ethnic or cultural reasons in the future becomes easier.

In conclusion, after secession from liberal democracy has occurred based on ethno-linguistic preference, both democratic principle and democratic procedure within the state have been weakened. The democratic state is no longer seen to be capable of accommodating societal difference. Rather, societal difference is the arbiter of whether the democratic state can prevail.

Hence, the erosion of democratic pluralism undermines the other principles of democracy. The principle of political toleration that treats all cultural communities equally, and all individuals regardless of community equally, is especially vulnerable.

This chapter assesses the thesis that, if the nation-state splinters along ethno-linguistic lines, democratic pluralism is at risk. In the twenty-first century, if the nation-state proves too weak a vessel to contain intercommunal conflict, then not only the principle of democratic pluralism but political toleration itself will have been cast a blow that augers poorly for the evolution of democracy.[3]

Parameters of the Thesis

Realism demands that different situations be treated differently. First, the thesis is for the most part limited to advanced industrial countries. Despite some success in the direction of pluralism during early economic development, the problems of development may overshadow what can be expected of pluralism.[4] For example, Lebanon, at one time held up as a paragon of democratic pluralism, was burdened by the struggle to lift itself out of the middle echelon of development while at the same time making political adjustments during an extremely troubled domestic and international interval of history. Despite a recent return to possible democratic rule in Lebanon, democratic pluralism should not be judged in the context of such hazards.

Second, democratic pluralism ought to be considered against the standard of countries that have established democratic roots. A lack of experience with democracy (democratic culture) seems to explain in part why democracy collapsed in Estonia in the 1930s but flourished in Finland.[5] Czechoslovakia, notwithstanding the regrets subsequently expressed in both the Czech Republic and Slovakia about the wisdom of the 'velvet divorce,' had been operating for some forty years under a system of communist dictatorship, perhaps ideal for covering up political fissures between communal groups, but not ideal for testing the principle of democratic pluralism.

Third, if violence is pervasive enough and intense enough, all considerations with respect to the niceties of democratic pluralism must be set aside. This qualification in judging the validity of democratic pluralism as a norm is not undermined by cases such as that of Wales where sporadic attacks on property, for example, are used to illustrate nationalist passion. But a case such as Bosnia in which there is long-standing massive violence and a tremendous loss of life among the Serb, Moslem, and Croat communities, or such as in Kosovo between the Serbian and Albanian communities, is hardly fertile ground in which to assess the merits of democratic pluralism.

Hence the argument on behalf of the superior status of democratic pluralism should only be made in the propitious context of (1) the wealth, education, and technological sophistication of advanced industrialism, (2) the long-standing democratic tradition of a polity, and (3) the absence of massive violence that would seriously distort concentration on pluralist norms. Similarly, the breakup of empire is not to be equated with divisive nationalism as problematic for democratic pluralism. Empire, unlike the state, because of its 'divide-and-rule' strategy and its political manipulation of dependent communities, is preconditioned for disintegration.

This is a cautious standard upon which to judge the validity of democratic pluralism as a working norm of political behaviour, and the performance of a large number of countries remains to be compared against it. The reality that most governments (among the sample of countries that qualify) have and will observe the rules of democratic pluralism is not sufficient however. If divisive nationalism takes root in some highly visible polities in the twenty-first century, the danger is as great to democratic institutions and to civility in general as any preceding threat, including that of the great totalitarian scourges of the early twentieth century. Divisive nationalism as a threat to democratic pluralism is merely a more subtle and a more selective threat, less easily criticized because it is more readily justified under the veil of self-determination and freedom of political expression.

Divisive nationalism strikes at the heart of modern democracy. It challenges the very notion of cultural toleration and social harmony. It says to a people that they are so unique, so linguistically fragile, so in need of political isolation for their prosperity that they cannot live under a single political roof with another cultural-linguistic grouping. Translated, this characterization of a communal fragment's situation means that its members believe their success and their fate is determined by that of another perhaps larger community, not primarily by their own energies and creativity. Such is the deceit of divisive nationalism.

Divisive Nationalism

Never more important is the lesson of Robin Winks concerning the value of comparative history.[6] Through the study of another polity, one obtains a better appreciation of the problems and possibilities of one's own nation. For liberal democracies everywhere, the fragility of democratic pluralism at home can perhaps best be understood by observing the challenges democratic pluralism faces abroad.

In some ways the great debate regarding democracy and culture is epitomized on the one hand by Francis Fukuyama's stand that democracy has ended history by superseding cultural nationalism, and on the other by the view of Samuel Huntington and of Shlomo Avineri that nationalism may curtail the spread of democracy.[7] Reconciling the two extremes is a middle view, such as that expressed by Ghia Nodia, that democracy and nationalism are compatible inside the framework of liberal democracy.[8] But the proviso is that democratic pluralism must prevail in liberal democracy as well. Liberal democracy itself is indeed under siege, and the best hope against cultural nationalism is liberal democracy in the form of democratic pluralism.

In fourteen of fifteen advanced-industrial countries, confidence in political democracy seems to have declined during the 1990s, according to a study by Robert Putnam, Susan Pharr, and Russell Dalton.[9] The evidence that citizens in the mature democracies seem to be losing confidence in their institutions has quite troubling implications for democratic pluralism. These governments will not be in a strong position to cope with any future challenges that divisive nationalism may pose to their political institutions. Conversely, the decline in confidence in political institutions is exactly the kind of facilitator that spurs divisive nationalism.

Powerless Subordinate or Active Co-participant?

Divisive nationalism possesses much in kin with the arguments of *dependencia*, so popular in intellectual circles during the 1970s, in which the prosperity of the 'periphery' was seen as only possible in response to and as a reflection of the more powerful 'core.' *Dependencia* created a sense of powerlessness and helplessness in the minds of its advocates. Their only escape from stagnation was held to be isolation from the larger economic system.[10] Import substitution with all of its barriers to trade and outside influence was the vehicle that would help attain economic growth.

Similarly, divisive nationalism argues that inside a polity one communal group will always be at the mercies of another, perhaps larger, communal group. Only by separation, so the argument is made, can the smaller communal group find the room to exercise its full potential for development and maturation. Like *dependencia*, divisive nationalism finds solace in withdrawal, not in engagement, and in identifying itself as a 'victim' rather than as a self-possessed, active, co-participant in a larger joint enterprise known as economic or political interdependence.

Like *dependencia*, divisive nationalism contains some of the anxiety sometimes emitted by liberal thought over the possible loss of political sovereignty either inside the international system (*dependencia*) or inside the larger state (divisive nationalism). But in a fuller sense, both *dependencia* and divisive nationalism undermine liberal value.

They undermine liberal value because liberalism, either the nineteenth-century Manchester style or the contemporary political liberalism variety, expresses cooperation, non-zero-sum relations, and absolute gains as being of paramount significance. The notion that one communal group, or one state within the contemporary international system, is able to exploit or subordinate a second group to the economic advantage of the first is strictly missing from the liberal ethos in a post-colonial world. Yet divisive nationalism, like *dependencia*, thrives on the assertion of exploitation, subordination, loss of political autonomy and the alleged collusion between members of elites to the vast detriment of the mass population. Divisive nationalism from this vantage point is both anti-liberal and a violation of the assumptions of democratic pluralism. Liberalism in the advanced-industrial democracy points the way, in contrast, to shared progress and to intercommunal communication and endeavour.

But suppose the only desire of the sovereigntists is to change the situation in which they find themselves in the minority to a situation in which they find themselves in the majority. Suppose the essence of the separatists' platform is to become 'masters of their own house.' Is there anything objectionable to the natural desire to 'govern oneself'?

On the surface, these goals are the most plausible of political objectives. They appear to correspond to the right of self-determination. They even seem to reinforce the principle of self-reliance and the desire to determine one's own fate, both political and economic, which is certainly a widely admired goal in North American society.

But let us examine the idea of becoming 'masters of one's own house' a bit more closely. Becoming master of one's own house is a perfectly plausible objective where a majority is not in control of its own existence and where a permanent minority is able to perpetuate its control of government, the market, or social rules. But once a more just equilibrium is attained, once equality has been achieved, once exploitation is at an end, to continue to assert the desire for 'mastery' and for 'one's own house' to the point of demanding political separation is quite another matter. At this point, assessment of other factors fuelling the drive for separation becomes essential.

For example, language does not seem to be the determining feature of separatist impulse in the Basque country or in Wales and Scotland, as opposed to Catalonia or Belgium. In the Basque country, only 28 per cent of the population speak Euskara, and in Wales fewer than 10 per cent of the population speak Welsh. In Catalonia, 86 per cent of the population speaks Catalan. Yet, ironically, Basque nationalism is very exclusionist (perhaps historically because of the relatively greater wealth of the Basque country than its poorer Spanish counterparts) and Catalan is quite inclusionist. In each enclave, however, it is the speakers of the language who loyally support the separatist political parties and the separatist cause.[11] Sons of Basque immigrants seem to be disproportionately represented in the terrorist groups associated with Euskadi Ta Askatasuna (ETA), perhaps as in all such terrorist organizations to prove their loyalty precisely because they cannot show lineage.[12]

In divisive nationalism, the house spoken of is a communal house of those who share the same culture, speak the same language, and live in the same neighbourhood. Even though other minorities may live there, it is not fundamentally a pluralist house composed of heterogeneous cultures and peoples (as discussed below in 'Self-Determination: The Pluralist Addendum').

To become master of one's own house suggests a past feudal master–subordinate peasant relationship. Two conclusions follow from this usage. First, assumed is that the prior political relationship was a clear communal hierarchy. It was a master–subordinate relationship in which the communal group was dominated and exploited. This was not a relationship of equality between communal groups. Nor was it a society where the individual, not the communal group, was the focus of rights and obligations. This is not the setting of modern pluralist democracy, but of colonialism, or at the very least a setting in which a colonial frame of mind about politics still persists.

Second, when placed in the context of opposed cultural-linguistic relations, the phrase 'become a master of one's own house' suggests to the listener that the future political relationship will be that of dominance and subordination once again. The only difference will be that the formerly downtrodden will now be those who downtread. There is no suggestion in the aphorism that equality is the objective, namely, a political or legal equality of individuals, or even an equality of cultural groups. Nor in this aphorism is there an intimation that democratic pluralism will be observed in the future, even if in the past its practice has been denied.

These observations highlight how cultural nationalism can challenge the very essence of liberal democracy. Findings on democratic satisfaction show that in very competitive political systems, the 'losers' are less happy than those in more consensual-type democracies; 'winners' are happier in strong majoritarian governments.[13] *But in democracy, there ought to be no permanent winners or losers. Moreover, cooperative outcomes ought to be the most prized.*

At the heart of becoming 'master of one's own house' through political secession is the notion that, despite minority opposition within the house, this house will become independent and the dominant cultural group will determine the rules and come to power.[14] The dominant cultural group may be less concerned about the interests and rights of other cultural groups inside the house. Celebrated is the triumph of the previously subordinate group that is now politically dominant. The observation that colonial dominance has long since been overthrown and that a new era of self-determination may already be in place is irrelevant. A lingering observation is that dominance–dependence relationships shall be the rule of political decision making into the future, with all the implications this holds for politics inside the new government and outside it vis-à-vis other governments.

The Paradox of Regional versus State Integration

One of the great puzzles of divisive nationalism is why it holds appeal in the context of regional integration where new rules and controls are likely to be imposed upon a separatist entity seemingly not so different in kind from those previously exercised within the larger state of which the entity once had been a member.[15] Why would the separatist exchange one set of interdependencies for another? Why should sovereignty associated with membership in a state be a problem for a communal group, but demands placed upon a separatist entity by regional integration not be a problem?

Either the obligations assumed under state sovereignty or regional integration are similar for the separatist entity, in which case separation itself makes no political sense, or the obligations are quite different and regional integration will demand less from the separatist fragment. In the latter case the implications ought to be spelled out so as not to disappoint partners who look forward to increasing regional integration.

The separatist fragment cannot have the situation both ways. It cannot claim that separation is vital if in the end, after secession, it must observe equivalent obligations under international regional integration. Likewise, if the level of obligation is different under statehood and under regional integration, then the separatist entity must admit that there is an upper limit to the amount and intensity of international integration it will tolerate in the future because it has no intention of approaching the level it had previously experienced under statehood. Other regional partners are entitled to know this sovereigntist constraint as they contemplate entrance of the separatist state into the framework of regional integration. As the level of integration increases over time, full support for regional integration at present may not mean full support for integration in the future. Which is the correct interpretation?

As it faces new levels of integration and controls on state sovereignty, the European Union countries are likely to feel these tensions ever more acutely.[16] Take for example the resignation of the entire twenty-member EU Commission over allegations of corruption on March 16, 1999. The members of the Commission resigned because they were caught between an increasingly truculent set of governments that were resisting loss of sovereignty and an increasingly assertive EU Parliament that was preparing itself for the June elections and was trying to demonstrate its increased sovereignty to the people, all in the name of democratic control. The Commission was being squeezed from both sides and could not simultaneously satisfy the governments that wanted to go slower and the Parliament that wanted to go faster. The Commission found that it could not have the situation both ways.

Similarly, secessionist entities cannot claim that separation is necessary to increase communal sovereignty and claim that entry into a regional trading bloc is logical if the outcome involves a significant transfer of sovereignty away from the separatist fragment in the future. If Scotland, Flanders, Catalonia, and Northern Italy all believe that secession is justified because the British, the Belgians, the Spanish and the Italians are demanding too much of them, but that transfers of sovereignty to the EU after secession are also justified because these transfers will place the same demands on them as they experienced under statehood, then why secede? What the separatist entity gains from secession will be lost to regional integration. The separatist leadership would need to be daft to accept such a bargain, and, of course, it is not daft. In each case, what the separatist leadership expects is that the degree of integration inside the European Union will be far *less* than what was experienced inside the prior state. Indeed, implicit in the behaviour of the secessionist entities is that, should such a degree of integration ever approach that of the existing nation-states, these entities would oppose that degree of integration and would perhaps have the support of other state governments as well.

This is the paradox of sovereigntist commitment. That commitment goes only so far in releasing them from the authority of the states in which they presently reside. Once outside the state as an independent actor, they will implicitly oppose further integration because this would put them, in sovereignty terms right back where they had been, this time under the control of larger neighbours (North America) or supranational institutions (European Union). Separatist entities, of course, are betting that regional interdependence and integration will never get this far. They are speculating that there will always be a sizeable gap between the degree of integration that might be expected of them within regions and the degree of integration they will insist upon within their own community.

Separation is designed to help secessionists escape state sovereignty and to increase their own sovereignty at the probable cost of the scope and pace of regional integration.[17] Newly secessionist actors, regardless of what they may tell the representatives of other state governments, cannot be on the forefront of change in favour of substantially tighter regional integration because they will accept the level of present regional integration. Indeed, they need this level because they must have access to an unfettered, larger market for the export of their goods and services. But when it comes to integration that will reduce sovereignty in the name of standard-setting or congruent public polices that affect cultural or political autonomy, however indirectly, secessionists will be obliged by procedural and electoral consistency to resist such trends.

The paradox of sovereigntist commitment is that it seeks a reduction of sovereignty within the original state through secession but accepts an increase in sovereign control externally through regional integration. It cannot do both things simultaneously. Beneath the paradox of sovereigntist commitment is a serious logical and political fallacy. That contradiction is likely in the end to be resolved in favour of retention of authority by the secessionist entity against the larger interests of supranational institutions or the other members of the region. There can be no other exit from an antinomy that is otherwise too large and too binding.

The Impact on Civility

Divisive nationalism carries another liability, the impact that it is likely to have on civility within the polis. The ancient Greek concept of civility (virtue) can scarcely be improved upon today.[18] It is not based on governmental enforcement of law, nor is it based on the identification with communal groups and their concept of societal constraint. It is based on the individual's acceptance of self-restraint. This self-restraint in turn, as it is amplified through society, means that society can operate with an internal harmony belying the heavy hand of the state. Democratic pluralism in a modern society of more than one culture or ethnic group epitomizes this understanding of government. The problem is that divisive nationalism opposes this Athenian concept of civility.

There are in at least three ways that divisive nationalism is likely to erode civility: (1) Extremism as experienced in the Basque country of Spain may occur. (2) Government reaction to extremism may be brutal as it was in Lebanon, India, Ethiopia, and Sri Lanka. (3) Even in the absence of violence or a violent governmental response to extremism, divisive nationalism may begin to poison the social and political atmosphere such that communal groups throughout society begin to demand greater accountability of their membership. Norms of heterogeneity within society may give way to homogeneity.[19] Attitudes towards 'the other' in society will harden.

Thus divisive nationalism may trigger attacks on democratic pluralism from a number of directions, depending upon the polarization of the society, the level of economic development, the recent history of arms use, and the commitment to democratic institutions. It is the third challenge to democratic pluralism, however, that is of the greatest interest to this assessment, even though this challenge is by far the most subtle.

If, as is assumed in this study, the society inside the advanced industrial states in the twenty-first century is becoming more heterogeneous and therefore more liberal in its social structure, then divisive nationalism in principle opposes this trend. Since the predominant reason for separation is cultural, that is, to maximize the purported interests of that culture relative to the more numerous members of another culture or cultures, divisive nationalism hurts. It establishes culture and language as the norm of political association. The impact upon civility is likely to reduce communication and interaction of all kinds between cultures. This withdrawal from the life of the political commons within the heterogeneous state is likely to redound poorly both to the members of the secessionist entity and to the members of the larger fragment. This rejection of civility is not just a short-term phenomenon associated with anger over the breakup of the state. The rejection of civility fundamentally arises out of the embrace of homogeneity and all that it entails socially and psychologically for each family and citizen.

The individual act that divisive nationalism most opposes in the name of the preservation of the culture, religion, ethnicity, language, or traditions of the group is intermarriage. In divisive nationalism, intermarriage is the antithesis of the social values that the separatist wants to inculcate in the society; intermarriage with a member of another cultural grouping is akin at the individual level to the perpetuation of state ties across cultural groupings at the state level. The shift towards homogeneity may not originate from an assault upon intermarriage. But divisive nationalism is bound to have a highly emotional impact at the individual level on the propensity to intermarry. It would seem that divisive nationalism and increasing civility within the polis follow two inevitably opposite trajectories.

Comparative history will be important in assessing each of the characteristics of divisive nationalism explored in this section. Ideally, one democracy's success in overcoming a particular divisive pull will guide other democracies in the effort to protect democratic pluralism itself.

Bogus Science of Primordial Causes for Ethnic Separatism

In scholarly literature there is a return to the application of social Darwinism in search of a 'genetic' explanation for the ethno-linguistic conflict. For example, harking back to long-discarded arguments by Herbert Spencer and followers, an effort is being made to distinguish two different 'genetic codes,' a code for *amity* towards in-group members, and a code of *enmity* for out-group members.[20] That there is no genetic or biological evidence for the existence of such codes, let alone delineation along such dubious behavioural lines, and that such 'sociobiology' stumbles on the evolutionary law denying the Lamarckian claim of 'an inheritance of acquired characteristics,' seem to have eluded notice of those using these arguments in sociology and anthropology.[21] This lack of evidence and contradiction with the fundamentals of evolutionary law must, however, be taken into consideration in evaluating any argument as scientific. In spite of the use of the evolutionary paradigm as basis, those arguments are completely bogus science.

While the argument is not made by Quebecers or about Quebec, the fear of 'primordial' cultural differences between communities has entered much of the debate about culture and politics where it is often manipulated by political elites for the purpose of obtaining or remaining in power.[22] Writing of Yugoslavia, Warren Zimmerman demolishes the myth that primordial ethno-linguistic differences among Serbs, Muslims, and Croats drove them to savage warfare.[23] Instead, he shows that self-interested elites and leaders used cultural difference to promote their own desire for control and political ascendancy, convincing militias that ethnic cleansing and other barbarity was essential to survival of the community. At the same time, they kept the enormity of these crimes from the critical gaze of the larger populations, an old trick of totalitarian rule.

After a careful review of the analytic literature on sociobiology, Frank Harvey writes, 'we are not yet equipped to move beyond analogy when applying evolutionary theory to international politics or conflict.'[24] This sage judgment holds meaning for the complexities of interpreting secessionist behaviour of communities within advanced-industrial democracy. Analysis must probe these complexities.

The separatist community is distinguished by linguistic or at least cultural difference from the members of the larger polity with which the community seeks to dissociate. Aims of the secessionist community are always tentatively expressed in 'civic' terms (a goal the community leaders sincerely would like to pursue but, as has been argued in the previous sections, cannot because of the limited nature of the secessionist enterprise). In fact, the appeal is much more narrowly cultural, for it is the cultural thrust that gives secession its emotive force. But this cultural focus alienates those who are of a different cultural orientation living on the territory of the secessionist community. To reflect the true complexity of the situation even more fully, not all of the members of the secessionist community who are of the same culture as the separatist leaders share in the ideal of separation. Finally, the elite, not the masses, carry forth the spark of separatist impulse. The elite must ignite a passion for separation within the mass base of their cultural community so that the minorities (who cannot for reasons of self-interest be convinced to join the separatist enterprise) can be outvoted.

Such a strategic and compositional complexity as this is a 'real world' example of the secessionist program. Primordial explanations and so-called evolutionary (social-Darwinist) explanations for separatist activity simply have no validity in explaining why a cultural community wishes to secede from a larger polity.

The Communitarian Challenge to Democratic Pluralism

In an elegant defense of communitarianism, Michael Sandel challenges the notion of universalism imbedded in liberal democracy:

> What egalitarian liberalism requires, but cannot within its own terms provide, is some way of defining the relevant community of sharing, some way of seeing the participants as mutually indebted and morally engaged to begin with. It needs a way of answering Emerson's challenge to the man who solicited his contribution to the poor – 'Are they *my* poor?'[25]

According to the communitarians, it is only 'natural' that an individual's affinities differ across groups and across institutions. Before helping the poor, from the perspective of communitarian thought, it is only natural to ask: Are they of my religion, my community, or my cultural grouping?

Most of an individual's generalized affinities will be stronger to family than to the ethno-linguistic community; or stronger to the community than to the overall polity of which the community is but one segment; and stronger to the polity than to the global international system. This stronger affinity has its roots in affection, comfort, familiarity, security, and responsiveness. Indeed, not only affinity but the sense of duty may also compel the individual to identify with local interests rather than global interests. Size may have something to do with these identifications as well. The local grouping, beginning with the family, is likely to be smaller and more intimate than the community or nation. Furthermore, none of these affiliations is undesirable or subject to approbation. As the communitarian point of view correctly emphasizes, each form of group participation has a role in shaping the overall identity of the individual.

It is easy to demonstrate the different affinities an individual holds for different groups. Enthusiasm for a university that a student has attended often is greater than the enthusiasm for another university that the student has never attended. Affinity for a local sporting team, rather than for other teams, is the basis for the creation of successful professional leagues such as the National Hockey League or the National Basketball Association. Without this preponderantly local identification, franchises could not survive, and without individual franchises that prosper on the local participation they receive, the professional sports association could not exist. Thus localized affiliation, support, and identification is almost a precondition for the kind of market necessary for the operation of entire industries.

But the proposition that affinities of an individual exist for groups, that the strength of these affinities may vary with the group, and that the strongest affinities may be associated with the groups that are most local, intimate, and smallest, does not necessarily translate into a *normative* rule concerning human preference or human behaviour. That the individual may find association with one group or the other indispensable for his or her personal identity may be indisputable. Such an association ought not to be discouraged or hindered. The opportunity to develop such an association and to exploit its benefits subject only to the rule that this opportunity should not come at the cost of another individual's opportunity ought to be recognized. But though these observations be true regarding the value of association between individual and group, the normative reality remains that a government has no obligation to strengthen one type of affinity rather than another or to foster a particular hierarchy of affinities across groups. The only obligation a government has is to allow the individual to choose the groups with which he or she wishes to affiliate, unimpeded, and with whatever degree of affinity that individual deems appropriate.

An analytic case can be made for the argument, however, that (1) where group affinities are strikingly different, (2) where society is composed of more than one regionally specific communal group, and (3) where the existence of cross-cutting affinities does not offset the striking difference in strength of different affinities, the capacity to hold the society together as an integrated unit can be very difficult.[26] Moreover, under the above conditions, the individual may find full participation and interaction within such a society very difficult. Where identity with family is paramount, affiliation with the other members of an ethnic community or religion may be somewhat sacrificed unless cross-cutting affiliations occur through schools, clubs, sporting teams, and businesses that help promote association with the larger community. Where identity with ethno-linguistic community is very strong and is localized within a single region or territory, affiliation with the larger polity may be diminished unless cross-cutting affiliations within and between universities, firms, occupational roles, political parties, unions, and church groups offset the primary affiliation with ethno-linguistic community.

Despite a laudable attention to the needs of community, moral motivation, and collective value in a society that sometimes appears excessively 'individualist,' the communitarian position is vulnerable to challenge for its failure to construct a common foundation within the overall polity for social and political cooperation. No society that fails to provide a way of resolving community division, that exacerbates competing communal ideas of social responsibility, and that encourages very limited and divergent domains of communal obligation, can long retain its integrity, or survive as a political unit.

But on normative grounds, the value and preference of communitarianism is also vulnerable. Perhaps an argument expressed in the tradition of a philosophic parable will help make the point.

Parable of the Waiting Room Suppose, for example, that a physician finds three patients in his waiting room, all of whom have arrived at the same time. One patient is the physician's brother. Another patient, though not a relative, is a member of the physician's own church congregation and speaks a language they share that is not the language of the majority population. The third patient is a recent immigrant to the community, who is poor, and who is racially different. Whom should the physician see first?

If the communitarian philosophy is followed, the answer is straightforward. Family is a priority; the doctor should care for his brother first. Next he should feel quite free to attend to the member of his own ethno-linguistic community, for the affinities to that community are strong. Finally, because affinities to an outsider are weakest, the physician should see and treat last the immigrant who also happens to be poor. This may actually be the preference ordering of some physicians in some countries today, which only adds reality to this situation.

Now of course various codes may exist to alter this preference ordering concerning medical care. The physician has probably sworn the Hippocratic oath to give care to those who need it most. So on these grounds he or she may decide to assist whomever appears to be most seriously ill or injured or otherwise in need of medical help. Likewise, in cases of emergency, this preference ordering may prevail over all others. In actual practice, all three patients probably did not enter the door of the waiting room simultaneously. So as a common courtesy, as well as a way of meting out fairness, the physician may ask his or her nurse who arrived first and attend to that person accordingly. If the physician is a strong liberal, or otherwise desirous of making a statement to his profession or community regarding his or her neutrality and integrity, the choice may be to see the poor, racially different immigrant first, while allowing his brother and colleague from the neighbourhood community to wait. All of these formulae for deciding whom to attend to first might override and at the same time simplify the physician's decision. But even with the last formula, the criterion of assisting the immigrant first on grounds of some type of affirmative action, the physician would still need to decide who subsequently had priority, family or ethno-linguistic community, and the formula provided would not be of much help in making this latter decision.

In the absence of any code or formula to simplify the task of deciding whom to see first, the physician nonetheless would be hard put to justify his decision on communitarian grounds. In most societies, if a physician chose to see his or her brother first and a member of his or her own church and ethno-linguistic community second while leaving the immigrant to wait, the physician at the very least would be accused of favouritism. On the other hand, what would happen if the physician were able to make the decision free from public observation, that is, behind the closed door to public scrutiny?[27] According to communitarian logic, nothing would change. Free of public scrutiny, the physician would be perhaps even more inclined to follow the hierarchy of his or her own preferences.

Yet from the perspective of goodness and justice for all members of the society, what would justify treating the brother before the member of the physician's own ethnic or linguistic community? What would justify treating either of these patients before any other member of the larger polity, or, for that matter, any other member of humanity. Nothing, not even affinity, could justify putting one man or woman ahead of any other.[28] All are equal before the law and before the hand of the physician. All have an equal bid to be healed according to an unbiased application of the principles of medicine.

And so it was in actual historical circumstance. Quebec francophones have no reason to doubt a history of unbiased generosity. The Sisters of St Ursuline in the shadow of the devastating defeat of the French forces of Montcalm by the British forces of Wolfe on the Plains of Abraham in 1759, knitted wool stockings for, and tended the wounded of, both the British and the French, side-by-side, during the icy winter that followed, with no regard for flag or country of national origin. Such altruism does exist more broadly within societies. Consider another parable.

Parable of the Campfire When, on the frontier, firewood was left for the next struggling traveller at a campsite along a winter path to preserve him or her from freezing and perhaps starvation, no question was asked regarding the age, sex, intelligence, wisdom, race, religion, or national origin of the recipient. All that was asked of the recipient of life-preserving, dry firewood was that he or she do the same for the next traveller.

What is remarkable is that this ethical assumption that dry firewood must be left for the next traveller, whomever he or she might be, is an unspoken and unwritten obligation.

Why does the first traveller leave firewood for a second person totally unknown to him or her? The first traveller need not fear any type of enforcement or penalty for failing to leave firewood. Nor would the first traveller face an unpleasant confrontation with the second traveller, whom in all probability the first traveller has never met and probably never will. Nor is the second traveller likely to be a member of the first traveller's family or specific ethno-linguistic community. Rather, this act of altruism is based partially on the Golden Rule 'Do unto others as you would have them do unto you' (The Old Testament; Kant; Rawls), partially on learned behaviour (Locke), and, in time, partially on habit (Hume). The altruism and generosity of the person who befriends someone unknown to him or her shapes the moral behaviour of the next person who may occupy the same campsite as well. That is where in this story, in a subtle way, moral learning takes place.[29] Conversely, this learning may also have been reinforced by a traveller's actual experience that, in a blinding snow storm on some bitterly cold evening after a long tiring day on the trail, a predecessor had *not* left enough dry firewood to start a life-preserving campfire.

While a proclivity exists to favour the member of a family, or of a community, or of a nation, before a mere member of humanity at large, education and ethics widen our beneficence to strangers. For although rights and duty may know limits imposed by law and politics, love, respect, and ultimate fairness ought to obey lesser limits of proximity or affinity. Michael Ignatieff argues that the citizen must love his or her own culture a little less and someone else's culture a little more.[30] As Ian Angus points out, the love of a mother for her children is never zero-sum.[31] Although every mother loves each child, that love is not diminished by sharing it across all children. Nor is that mother ever expected to choose one child over another, or to provide love to one child and to deny it to another. So it is within society, honoured perhaps more in the breach than the practice, one person is not expected to benefit from the generosity of another human being because of affinity, while a second person is denied that benefit. Nor must the love of one culture exclude that of another. Communitarianism can provide no guide in the distribution of the 'good' within the polity.

As the debate between communitarians and liberals ultimately must admit, all communal identity is not without egoism, and all individualism does not manifest egoism. Communities can sometimes suffocate the expression of idea, and individuals can sometimes reach out. Carlos Fuentes, contemplating Latino diversity, tells communities to reach out: 'All together now, keep your eyes open beyond yourselves ... where those who are different are waiting to demonstrate that they are as human as we.'[32]

Analysis thus takes us back full circle to the discussion in chapter 1 of 'How Democratic Pluralism Amends Communitarianism.' Communitarianism has provided a great analytic service by preventing a 'heavy' liberalism from reaching too deeply into the norms, preferences, and behaviours of ethnic and cultural communities and of denying them their place and origin as a base for generating societal value. But what communitarianism ultimately has been unable to provide is a resolution to the unity problem within society. Indeed, by stressing difference and diversity rather than 'overlapping consensus,' communitarianism has aggravated already too sensitive communal differences within the polity.

It is 'just as natural' at every level of society to emphasize affinity between groups as it is to emphasize affinity between members within a group. This is the message of democratic pluralism, which translates the world of cultural and linguistic preference and difference into the world of politics. Democratic pluralism permits communal groups, often territorially based, to fully develop their identity and to fully express their sense of self. Democratic pluralism provides the political space in which community is able to articulate idea and practice. It also supplies a conceptual framework in which to manage communal adversity in polities that both tolerate pluralism and are deeply committed to democracy. In a word, democratic pluralism is an answer to the unity problem that communitarianism raises but cannot itself resolve outside the give and take of political exchange and compromise.

Self-Determination: The Pluralist Addendum

Subsequent to the enunciation of the doctrine of self-determination, Woodrow Wilson began to have self-doubts about the Pandora's Box he had opened.[33] Recognizing these shortcomings in the notion of self-determination, political theorist Robert Dahl tries to reconcile the concept of self-determination and the concept of representation, bringing the argument of liberal democracy directly back to the fundamental challenge raised by Alvin Rabushka and Kenneth Shepsle in 1972: 'Is the resolution of intense but conflicting preferences in the plural society manageable in a democratic framework?'[34] Cultural nationalism today forces us to confront warnings, harking back to a much earlier era, that liberal democracy was vulnerable to attack from within. In highly divided societies with intensely felt differences, where the appeal of self-determination may be especially strong, liberal democracy faces deep problems and needs new ground rules of operation.

If self-determination is the right to live under laws that one chooses, and if democracy maximizes the prospect of self-determination, then, according to Robert Dahl, three conditions are necessary for achieving political harmony:[35] (1) Every citizen should know about a law before it is enacted. (2) Chance for discussion of the law will facilitate deliberation and compromise that may result in the best possible law for all concerned. (3) Since unanimity is unlikely, majority rule will prevail. Presumably, safeguards of rights that are shared by all, but may be of greatest concern to minorities, will also accompany any decision made by majority rule.

What is most interesting about Dahl's notion of self-determination is that it is written from the classical liberal perspective of the individual. But self-determination in the twentieth century has almost always been exercised by the collective, by a communal group with a geographical centre of gravity seeking political autonomy. Moreover, the polity itself is thus often composed of a majority communal group and one or more minority communal groups vying with each other to some extent for power and sometimes for rights. In this contemporary situation involving the self-determination of communal groups rather than just of the individual in the classical liberal paradigm, a *pluralist addendum* to Dahl's plausible defence of self-determination must be conceived.

How does one get from the individual to the collective, from the *preferences* of the individual to the *preferences* of the collective, indeed from an ethic that treats the individual and the collective separately to an ethic that fully comprehends their mutual contribution to representation and to participation within the context of democratic pluralism?

Utilitarian approaches work within very sharp limits of application, undoubtedly stretched to those limits at least in modern economic analysis. However, where absolutes are involved, the comparative calculus of utility almost by definition fails. Interpersonal preferences can be added where the quality of information is high and not too complex. But the utilities of collective groups are not properly encompassed because much of the non-additivity and the incongruity of collective preferences gets left out.

Yet, in real life, democracy must encompass those collective preferences of ethno-linguistic communities and somehow find representation in the polity without doing injustice to the preferences of the individual inside or outside the group. In practice, democracy tries to improve upon 'one man/one woman, one vote' with various procedural and institutional contrivances that offset the most obvious sources of collective disagreement. Power of the collective group normally determines whether the interests of that group are taken seriously enough to make a procedural or institutional exception to 'one man/one woman, one vote.'

Some of those familiar exceptions include a system made up of layers of government; the provision of two senators per U.S. state, regardless of the state's population, to protect the interests of the smaller states; the retention of certain federal powers in Canada and the United States, including the power of the purse to ensure that a high minimum standard of service (including in the poorer areas) is provided across the country; admission that Quebec is a 'unique' society to guarantee that its collective cultural being is acknowledged.

Within the aforesaid limits of the utilitarian paradigm, a pluralist addendum to the notion of self-determination based on the rights of the individual must be included in the theory of democratic pluralism.

Harmony among communal groups is achieved by optimizing self-determination within the polity across these groups, according to the pluralist addendum. Both the individual and the communal group can benefit from this manner of achieving optimal rights. If a value is placed upon living within the welfare, security, and borders of the state as a whole (i.e., in a state that is larger than that associated with only a single communal group), then the difference between the optimal benefits to the individual in such a larger state and the maximal benefits in the smaller communal or ethnic state will be more than repaid.

Since, as already shown in chapter 6, there are greater economic benefits from living in the larger polity with the larger more integrated market, it should follow that these benefits will more than repay the individual member of a communal group who receives optimal rather than maximal advantage by retaining unity instead of seceding. Harmony among communal groups within a larger unified polity is not only politically feasible, it can be achieved at no additional net cost.

Minimizing the Net Communal Deficit

It is possible that there may be a difference, a *net communal deficit* perhaps, caused by accepting optimal benefit (within a state of more than two communal groups) rather than maximal benefit (in a state with only one communal group). But the argument made here is that this net communal deficit, exacted because of the need to live harmoniously with other communal groups inside a single state, is small to negligible in a well-run pluralist democracy. Moreover, according to

the logic of this notion of the pluralist addendum, the economic benefits of living inside the larger state with its more ample market more
than compensates any individual living within a communal group
who will be disadvantages by the possible net communal deficit. This
deficit – the difference between the benefits arrived at through optimizing benefits across several communal groups inside the single state
as opposed to maximizing benefits inside a smaller homogeneous state
composed of one communal group alone – is likely to be more than offset by the economic advantages of living inside a much larger state. A
larger state has greater potential for an increase in the rate of purchasing power parity, that is, for an increase in the rate of capacity to generate per capita welfare. Jobs, income, and economic welfare more than
make up for having to co-exist inside a polity with other communal
groups, which live predominantly in their own geographic regions.

But the net communal deficit argument may take one further turn.
An advocate of separatism may assert that the net communal deficit is
not small because economic benefits have been used to trade off
against cultural costs. What are these alleged cultural costs? At its raw-
est edge, a cultural cost some separatists believe, though seldom will
admit, is the cost of living next to someone culturally or ethnically different. This is equivalent to the desire to discriminate. The other cultural cost that the separatist may feel but not want to admit is the
preference to be in the majority rather than the minority. In the larger
polity the separatist will be in a cultural minority; after separation that
same individual will be a member of a cultural majority.

On the one hand, these sentiments are anti-pluralist. That such anti-
pluralist notions can stand side-by-side with more liberal preferences
regarding education, health care, pension rights, or access to services is
a great puzzle. Yet members of communal groups can discriminate on
some dimensions of cultural-linguistic behaviour and pursue immacu-
lately liberal preferences on other dimensions of public policy.

On the other hand, cultural and political benefits flow from contact
and intercommunication with individuals of different communal orientation as well. Cultural interaction among children and young
adults broadens knowledge and perspective. Creativity flourishes.
Self-awareness grows. The total output of productivity in many fields
of endeavour is likely to be greater than in a more homogeneous community. (Every great 'national' European cathedral, for instance,
resulted from Europe-wide skills and craftsmanship fed by ideas and
innovation from the non-European world.) Greater opportunity for

specialization occurs in the larger community possessing a wider variety of culturally specific skills and aptitudes. Politically, the openness to new ideas, to change, and to dialogue strengthens the capacity for honest government. Local monopolies that quell innovation and change are less likely in a society composed of multiple ethnic and cultural communities than in those dominated by a few families of similar cultural outlook such as in some countries in the third world.

If elimination of a possible net communal deficit is claimed to follow some kind of trade-off of cultural preference for exclusivity against economic benefit, the analyst must be certain that the claimed cultural preferences are not bogus anti-pluralist or even discriminatory preferences. Liberal behaviour elsewhere in the society is not sufficient to act as a counterweight to such preferences. Fortunately, any net communal deficit that is said to persist inside a unified state composed of more than a single communal group can find ample trade-offs that are both politically legitimate and culturally satisfying.

The argument that the net communal deficit of living with other communal groups inside a single community can be minimal is strengthened by two further observations. First, in many areas of the world, although thankfully not in North America, the matter of external security is also a problem. We might call this problem the 'Leviathan problem.' Larger size contributes to political survival. Leviathan considerations may make larger political size important in defensive military terms.

The other observation is that the foregoing analysis has actually simplified reality to the advantage of those who wish to secede. The reason for this bias is that in reality a communal group that chooses to opt out of a larger polity will not escape the need to coexist with minority groups. A dominant communal group within a secessionist fragment will find itself locked in possible contention with further minority groups of a different ethnic, linguistic, or cultural complexion inside the fragment that has so recently separated.

To say, then, that the size of the net communal deficit is very large when the actual opportunity costs of statehood for the newly independent communal group are also quite large, because of the need to live in harmony with its own minority groups, is to exaggerate the burden of living beside other communal groups inside the larger original polity.

If the law treats all individuals equally, then whether the individual lives in a majority community or in a minority community will not matter. To quote Hurst Hannum, Professor of International Law at the Fletcher School of Law and Diplomacy:

> 'internal' self-determination implies finding appropriate levels of democratic self-government to guarantee effective participation by all in the economic and political life of the country. These purposes may often be realized within less-than-independent political entities. Strong national cultures can continue to survive even without their own states, such as the Catalans, Scots, Welsh, Indian Tamals, Quebecois, Tibetans, and many indigenous peoples – so long as the human rights of their members are protected.[36]

Moving from minority status to majority status will not confer any disproportionate benefits on the individual or the group following secession.

Self-determination and pluralism are thus made compatible even where communal groups, not individuals, are the object of self-determination, because the size of the net communal deficit is small to negligible and is in any case fully compensated by increased economic welfare associated with the benefits of larger economic size and the potential for growth in per capita welfare. As well, any possible net communal deficit is negligible because of the increased creativity, productivity, and openness that interaction with people of different cultural origins brings to a society.

If diverse levels of government cannot cooperate within democracy, how can these entities, after secession, be expected to cooperate as independent states?[37] If different ethnic communities cannot solve their problems harmoniously inside a polity, how can they be expected to interact successfully, after separation, inside some larger regional grouping? If justice fails inside a federal democracy, that failure will plant seeds of injustice throughout the polity and indeed throughout the international system.

India, like Canada a Commonwealth member, is attempting in a noble struggle to show that its more than 100 major language and cultural groupings can make democratic pluralism work. Likewise Russia, facing the prospect of ever greater pressures for breakup from indigenous peoples geographically concentrated, needs inspiration from the West to show that democratic pluralism can succeed. These great civilizations will profit from the knowledge, more so than from aid monies or rhetoric, that democratic pluralism in North America is a reality. Interdependence among democracies diffuses the fruits of good policy. But as the Asian financial crisis of 1998–9 shows, and as the tragic history of Kosovo reminds us, interdependence can also spread the sour harvest of incompetence, inattentiveness, and bad policy.

Problems involving communities of differing culture and language ought to be resolved where those problems originate, at the level of society and government that understands the problems most acutely and that possesses the authority to deal with those problems most directly. The international community offers no insight to heal communal strife that the polity itself does not contain. Federal governments cannot abdicate this responsibility by allowing civility to deteriorate to the point where communities demand to leave. Because they are not likely to fare any better as separate states than as a member of a larger polity, especially when bargaining leverage is given its due, communities must genuinely try to resolve their differences inside the democratic polity.

This is the modest conclusion to which this study has come. In the twenty-first century, breakup of the nation-state is not the answer to society's shortcomings. Even when the ballot box rather than the sword is the instrument, divisive nationalism threatens the principle of democratic governance, for cultural-linguistic difference has proven more convincing than democratic pluralism inside a single unified polity.

Confronting the Challenge to Democratic Pluralism

Divisive nationalism cuts to the heart of democratic pluralism. Culture and language are raised to a plane that surmounts all other divisions of society. Culture and language become the overwhelming rationale for state organization and political autonomy. This inevitably creates tension within the resulting political entity once separation has occurred because minority ethnic and cultural groups trapped inside the new state will anticipate, not without some justification, that if cultural difference is powerful enough to break up a democratic polity, cultural difference may be used as well to make policy disadvantageous to groups outside the dominant culture. A response that says citizens who are not happy with the new cultural/political orientation of the separatist state can leave is distinctly uncivil, and arguably illiberal.

Divisive nationalism is for another reason the enemy of democratic pluralism. Tyranny is the classical justification for political withdrawal or rebellion. But tyranny inside a democratic polity is not only unlikely, it is a contradiction. Therefore divisive nationalism cannot be justified on the grounds of tyranny. It is instead justified on the grounds of cultural-linguistic preference, namely, the preference not to share governance with those who look, act, dress, believe, or speak differently. Also implied is the preference not to associate or communicate intensely with those from another culture. Since democratic pluralism is founded on exactly the opposite assumptions of societal organization, divisive nationalism attempts to turn the clock back to a more austere, more archaic form of social and political organization, that of the supposedly homogeneous state. Everywhere in the advanced-industrial world of market-oriented democracies, the trend is towards increasing cultural diversity because of immigration and differential birth rates. The effort to recreate a kind of society that time has passed by is bound to be stressful for international society.

Paradoxically, North America has gradually evolved a form of political and social organization that is open, liberal, tolerant, and accepting of religious and cultural difference. Divisive nationalism smites this effort by North America to act as a beacon for liberal social and political organization. Democratic pluralism in both Canada and the United States (and implicitly in Mexico, though in more complex ways) has been contrasted with a narrower understanding of social and political organization in the Old World that sought greater homogeneity.[38] A further paradox is that the European Union holds out the possibility that Europe will be composed of more closely interdependent nation-states whose present-day degree of cultural interpenetration may begin to exceed that of North America. Yet divisive nationalism in Europe threatens this vision as much as it may threaten the reality of democratic pluralism in North America.

North Americans have always regarded themselves as a city on a hill with institutions and values that others may want to emulate. Canadians, no less than U.S. citizens, share this propensity for pride in their political and social ethos. Yet nowhere else is this pride more justified than in terms of the principles of democratic pluralism. For it is in this set of socio-political undertakings where the North American experiment most shines.

Canadians, Mexicans, and Americans must be able to demonstrate to other polities, including the transition governments of formerly communist countries and the developing countries, that these three governments have made democratic pluralism work. By demonstrating that democratic pluralism is a success in their own countries,

North Americans can help protect democratic pluralism from risk worldwide.[39] It does matter how federal Canada, Quebec, and the other provinces deal with their own experience with divisive nationalism, however unique and however benign.

Confronting the contemporary challenges of divisive nationalism to democratic pluralism and focusing on the case of Canadian unity, this study comes to the following conclusions. First, although states worldwide may be affected negatively by divisive nationalism, and some states will surely breakup, overall the state will survive as an institution. Some states may become stronger for having surmounted a bout with divisive nationalism and prevailed. Other states and state populations may suffer grievously through the effects of secession. Higher economic and political cost associated with smaller size and lesser leverage may cause other states increased vulnerability.

But the greatest impact of state fragmentation will be, according to the argument of this study, on the principle and process of democratic pluralism. Democratic pluralism is fragile. It has not enjoyed a long history of success. It has matured largely under the fairly sheltered conditions of liberal democracy. It has flourished among immigrant populations of the New World, highlighting the condition of the twenty-first century when all states are becoming 'new' in their characteristics of mixed ethnic, cultural, and linguistic bases. Immigration, emigration, differential growth rates across populations of differing cultural background – all contribute to the mixing of populations within states worldwide. That is why success for democratic pluralism is such an essential attribute of future world politics.

North America is the beacon for democratic pluralism. This is where democratic pluralism has reached its highest affirmation. North America has been the 'great experiment' in cultural harmony and ethnic toleration where the political conditions were thought ideal. For these reasons the success of the experiment in democratic pluralism will carry such weight elsewhere in the global system.

If democratic pluralism continues to flourish in North America, Canada and the United States will remain truly a model for other countries to follow. But if secession occurs, democratic pluralism worldwide will suffer, for the model itself will have failed and democratic pluralism will be regarded as a 'damaged good' not worthy of consideration. Homogenization of culture within increasingly fragmented and increasingly isolated populations will become the norm for state organization.

If divisive nationalism is the recipe for dealing with the growing reality of mixed populations and cross-cutting ethnic and linguistic communities, what will be the cost for international society? If democratic pluralism fails in North America, where else can this grand experiment prevail? In the new millennium, the people of Canada can leave no greater gift to humanity than the knowledge, based on a history of shared political culture, that democratic pluralism works.

Notes

1: Challenges to Democratic Pluralism

1 James Mayall, *Nationalism and International Security* (Cambridge: Cambridge University Press, 1990), 65–9.
2 Manus I. Midlarsky, *The Internationalization of Communal Strife* (New York: Routledge, 1992), 5.
3 E.J. Hobsbawm, *Nations and Nationalism since 1780: Program, Myth, Reality* (Cambridge: Cambridge University Press, 1990; Cando Ed., 1991), 164.
4 G. Bingham Powell, Jr., *Contemporary Democracies: Participation, Stability, and Violence* (Cambridge, MA: Harvard University Press, 1982); Ted Robert Gurr and Barbara Harff, *Ethnic Conflict in World Politics* (Boulder: Westview Press, 1994).
5 Benjamin Barber, *Strong Democracy: Participatory Politics for a New Age* (Berkeley: University of California Press, 1984), 213–60.
6 Robert Putnam, *Making Democracy Work: Civic Traditions in Modern Italy* (Princeton: Princeton University Press, 1993), 73–82.
7 Amy Gutmann and Dennis Thompson, *Democracy and Disagreement* (Cambridge, MA: Harvard University Press, 1996), 39–51.
8 William H. McNeill, *Polyethnicity and National Unity in World History* (Toronto: University of Toronto Press, 1986), 82.
9 *Webster's Third New International Dictionary* (New York: G and C Merriam and Co., 1976).
10 James Fishkin, *The Voice of the People* (New Haven: Yale University Press, 1995); Robert A. Dahl, *On Democracy* (New Haven: Yale University Press, 1998).
11 Fishkin, *Voice of the People*, 53. Thomas Hobbes allowed rebellion in only the most extreme of circumstances where the sovereign seeks to 'kill, wound,

or imprison a subject.' Though too confining by today's understanding of
sovereignty and rights, this doctrine serves to reveal the limitations placed
on the right of resistance or secession. Thomas Hobbes, *Leviathan*, with an
introduction by John Plamenatz (New York: Meridian, 1963), 47–8, 299–300.

12 Michael Walzer, *On Toleration* (New Haven: Yale University Press, 1997), 10.

13 In an open one-page letter, the pastor of a Baptist Church in Chattanooga,
Tennessee, following the tragic murder of students in Colorado by two
deranged fellow students, repeatedly made an equation between loss of
'the Judaeo-Christian ethic' and pluralism, and between the lack of 'moral
absolutes' and pluralism. Reverend James E. Gibson, II, *Washington Post*,
10 May 1999, A17.

14 James Kurth, 'America versus the West,' *Watch on the West* (Foreign Policy
Research Institute) 1, no. 1 (October 1997), 1–2.

15 Cary J. Nederman, 'Freedom, Community, and Function: Communitarian
Lessons of Medieval Political Theory,' *American Political Science Review* 86,
no. 4 (December 1992), 977–86.

16 David S. Landes, *The Wealth and Poverty of Nations: Why Some Are So Rich
and Some Are So Poor* (New York: W.W. Norton and Company, 1998).

17 Jack L. Granatstein, *Canada 1957–1967: The Years of Uncertainty and Innovation* (Toronto: McClelland and Stewart, 1986); David J. Bercuson and Barry
Cooper, *Deconfederation: Canada without Quebec* (Toronto: Key Porter, 1991).

18 Nederman, 'Freedom, Community, and Function,' 983. The author's study
of medieval political theory provides many insights into the contemporary
relationship between individual and community.

19 Anthony Smith, 'National Identity and the Idea of European Unity,' *International Affairs* 68 (January 1992), 55–76.

20 Leo Driedger, *Multi-Ethnic Canada: Identities and Inequalities* (Toronto:
Oxford University Press, 1996), 146; J.W. Berry, R. Kaylin, and D.M. Taylor,
Multiculturalism and Ethnic Attitudes in Canada (Ottawa: Minister of Supply
and Services, 1977).

21 John Richards, 'Language Matters: Ensuring that the Sugar Not Dissolve in
the Coffee,' in David R. Cameron, ed., *The Referendum Papers: Essays on
Secession and National Unity* (Toronto: University of Toronto Press, 1999),
84–143.

22 John Kenneth Galbraith, *The Scotch* (Baltimore: Penguin 1966), 12.

23 Randolph M. Siverson and Harvey Starr, *The Diffusion of War: A Study of
Opportunity and Willingness* (Ann Arbor: University of Michigan Press,
1991).

24 Yael Tamir, *Liberal Nationalism* (Princeton: Princeton University Press, 1993),
70–5.

25 Iris Marion Young, *Justice and the Politics of Difference* (Princeton: Princeton University Press, 1990).

26 Bhikhu Parekh, *Rethinking Multiculturalism: Cultural Diversity and Political Theory* (London: Macmillan, 2000).

27 Lawrence Cahoone, 'Thick or Thin: Liberal Culture or Cultured Liberalism' (paper presented at the American Political Science Association Meeting, Washington, DC, August 31–September 3, 2000), 10.

28 Alexander Wendt, 'Collective Identity Formation and the International State,' *American Political Science Review* 88, no. 2 (June 1994), 394, 390.

29 Pierre Hassner, 'Beyond Nationalism and Internationalism: Ethnicity and World Order,' in Michael E. Brown, ed., *Ethnic Conflict and International Security* (Princeton: Princeton University Press, 1993), 135.

30 Timothy Garton Ash, 'Europe's Endangered Liberal Order,' *Foreign Affairs* (March/April 1998), 63.

31 Alvin Rabushka and Kenneth A. Shepsle, *Politics in Plural Societies: A Theory of Democratic Instability* (Columbus, OH: Charles E. Merrill, 1972), 217.

32 See Rabushka and Shepsle, *Politics in Plural Societies*, 18–19; Lewis Coser, *The Functions of Social Conflict* (Glencoe: Free Press, 1956), 78–9; Seymour Martin Lipset, *Political Man: The Social Bases of Politics* (Garden City: Anchor Books, 1963), 77. William Kornhauser, *The Politics of Mass Society* (New York: The Free Press, 1959).

33 Arend Lijphart, *Democracy in Plural Societies: A Comparative Exploration* (New Haven: Yale University Press, 1977), 25–43.

34 Robert A. Dahl, *On Democracy* (New Haven, CT: Yale University Press, 1998), 194.

35 Ibid., 195. Emphasis in the original.

36 Samuel Huntington, *The Clash of Civilizations and the Remaking of World Order* (New York: Simon and Schuster, 1996), 261; Dragomir Vojnic, 'Disparity and Disintegration: The Dimension of Yugoslavia's Demise,' in Payam Akhnavan and Robert Howse, eds., *Yugoslavia, the Former and Future* (Washington, DC: The Brookings Institution, 1995).

37 Richard D. Alba, *Ethnic Identity: The Transformation of White America* (New Haven, CT: Yale University Press, 1990), 12. Daniel Patrick Moynihan, *Pandaemonium: Ethnicity in International Politics* (Oxford: Oxford University Press, 1993), 191, reports that in Alba's study, 75 per cent of the marriages among whites in the United States 'involve some degree of ethnic boundary crossing,' and that about half of them 'occur between individuals whose ancestries differ completely.'

38 V.P. Gagnon, Jr., 'Serbia's Road to War,' in Larry Diamond and Marc F.

Plattner, eds., *Nationalism, Ethnic Conflict and Democracy* (Baltimore: Johns Hopkins University Press, 1994), 117–31.

39 Karl Mannheim, *Ideology and Utopia* (New York: Harcourt, Brace and World, Inc., 1936), 25.

40 A huge literature about identity has emerged with a bearing on the secessionist mentality. The following are indispensible sources: John R. Gillis, ed., *Commemorations: The Politics of National Identity* (Princeton: Princeton University Press, 1994); Eric Hobsbawm and Terence Ranger, eds., *The Invention of Tradition* (Cambridge: Cambridge University Press, 1983); Benedict Anderson, *Imagined Communities: Reflections on the Origin and Spread of Nationalism* (Norfolk: The Thetford Press, 1983). See also Smith 'National Identity and the Idea of European Unity,' and Wendt, 'Collective Identity Formation and the International State.'

41 Parsons was an acute observer of 'emancipation' from patterns and symbols of traditional thought as nationalism proceeds, involving intellectualism, urbanism, the market system, and large-scale organization and the literature and the arts. Talcott Parsons, 'The Sociological Aspects of Fascist Movements,' in *Sociological Theory* (New York: The Free Press, 1954), 135–6.

42 R.M. MacIver, *The Modern State* (Oxford: Oxford University Press, 1964), 437.

43 *The Economist*, 9 September 2000, 98; Shang-Jin Wei, 'Natural Openness and Good Government,' working paper, National Bureau of Economic Research, Cambridge, MA, June 2000.

44 Alfred W. Crosby, 'Expansion and Collision,' *University of Helsinki Quarterly* 16, no. 1 (1998), 35–6; Frances Karttunen, 'Raising the Alarm for Endangered Languages,' *University of Helsinki Quarterly* 16, no. 1 (1998), 37–8.

45 Aristotle, *The Politics*, trans. T.A. Sinclair (Baltimore: Penguin Classics, 1962), 237. According to Tawney, North America enjoyed the inverse of the Aristotelian problem of too much numerical equality and not enough equality by merit. Here economic inequality existed side-by-side with social equality, which gave the society what he called its 'charm.' R.H. Tawney, *Equality* (London: Unwin, 1964), 79.

46 In this regard, see Melvin Ember, Carol R. Ember, and Bruce Russettt, 'Inequality and Democracy in the Anthropological Record,' 110–32, and Steve Chan, 'Democracy and Inequality: Tracking Welfare Spending in Singapore, Taiwan and South Korea,' 227–43, in Manus Midlarsky, ed., *Inequality, Democracy, and Economic Development* (Cambridge: Cambridge University Press, 1997).

47 Alexis de Tocqueville, *Democracy in America: Selections* (Chicago: The Great Books Foundation, 1945), 102. See also Jean-Jacques Rousseau, *The*

Social Contract and Discourses, trans. G.D.H. Cole (London: Everyman, 1913), 205.

48 Tocqueville, *Democracy in America: Selections*, 30. Also, Alexis de Tocqueville, *Democracy in America*, trans. George Lawrence (New York: Doubleday, 1969), 189–95.

49 Alan Hendrikson and Hans Binnerdijk, 'Back to Bipolarity?' *Strategic Forum*, no. 161 (May 1999), 4.

50 Four excellent edited collections on the internationalization of conflict mirror the preoccupations of world order in the post–Cold War era: David Lake and Donald Rothchild, eds., *The International Spread of Ethnic Conflict: Fear, Diffusion, and Escalation* (Princeton: Princeton University Press, 1998); Michael E. Brown, ed., *Ethnic Conflict and International Security* (Princeton: Princeton University Press, 1993); Manus I. Midlarsky, ed., *The Internationalization of Communal Strife* (London: Routledge, 1992); Michael E. Browne, ed., *The International Dimensions of Internal Conflict* (Cambridge, MA: MIT Press, 1996).

51 Will Kymlicka, *Multicultural Citizenship: A Liberal Theory of Minority Rights* (Oxford: Clarendon Press, 1995), 188–9.

52 Ibid., 186.

53 John Stuart Mill, "On Liberty," ch. 2, in John Stuart Mill, *Utilitarianism, Liberty, and Representative Government* (London: J.M. Dent and Sons, Ltd., 1948), 79.

54 Hurst Hannum, 'The Specter of Secession: Responding to Claims for Ethnic Self-Determination,' *Foreign Affairs* (March/April 1998), 16.

55 Ibid., 17.

2: A U.S. Perspective on Canadian Unity

1 This speech was made on board the *Arabella* as it sailed for what would become New England.

2 George Grant, *Lament for a Nation* (Ottawa: Carleton University Press, 1989), ch. 5, 53–67.

3 John Winthrop was perhaps inspired by a passage in the Sermon on the Mount: 'A city that is set on a hill cannot be hid.'

4 Consider Stephen Clarkson, *Canada and the Reagan Challenges: Crisis in the Canadian–American Relationship* (Toronto: James Lorimer, 1962).

5 In perhaps the toughest critique ever by an American, former U.S. Secretary of State Dean Acheson, himself of Canadian ancestry, warned of the effects of Canadian regionalism. 'Stern Daughter of the Voice of God,' in Livingston T. Merchant, ed., *Neighbors Taken For Granted: Canada and the United States* (New York: Praeger, 1966), 134–5.

6 Abetted by the distribution of an abbreviated version of 'Will Canada Unravel?' *Foreign Affairs* 75, no. 5 (September/October 1996), 104, taking one sentence out of context led to a great misunderstanding. The article read as follows: 'Washington would increasingly take on the jobs of peacemaker, adjudicator, rule-maker, and police officer. These are not roles that the United States should seek. Nor are they responsibilities Washington would necessarily be able to carry out better than any of the Canadian provinces or the Canadian federal government.' In the September 15 Canadian Press account of the article, the second and third sentences were not included. Likewise, in John Butcher's letter to the editor in *Foreign Affairs* 76, no. 1 (January/February 1997), 169, the first sentence is quoted as my 'position' even though my subsequent two sentences totally reject that position. A Montreal radio station even asked me to appear on their show to defend the article 'on policing Canada'! The Canadian Press did send a full retraction out on the news wire, although by then the misinterpretation had had wide impact.

7 See J. L. Granatstein, *A Man of Influence: Norman Robertson and Canadian Statecraft 1929–68* (Toronto: Deneau, 1981), 336–56; John F. Hilliker, 'Diefenbaker and Canadian External Affairs,' in J. L. Granatstein, *Canadian Foreign Policy: Historical Readings* (Toronto: Copp, Clark, Pitman, 1986), 183–97.

8 Joseph Nye's classic treatment of the U.S.–Canada relationship highlights why the relationship is different (but not utopian) from many other relationships between foreign governments. He examines the outcome of some thirty-one disputes between the two countries. His thesis, with which I agree, is that there is an absence of force in the relationship but not an absence of power. Joseph S. Nye, Jr., 'Transnational Relations and Interstate Conflicts: An Empirical Analysis,' in Annette Baker Fox, Alfred O. Hero, Jr., and Joseph S. Nye, Jr., eds., *Canada and the United States: Transnational and Transgovernmental Relations* (New York: Columbia University Press, 1976), 399.

9 Seymour Martin Lipset, *Continental Divide: The Values and Institutions of the United States and Canada* (New York: Routledge, 1990), 2.

10 George Washington, 'Observe Good Faith Towards All Nations,' September 17, 1796, in Brian MacArthur, ed., *The Penguin Book of Historic Speeches* (London: Penguin, 1995, 1996), 206–12.

11 Robert J. Barro, *Getting It Right: Markets and Choices in a Free Society* (Cambridge: MIT Press, 1996), 26–8.

12 The southern market of the United States was also, according to Hamilton, capable of establishing manufacturing industry, a point that seemed to stir southerners themselves to indifference. 'Alexander Hamilton,' in Samuel

Eliot Morison, *The Oxford History of the American People* (New York: Oxford University Press, 1965), 325.

13 For example, Pierre-Paul Proulx, 'Le pourquoi économique de la souveraineté et les coûts du fédéralisme pour le Québec,' *Choix: Serie Québec-Canada*, IRPP (Institute for Research on Public Policy) 1, no. 11 (June 1995), 21–36.

14 Max Weber did not. Instead he stressed the 'individualistic idea of the "inalienable rights of men."' Max Weber, 'The New Despotism,' as translated from 'On the Status of Middle Class Democracy,' trans. Benjamin K. Bennett *Archiv füer Sozialwissenschaft and Sozialpolitik*, 1906, cited in *The Western World in the Twentieth Century* (New York: Columbia University Press, 1961), 36. See in contrast, S.F. Wise and Robert Craig Brown, *Canada Views the United States: Nineteenth-Century Political Attitudes* (Toronto: MacMillan, 1967), 56–7.

15 Mark Miringhoff and Marque-Louisa Miringhoff, *The Social Health of a Nation: How America Is Really Doing* (Oxford: Oxford University Press, 1999).

16 Barry Glassner, *The Culture of Fear* (New York: Basic Books, 1999).

17 'For man, when perfected, is the best of animals, but, when separated from law and justice, he is the worst of all.' Aristotle, *Politics*, Book I, chs. 2–3, trans. Benjamin Jowett, reprinted in *The Great Books*, Vol. 2 (Chicago: The Great Books Foundation, 1955), 5.

18 Unlike some other differences, differences in the way Canada and the United States treat women, minorities, and immigrants seem to have dwindled. Lipset, *Continental Divide* (New York: Routledge, 1990), 192.

19 John Hall and Charles Lindholm, *Is America Breaking Apart?* (Princeton: Princeton University Press, 1999).

20 Giles Gherson, 'Canadian Continentalism and Industrial Competitiveness,' in Fen Osler Hampson and Christopher J. Maule, eds., *A New World Order? Canada Among Nations: 1992–1993* (Ottawa: Carleton University Press, 1992), 155–73.

21 Even trade between individual regions of the United States and Canada is quantitatively significant. See The Honorable Lloyd Axworthy, Minister of Foreign Affairs, *Canada and the United States in a Changing World* (Los Angeles: The World Affairs Council, 1997).

22 Charles F. Doran, 'Trade Dispute Resolution "On Trial": Softwood Lumber,' *International Journal* 51 (Autumn 1996), 709–33; Charles F. Doran and Timothy J. Naftali, 'U.S.–Canadian Softwood Lumber: Trade Dispute Negotiations,' *Foreign Policy Institute Case Studies*, No. 8, School of Advanced International Studies (Washington, DC: Johns Hopkins University Press, 1987).

23 Gilbert R. Winham and Heather A. Grant, 'NAFTA: An Overview,' in Donald Barry, ed., *Toward a North American Community: Canada, the United States, and Mexico* (Boulder: Westview Press, 1995), 18.

24 See for a very clear exposition W. Max Corden, 'The Revival of Protectionism in Developed Countries,' in Dominick Salvatore, ed., *The New Protectionist Threat to World Welfare* (New York: North-Holland, 1987), 45–68; James C. Ingram and Robert M. Dunn, Jr., 'The Theory of Protectionism: Tariffs and other Barriers to Trade,' ch. 6, *International Economics*, 3rd ed. (New York: John Wiley and Sons, 1993), 113–39.

25 Indeed, former Prime Minister Mulroney sold free trade to Quebec for the opposite reasons. Graham Fraser, *Playing for Keeps: The Making of the Prime Minister, 1988* (Toronto: McClelland and Stewart, 1989), 354–75. The prior watershed of 1957 in terms of 'foreign ownership' politics had disappeared. Richard Gwyn, *The 49th Paradox: Canada in North America* (Toronto: McClelland and Stewart, 1985), 103–17.

26 Maria Isabel Studer and Jean-Francois Prud'homme, 'Quebec–Mexico Relationships: A New Partner,' in Guy Lachapelle and Stephen Blank, *Quebec Under Free Trade: Making Public Policy in North America* (Quebec City: Presses de l'Université du Québec, 1995), 103–28.

27 Charles F. Doran, 'When Building North America, Deepen before Widening,' in Charles F. Doran and Alvin Paul Drischler, eds., *A New North America: Cooperation and Enhanced Interdependence* (Westport, CT: Praeger, 1996), 65–90.

28 For a neat theoretical discussion, see James R. Markusen, James R. Melvin, William H. Kaempfer, and Keith E. Maskus, *International Trade Theory and Evidence* (New York: McGraw Hill, 1995), 314–20; David Leyton-Brown, 'Canada–U.S. Trade Disputes and the Free Trade Deal,' in Maureen Appel Molot and Brian W. Tomlin, 'A World of Conflict,' *Canada Among Nations* (Toronto: James Lorimer and Sons, 1988), 161–77.

29 Keith G. Banting, 'Social Policy in a North American Free-trade Area,' in Doran and Drischler, *A New North America*, 91–112. Lawrence Martin interprets these processes as less benevolent. 'Continental Union,' in Charles F. Doran and Ellen Babby, 'Being and Becoming Canada,' Special Issue of *The Annals* of the American Academy of Political and Social Science 538 (March, 1995), 143–50.

30 Timothy J. McKeown, 'What Forces Shape American Trade Policy?' in Charles F. Doran and Gregory Marchildon, eds., *The NAFTA Puzzle: Political Parties and Trade in North America* (Boulder: Westview Press, 1994), 65–86.

31 Sidney Weintraub, 'Next Steps: Policy Options after NAFTA,' in Doran and Drischler, *A New North America*, 131–50.

32 Denis Stairs, 'The Canadian Dilemma in North America,' in Joyce Hoebing, Sidney Weintraub, and M. Delal Baer, eds., *NAFTA and Sovereignty Trade-offs for Canada, Mexico, and the United States* (Washington, DC: The Center for Strategic and International Studies, 1996), 31; John Herd Thompson and Stephen J. Randall, 'Canada in the American Empire, 1947–1960,' *Canada and the United States: Ambivalent Allies* (Montreal: McGill-Queen's University Press, 1994), 184–213.

33 James A. Baker III, 'The Shield Becomes the Sword,' *The Politics of Diplomacy* (New York: G.P. Putnam's Sons, 1995), 366–7.

34 This is what Henry Kissinger terms 'the reach of international relations.' Technology has transformed it. *Diplomacy* (New York: Simon and Schuster, 1994), 808.

35 Steven Vogel, 'The Power Behind the "Spin-ons": The Military Implications of Japan's Commercial Technology,' in Michael Borrus, Wayne Sandholtz, Steve Weber, and John Zysman, eds., *The Highest Stakes: The Economic Foundations of the Next Security System* (New York: Oxford, 1992), 55–80.

36 Charles F. Doran, *Systems in Crisis: New Imperatives of High Politics at Century's End* (Cambridge: Cambridge University Press, 1991), 237–59.

37 Joseph T. Jockel, 'Command and Control Arrangements for North American Aerospace Defense,' *Security to the North: Canada–U.S. Defense Relations in the 1990s* (East Lansing, MI: Michigan State University Press, 1991), 144–61.

38 Richard Rosecrance and Arthur A. Stein, 'Beyond Realism: The Study of Grand Strategy,' in Richard Rosecrance and Arthus A. Stein, eds., *The Domestic Bases of Grand Strategy* (Ithaca: Cornell University Press, 1993), 11–15.

39 Standing Senate Committee on Foreign Affairs, Report of the Sub-Committee on National Defence, *Canada's Maritime Defence*, Appendix C: Canada's Naval Forces (Ottawa: Supply and Services, May 1983), 11–115.

40 D.W. Middlemiss and J.J. Sokolsky, *Canadian Defence: Decisions and Determinants* (Toronto: Harcourt Brace Jovanovich, 1989), 170–74; contrast with Peter C. Dobell, *Canada's Search for New Roles: Foreign Policy in the Trudeau Era* (London: Oxford University Press, 1972), 149.

41 Joseph T. Jockel and Joel J. Sokolsky, *Canada and Collective Security: Odd Man Out*, The Washington Papers, Center for International and Strategic Studies (Westport: Praeger, 1986), 80–90.

42 Strategically the city on the hill metaphor has two meanings. It corresponds to the notion of the Rankean Great Power in that it is militarily capable of standing alone. But the metaphor also implies that the 'city' is the territorial base for interdependent relations abroad that benefit from this confidence

and generous outlook. Consider William T.R. Fox, 'North America: Two Three, or One?' *A Continent Apart: The United States and Canada in World Politics* (Toronto: University of Toronto Press, 1985), 3–17. For how Quebec is seen in contemporary security terms, consider Patrick Clawson, ed., *1997 Strategic Assessment: Flashpoints and Force Structure* (Washington, DC: Institute for Strategic Studies, 1998), 74–5. Of course the 'city on the hill' metaphor can have other motivational meanings such as Margaret Atwood's notion of the island as a 'sense of security.' *Survival* (Toronto: Anansi, 1972), 33.

43 Gary Hamel and C. K. Prahalad, 'Strategic Intent,' in Percy Barnevik and Rosabeth Moss Kanter, eds., *Global Strategies* (Cambridge: Harvard Business Review, 1994), 22.

44 Robert Bothwell, 'Has Canada Made a Difference? The Case of Canada and the United States,' in John English and Norman Hillmer, eds., *Making a Difference? Canada's Foreign Policy in a Changing World* (Toronto: Lester Publishing, 1992), 1–4.

45 According to James Driscoll, in one of the more than thirty articles written about or in response to 'Will Canada Unravel?' the concept of regional affiliation 'only makes sense if you assume the Monroe Doctrine kicks in.' Quoted in Alan Martin, *Gemini News* (Ottawa: News-Scan International Ltd., Feb. 11, 1997). But, of course, the favoured strategy is the opposite of the Monroe Doctrine. It is internationalism.

46 For a somewhat more pessimistic account of the U. S. role in contemporary geostrategy, consider Ludwig Dehio, *The Precarious Balance: Four Centuries of the European Power Struggle* (New York: Vintage, 1965), 281–4. In the Canadian context, see Harald von Riekhoff and Hanspeter Neuhold, eds., *Unequal Partners: A Comparative Analysis of Relations Between Austria and the Federal Republic of Germany and Between Canada and the United States* (Boulder: Westview Press, 1993).

47 Doran, *Systems in Crisis* (Cambridge: Cambridge University Press, 1991), 69–79.

3: Will Quebec Secede?

1 'Strange people, all these foreigners,' Le Gardeur continued, but with less animation. 'Very strange; not one bit like us ...' in Gabrielle Roy, *The Cashier*, trans. Harry Binsse (Toronto: McClelland and Stewart, 1987), 118; Ellen Babby, *The Play of Language and Spectacle* (Toronto: ECW Press, 1985), 49–70.

2 Leon Dion, 'Towards a Self-Determined Consciousness,' in Dale C. Thompson, ed., *Quebec: Society and Politics (Views from the Inside)* (Toronto: McClel-

land and Stewart, 1973), 26–38; W.L. Morton, *The Canadian Identity*, 2nd ed. (Toronto: University of Toronto Press, 1972); Anthony D. Smith, *National Identity* (London: Penguin, 1991); Ramsey Cook, 'Nation, Identity, Rights: Reflections on W.L. Morton's *The Canadian Identity*,' *Canada, Quebec and the Issues of Nationalism*, 2nd ed. (Toronto: McClelland and Stewart, 1986), 221–36; Ian Angus, *A Border Within: National Identity, Cultural Plurality, and Wilderness* (Montreal: McGill-Queen's University Press, 1997).

3 'Quebec Premier Lucien Bouchard yesterday told the National Assembly he is dedicated to the separatist option and insisted that Quebec voters will decide in the next provincial election whether there will be another referendum.' *The Globe and Mail*, 3 April 1996. This was later modified to mean that a referendum will be held 'only when it is winnable.' See also Kenneth McRoberts, *English Canada and Quebec: Avoiding the Issue*, Robarts Centre for Canadian Studies Lecture Series (Toronto: York University, 1991), 39–50; Charles Taylor, 'Alternative Futures: Legitimacy, Identity, and Alienation in Late-Twentieth-Century Canada,' in Alan Cairns and Cynthia Williams, eds., *Constitutionalism, Citizenship and Society in Canada* (Toronto: University of Toronto Press, 1985).

4 Robert Bothwell, *Canada and Quebec: One Country, Two Histories* (Vancouver: University of British Columbia Press, 1995); Robert Young, *The Secession of Quebec and the Future of Canada* (Montreal: McGill-Queen's University Press, 1995); Pierre Martin, 'Générations politiques, rationalité économique et appui à la souveraineté au Québec,' *Canadian Journal of Political Science* 27, no. 2 (June 1994), 345–59; Andre Blais, Pierre Martin, and Richard Nadeau, 'Attentes économiques et linguistiques et appui à la souveraineté du Québec: Une analyse prospect et comparative,' *Canadian Journal of Political Science* 27, no. 4 (December 1994), 637–57; Pierre Fournier, *Autopsie du lac Meech: La souveraineté est-elle inévitable?* (Montreal: VLB, 1991).

5 See, for example, the argument presented in Viva Ona Bartkus, *The Dynamic of Secession* (Cambridge: Cambridge University Press, 1999), 189–201.

6 Fernand Ouellet argues that these patterns had deep roots in the early nineteenth century and were often the result of choice rather than exclusion. French Canadian businessmen were not as receptive to technological innovation as English businessmen, he claims. He also argues that the French Canadian who made a fortune in the fur trade was more likely to invest it in an 'unproductive investment' such as a seigneury than in business. *Lower Canada 1791–1840: Social Change and Nationalism* (Toronto: McClelland and Stewart, 1980), 329. The trouble with this interpretation is that it is so much at odds with the later Quebec entrepreneurial spirit. A competing interpretation explains francophones' post-Conquest exclusion from the fur

trade in terms of their lack of trading links with the new metropolis and
their inability to compete with the British newcomers, who had much
greater capital resources. See Ronald Rudin, 'Revisionism and the Search
for a Normal Society: A Critique of Recent Quebec Historical Writing,'
Canadian Historical Review 73 (1992).

7 One of the contentious issues has always been immigration policy. See Irv-
ing Abella and Harold Troper, *None is Too Many: Canada and the Jews of
Europe 1993–1948* (Toronto: Lester and Orpen Dennys, 1983), 264–7.

8 Bouchard's opposition to a unilingual language policy for Quebec is a case
in point. It complements Bourassa's dual sign policy reflecting continuity
of position. For an easily read introduction to language rights under the
Charter, see the following: Ian Greene, 'Language Rights,' *The Charter of
Rights* (Toronto: James Lorimer, 1989), 186–207; Gerard Pelletier, '1968: Lan-
guage Policy and the Mood in Quebec,' in Thomas S. Axworthy and Pierre
Elliott Trudeau, eds., *Towards a Just Society: The Trudeau Years* (Markham,
ON: Viking, 1990), 203–6; Michael Ignatieff, *Blood and Belonging: Journeys
Into the New Nationalism* (Toronto: Penguin, 1993), 169.

9 Paul Martin, Sr., described Canada as a 'border people.' William R. Young,
ed., *Paul Martin: The London Diaries 1975–1979* (Ottawa: University of
Ottawa Press, 1988).

10 Paul Romney, personal communication, August 25, 2000. See also Paul
Romney, *Getting It Wrong: How Canadians Forgot Their Past and Imperilled
Confederation* (Toronto: University of Toronto Press, 1999).

11 Reg Whitaker, 'Quebec's Self-determination and Aboriginal Self-govern-
ment: Conflict and Reconciliation?' in Joseph H. Carens, ed., *Is Quebec
Nationalism Just? Perspectives from Anglophone Canada* (Montreal: McGill-
Queen's University Press, 1995), 206–9; Mary Ellen Turpel, 'Does the Road
to Quebec Sovereignty Run through Aboriginal Territory?' in Daniel
Drache and Roberto Perin, eds., *Negotiating with a Sovereign Quebec* (Toronto: James Lorimer, 1992), 93–106; Grand Council of the Crees, *Sovereign
Injustice: Forcible Inclusion of the James Bay Crees and Cree Territory into a Sov-
ereign Quebec* (Nemaska: Grand Council of the Crees, 1995), 46–67.

12 For an intelligent discussion of the 1970s ownership debate, see A.E. Safar-
ian, *Foreign Ownership of Canadian Industry* (Toronto: University of Toronto
Press, 1973).

13 See, for example, *Canada 1996: Agenda/Engagement Calendar* (Willowsdale,
ON: Firefly Books Ltd., 1995).

14 Roger Gibbons, 'Western Canada in the Wake of the Events of 1995,' in John
E. Trent, Robert Young, and Guy Lachapelle, *Quebec-Canada: What is the
Path Ahead?* (Ottawa: University of Ottawa Press, 1996), 255–62.

15 E.J. Hobsbawm, *Nations and Nationalism Since 1780: Programme, Myth, and Reality* (Cambridge: Cambridge University Press, 1991), 119.

16 Peter Morici, *A New Special Relationship: Free Trade and U.S.-Canada Economic Relations in the 1990s* (Halifax: Institute for Research on Public Policy, 1991), 147–50; Francois Rocher and Richard Nimijean, 'Global Economic Restructuring and the Evolution of Canadian Federalism and Constitutionalism,' in Francois Rocher and Miriam Smith, eds., *New Trends in Canadian Federalism* (Toronto: Broadview Press, 1995), 211–33.

17 Highly politicized and partisan, this book is nonetheless quite revealing of procedure: Pierre Arbour, *Quebec Inc. and the Temptation of State Capitalism* (Montreal: Robert Davies Publishing, 1993).

18 Thomas J. Courchene, 'Mons Pays, C'est l'Hiver,' *Canadian Public Policy* 17, no. 1 (March 1991), 4.

19 National Executive Council of the Parti Québécois, *Quebec in the World: The PQ's Plan for Sovereignty*, trans. Robert Chodos (Toronto: James Lorimer, 1994), 61.

20 Ottawa, Royal Commission on the Economic Union and Development Prospects for Canada, *Report* (Ottawa: Supply and Services, 1985).

21 Pierre-Paul Prouxl, 'Economic Integration, Its Effects on the Allocation of Powers, and Economic Policy Challenges for Quebec and the Rest of Canada,' in John E. Trent, Robert Young, and Guy Lachapelle, eds., *Quebec-Canada: What is the Path Ahead?* (Ottawa: University of Ottawa Press, 1996), 185.

22 House Committee on International Relations, Subcommittee on the Western Hemisphere, *The Issue of Quebec's Sovereignty and Its Potential Impact on the United States*, 104th Cong., 2nd sess., 1996, 8–9, 34–6.

23 Gellner's explanation is that all nationalism is contrived and that time is required to contrive. 'It is nationalism which engenders nations ...' Ernest Gellner, *Nations and Nationalism* (Ithaca: Cornell University Press, 1994), 55. See Pierre Elliott Trudeau's early denunciation of separation, *Federalism and the French Canadians* (Toronto: Macmillan of Canada, 1968), 209–11, together with the following sources, for a mature and thorough assessment of this and other aspects of nationalism pertaining to Quebec and Canada: Alain-G. Gagnon and Joseph Garcia, 'Quebec and the Pursuit of Special Status,' in R.D. Olling and M.W. Westmacott, eds., *Perspectives on Canadian Federalism* (Scarborough, ON: Prentice-Hall Canada Inc., 1988), 304–25: Kenneth McRoberts, 'Is Separatism the Only Answer?' ch. 10 in *Misconceiving Canada: The Struggle for National Unity* (Don Mills, ON: Oxford University Press, 1997), 245–76.

24 Walker Conner, 'When Is a Nation?' *Ethnic and Racial Studies* 13, no. 1 (January 1990), 92–100. For a discussion of the role of time and Canadian his-

tory, consider John Conway, 'An "Adapted Organic Tradition,"' *In Search of Canada*, Special Issue, *Daedalus*, *Journal of the American Academy of Arts and Sciences* 117, no. 4, (Fall 1988), 381–96; and Robin Winks, *The Relevance of Canadian History* (Lanham, MD: University Press of America, 1988). For one of the best historical accounts of the dual evolution of nations within a single state, see Robert Bothwell, *Canada and Quebec: One Country, Two Histories* (Vancouver: University of British Columbia Press, 1995), especially ch. 5, 'The Awakening of Quebec: The Quiet Revolution,' 79–96.

25 See Donald Horowitz, 'The Logic of Secession,' *Ethnic Groups in Conflict* (Berkeley: University of California at Berkeley, 1985), 230–6.

26 Charles Taylor, 'Transformations in Religious Experience,' The William James Lecture, *Harvard Divinity Bulletin* 28, no. 4 (Winter 1999), 20.

27 A historian who appreciates this point is E.J. Hobsbawm, *Nations and Nationalism Since 1780*, 166. See also Colin Campbell, *Governments under Stress* (Toronto: University of Toronto Press, 1983). This sense of guilt translates into the wording of the 1995 Referendum Question since the authors knew that most Quebecers felt guilty about breaking up Canada. Hence the important qualification to the declaration of sovereignty, 'after having made a formal offer to Canada for a new Economic and Political Partnership.' See also Mildred A. Schwartz, 'Politics and Moral Causes in Canada and the United States,' in Richard S. Thomasson, ed., *Comparative Social Research*, Vol. 4 (Greenwich, CT: JAI Press, 1981), 65–90.

28 Louis Hartz, *The Founding of New Societies* (New York: Harcourt, Brace and World, 1964).

29 Ronald Inglehart, *Modernization and Post Modernization: Cultural, Economic, and Political Change in 43 Countries* (Princeton: Princeton University Press, 1997); Alex Inkeles and David H. Smith, *Becoming Modern: Individual Change in Six Developing Countries* (Cambridge: Harvard University Press, 1974); Mildred Schwartz, 'The Environment for Policy-making in Canada and the United States,' *Canada–U.S. Prospects* (Montreal: C.D. Howe Institute; Washington, DC: National Planning Association, 1981); Kenneth Norrie, 'Is Federalism the Future: An Economic Perspective,' in Karen Knop, Sylvia Ostry, Richard Simeon, and Katherine Swinton, eds., *Rethinking Federalism: Citizens, Markets, and Governments in a Changing World* (Vancouver: University of British Columbia Press, 1995), 135–53.

30 From an outsiders point of view, (some) francophones in Quebec seem to fear English Canada, and (some) English-speaking Canadians seem to fear American culture. Ramsey Cook, 'Cultural Nationalism in Canada,' *Canada, Quebec and the Uses of Nationalism*, 2nd ed. (Toronto: McClelland and Stewart, 1995), 172–95.

31 Michel Seymour, 'At the Heart of Sovereigntist Thought' (Montreal: Bloc Québécois, October, 1999), 4.

32 Ibid.

33 *The Main Proposal* was available on the Bloc Québécois Web's site <http://www.blocquebecois.parl.gc.ca>, copy obtained on December 5, 1999. The document is the product of four think tanks, which comprised over fifty events, and it was 'submitted for debate and amendment where necessary' at the Bloc Québécois convention of January 28–30, 2000, Quebec City.

34 Michael Mandlebaum, 'Conclusion,' in Michael Mandlebaum, ed., *The New European Diasporas: National Minorities and Conflict in Eastern Europe* (New York: Council on Foreign Relations Press, 2000), 300.

35 Charles Taylor, 'Sharing Identity Space,' in Trent, Young, and Lachapelle, eds., *Quebec-Canada: What Is the Path Ahead?* 123.

36 Ibid.

37 'Election Will Test Support for Sovereignty: Parizeau,' *The Globe and Mail*, 30 October 2000, A1, A8.

38 Alain Gagnon claims that the constitutional question has driven every other issue off the party landscape in Quebec since 1960, including ideology. Lecture presented at Johns Hopkins University, School of Advanced International Studies, Washington, DC, February 14, 1997.

39 Time changes much. 'The BQ [Bloc Québécois] has often indicated that it will remain in Ottawa for no more than one mandate.' Rejean Pelletier, 'The Structures of Canadian Political Parties,' in A. Brian Tanquay and Alain-G. Gagnon, *Canadian Parties in Transition*, 2nd ed. (Toronto: Nelson Canada, 1996), 148.

40 Louis Massicotte, 'Changing the Canadian Electoral System,' *Choices, IRPP* 7, no. 1 (February 2001), 1–25.

41 In a personal communication with the late Robert Bourassa, he confided that one of the most difficult problems with making the economic cost argument against Quebec separation was not that the costs would not exist but that the whole topic was regarded in Quebec as 'negative' and that the bearer of bad news would be regarded as having a negative (non-positive, non-upbeat) image as well.

42 Rheal Seguin, 'PQ Government Produces 26 Studies on Sovereignty,' *The Globe and Mail*, 30 September 1995; Susanne Craig, 'Office Vacancies Fall Slightly in Most Cities but Rents Not Moving,' *Financial Post*, 14 October 1995, 8.

43 Richard Mackie, 'Sovereignty Puts 90,000 Jobs at Risk, Johnson Predicts,' *The Globe and Mail*, 11 October 1995, A3.

44 Earl H. Fry, 'Quebec, Canada, and the United States: The Economic Dimension,' *The American Review of Canadian Studies* (Winter 1995), 497–517;

Edward P. Neufeld, 'Quebec Separation and the Public Debt,' *C.D. Howe Institute Commentary* (July 1995).

45 Alan Freeman and Patrick Grady, *Dividing the House: Planning for a Canada without Quebec* (Toronto: HarperCollins, 1995), 150–3.

46 Ibid., 149–50.

47 This point is challenged by Lucien Bouchard on grounds that the U.S. 'needs NAFTA.' 'A Talk with Quebec's Top Separatist: Premier Bouchard on Sovereignty and Business Confidence,' *Business Week*, 17 June 1996, 56. Also consider the interesting examination of Massachusetts Governor Paul Celluci's tilt towards Quebec allegedly because of pressure from Hydro-Québec and lobbying dollars, in 'The Separatist Connection,' *The American–Canada Watch* 4, nos. 4–5 (June–July 1998), 6–12. My own judgment is that the explanation is more complex and less political than this account suggests.

48 Charles E. Roh, Jr., *The Implications for U.S. Trade Policy of an Independent Quebec*, Quebec Series, Center for Strategic and International Studies, Americas Program (Washington, DC: October 5, 1995).

49 Some of the matters at issue are whether all of the states in the international system or only the advanced industrial states are the correct referents, whether the correct methodology is linear or non-linear, and whether market size is to be indexed by GDP or population.

50 Robert Bourassa, interview by author, Washington, DC, September 1995.

51 Private communication with a Canadian polling firm, 1994.

52 Charles F. Doran, 'Will Canada Unravel?' *Foreign Affairs* (September/October 1996), 104.

53 In Quebec political opinion polls, the category '18 to 25' reveals *twice* the level of support for separation of that reflected in the age category '55 and over.'

54 Edouard Cloutier, 'Les tendances de l'opinion publique,' in *L'année politique au Québec, 1987–1988* (Montreal: Editions Québec/Amérique, 1989), 167–74; see also, Harold D. Clarke and Allan Kornberg, 'Support for the Canadian Federal Progressive Conservative Party Since 1988: The Impact of Economic Evaluations and Economic Issues,' *Canadian Journal of Political Science* 25, no. 1 (March 1992), 29–53.

55 Some 13,000 francophones and 14,000 anglophones move to Quebec each year from elsewhere in Canada. Marcel Côté and David Johnston, *If Quebec Goes: The Real Cost of Separation* (Toronto: Stoddart, 1995), 61.

56 Of the 620,000 anglophones remaining in Quebec, nearly half would leave after separation according to opinion poll results. Freeman and Grady, *Dividing the House: Planning for a Canada without Quebec*, 231.

57 Martin Lubin, 'Quebec-Only Political Parties, Federal and Provincial' (paper presented at the 51st Annual Meeting of the New York State Political Science Association, New York City, April 18–19, 1997), 10.

58 In the 1995 Referendum, 4,669,500 people voted. The margin of victory amounted to 53,500 votes. Seven per cent of the segment of the population who went to the polls equals 327,000 voters. It is quite easy to see the effect of 'voting by one's feet' in contemporary Quebec. Raymond Breton, 'Multiculturalism and Canadian Nation-Building,' in Alan Cairns and Cynthia Williams, eds., *The Politics of Gender, Ethnicity, and Language in Canada* (Toronto: University of Toronto Press, 1986).

59 Paul R. Brass, 'Elite Competition and Nation-Formation,' *Ethnicity and Nationalism: Theory and Comparison* (New Delhi: Sage, 1991), 69–108.

60 'The proportion of Quebec's SMEs (Small Manufacturing Enterprises) using at least one advanced technology has almost caught up with the American figure ...' Pierre-André Julien, 'United States/Canada Free Trade Agreement and Quebec Small Business Behaviour,' in Guy Lachapelle, *Quebec under Free Trade: Making Public Policy in North America* (Montreal: Presses de l'Université du Québec, 1995), 188.

61 For a discussion of issue formation and dissipation see W.T. Stanbury, *Business-Government Relations in Canada* (Toronto: Methuen, 1986), 218–21. For a broader context, consider James E. Alt, 'Leaning into the Wind or Ducking the Storm? U.S. Monetary Policy in the 1980s,' in Alberto Alesina and Geoffrey Carliner, eds., *Politics and Economics in the Eighties* (Chicago: University of Chicago Press, 1991), 41–77.

62 'Sovereignty association is only a stop-gap measure to make separation less abrupt and traumatic, and thus to make it more salable to the majority in the province.' Charles Taylor, *Reconciling the Solitudes: Essays on Canadian Federalism and Nationalism* (Montreal: McGill-Queen's Press, 1993), 57.

63 For an informed and very astute assessment of the 'distinct society' argument politically and legally, see Peter H. Russell, *Constitutional Odyssey: Can Canadians be a Sovereign People?* (Toronto: University of Toronto Press, 1992), 181–9.

64 'The erosion of national sovereignties will often occur more smoothly by increment than by spectacular leaps forward.' Pierre Marc Johnson and André Beaulieu, *The Environment and NAFTA: Understanding and Implementing the New Continental Law* (Washington, DC: Island Press, 1996), 258.

65 Dalton Camp, 'Mr. Chrétien Lacks Company,' *Whose Country is this Anyway?* (Vancouver: Douglas and McIntyre, 1995), 204–5.

4: Could English Canada Unravel?

1 Howard Schneider, 'Canada Drops U.S. Shows In Effort to Build Identity,' *The Washington Post*, 29 September 1996, A30.

2 Bogdan Kipling, 'Subsidiarians,' *The Chronicle-Journal*, 17 August 1996.

3 Graham Fraser, 'Some Americans, At Least, Paying Attention to Canada-Quebec Rift,' *The Globe and Mail*, 23 September 1996, A18.

4 Canadian Press story, September 15, 1996, was printed in a number of newspapers across Canada: Robert Russo, 'Article's Prediction of Canada Split Sparked Congressional Hearing,' *The Montreal Gazette*, 16 September 1996, A6; 'Alarm on Canada Has Washington Watching,' *The Province*, 16 September 1996, A2. Correction was made on September 17, 1996.

5 Andrew Phillips, 'Worry in Washington,' *Maclean's* (September 23, 1996), 19; Tom Campbell, 'When Canada's Turmoil Becomes the Americans' Business,' *The Globe and Mail*, 24 September 1996, A23.

6 Anthony De Palma, 'For Canada, Is U.S. Gaze Offensive or Friendly?' *The New York Times*, 28 September 1996.

7 Fern Callan, 'Will Canada Unravel?' 'Globe: Canada's Web Site,' *National Issues Forum* (September 12, 1996).

8 George Bain, 'How to Prepare For Life Without Quebec,' *The Globe and Mail*, 18 September 1997, 21.

9 The article was excerpted or reprinted in whole in *The Los Angeles Times* and in *The Globe and Mail*, on 17 September 1996, 15; it was also on an Internet Web site.

10 Thomas d'Aquino, 'The Case for Canada: An Optimistic Perspective on Canada's Political and Economic Prospects' (Address), The Paul H. Nitze School of Advanced International Studies, Centre of Canadian Studies, Johns Hopkins University, Washington, DC, February 13, 1997.

11 Jeffrey Simpson, 'Losing the "Quebec Problem" Would Create An "Ontario Problem,"' *The Globe and Mail*, 21 September 1996.

12 Gordon Gibson, 'An Outsider Sounds An All-Canada Wake-Up Call,' *The Globe and Mail*, 21 September 1996, D2.

13 Allan Gotlieb, 'South of the Border,' *The Ottawa Citizen*, 27 April 1997, 2.

14 'In all his life, he had never seen an English-Canadian and a French-Canadian hostile to each other face to face. When they disliked, they disliked entirely in the group.' Hugh MacLennan, *Two Solitudes* (New York: Popular Library, 1945), 352.

15 Of the 180 countries, only two come to mind that have territories divided by another state – Pakistan by India, and Azerbaijan by Armenia. Although each has been troublesome, neither is an example relevant to Quebec. The larger

reality is that territories become independent or they attach themselves to an adjacent polity. Because territories in Canada do not need to worry about security, however, perhaps there is less need to seek attachment.

16 Dalton Camp reports a conversation with Jacques Parizeau who, on the one hand, laments a monetary policy made to fit Ottawa's interests, but on the other hand shows the shortcomings of trying to go it alone with a separate currency for Quebec. 'Me and Mr. Parizeau,' *Whose Country is this Anyway?* (Vancouver: Douglas and McIntyre, 1995), 102–5.

17 This, of course, was the feeling of French-Canadians after the Conquest when the French governing and commercial elite returned to France, generating a sense of abandonment. Francis Parkman, *France and England in North America*, Vol. II (New York: Literary Classics, 1983), 1454.

18 Three prior attempts at Confederation with Newfoundland had failed, usually because of financial matters, and its entry in 1949 was a near thing based on a run-off plebiscite. Robert Bothwell, Ian Drummond, and John English, *Canada Since 1945: Power, Politics, and Provincialism* (Toronto: University of Toronto Press, 1981), 148–9.

19 Exemption of Canada, the United States, and France from the international requirement of a 40 per cent reduction in the take of silver hake, menhaden, mackerel, red fish, herring and red hake in 1975, for example, did little to stem the decline in these fish stocks. Barbara Johnson, 'Canadian Foreign Policy and Fisheries,' in Barbara Johnson and Mark W. Zacker, *Canadian Foreign Policy and the Law of the Sea* (Vancouver: University of British Columbia, 1977), 87.

20 David Leyton-Brown, 'Canadianizing Oil and Gas: The National Energy Program, 1980–83,' in Don Munton and John Kirton, *Canadian Foreign Policy: Selected Cases* (Scarborough, ON: Prentice-Hall, 1992), 299–310.

21 'An American Newfoundland, King feared, would not merely enfilade the St. Lawrence and outflank Canada's Atlantic gateway; in the long run it might well threaten confederation entire. The loss of Newfoundland, the realization that Canada was hemmed in on the east by another giant stride of Manifest Destiny, would inflict a grave, perhaps fatal, psychic wound on the Canadian people, would make them despair of their long continental labours when they could not hold the most vital strategic point in their natural geography. King's fears may have been excessive, but he held them tenaciously.' Bruce Hutchison, *Struggle for the Border* (New York: Longmans, Green, and Co., 1955), 471.

22 See the discussion in Lansing Lamont's beautifully written book on Canada's troubles, *Breakup: The Coming End of Canada and the Stakes for the United State* (New York: Norton, 1994), 220.

23 Jozef M. van Brabant, 'Technology Transfer and Regional Integration in the East,' in Gustav Schmidt, ed., *Ost-West-Bezeiehungen: Konfrontation and Detente*, Band I (Bochum: Universitaetsverlag Dr. N. Brockmeyer, 1993), 145–62.

24 Giorgio La Malfa, 'Italy: New Dilemmas an Old Evasions,' in David Calleo and Claudia Morgenstern, eds., *Recasting Europe's Economics: National Strategies in the 1980s* (Lanham, MD: University Press of America, 1990), 138–42.

25 'Moynihan Pomises Something Different on Welfare,' *The New York Times*, 14 May 1995.

26 Jean-Marie Guehenno, *The End of the Nation-State*, trans. Victoria Elliott (Minneapolis: University of Minnessota Press, 1995), 12.

27 For a thorough critique, see Peter Brimelow, *The Patriot Game: National Dreams and Political Realities* (Toronto: Key Porter Books, 1986).

28 For insight on how the Senate is used as a 'patronage payoff,' see Christina McCall-Newman, *Grits* (Toronto: Macmillan of Canada, 1982), 313.

29 According to Thomas J. Courchene, with Quebec gone, 'the taste for regional redistribution is likely to erode.' '"Staatsnation vs. Kulturnation": The Future of ROC,' in Kenneth McRoberts, *Beyond Quebec: Taking Stock of Canada* (Montreal: McGill-Queen's University Press, 1995), 389.

30 For an estimate of the effect of financial transfers per province, see *L'évolution des finances publiques au Québec, au Canada et dans certains pays de l'OCDE* (Quebec City: Bibliothéque nationale du Québec, 1996).

31 'The Call of the Wild in Western Canada,' *Business Week* (December 18, 1995).

32 Donald J. Savoie, 'The Continuing Struggle for a Regional Development Policy,' in Peter M. Leslie, ed., *Canada: The State of the Federation: 1985* (Kingston, ON: Institute of Intergovernmental Affairs, Queen's University, 1998), 144–9.

33 Alvin Finkel, *The Social Credit Phenomenon in Alberta* (Toronto: University of Toronto Press, 1989). The future of the Reform Party (now the Canadian Alliance) is its capacity to achieve national appeal, even though this effort may alienate the regional voter. See Tom Flanagan, 'Going National,' ch. 5, *Waiting for the Wave: The Reform Party and Preston Manning* (Toronto: Stoddart, 1995), 73–98.

34 T. Harry Williams, Richard N. Current, Frank Freidel, 'Protest and Reaction,' *A History of the United States (Since 1865)* (New York: Alfred A. Knopf, 1961), 186–203.

35 David Laycock, *Populism and Democratic Thought in the Canadian Prairies* (Toronto: University of Toronto Press, 1990).

36 V.C. Fowke, *The National Policy and the Wheat Economy* (Toronto: University of Toronto Press, 1978), 112.

37 Donald Creighton, *Canada's First Century* (Toronto: Macmillan of Canada, 1970), 75; Jakob Johann (Ben) Forster, *A Conjunction of Interests: Business, Politics and Tariffs, 1825–1879* (Toronto: University of Toronto Press, 1986).

38 Donald C. MacCharles, 'Canada in a Global Economy,' in Alan M. Rugman, ed., *International Business in Canada: Strategies for Management* (Scarborough, ON: Prentice-Hall, 1989), 12–54.

39 James C. Ingram and Robert M. Dunn, Jr., 'The Infant Industry Argument,' *International Economics*, 3rd ed. (1993), 148–51.

40 Fowke, *The National Policy and the Wheat Economy*, 72.

41 Ibid., 125.

42 Eric A. Uslaner, *Shale Barrel Politics: Energy and Legislative Leadership* (Stanford, CA: Stanford University Press, 1989); James A. Desveaux, *Designing Bureaucracies: Institutional Capacity and Large-Scale Problem Solving* (Stanford: Stanford University Press, 1995).

43 David Kilgour, *Uneasy Patriots: Western Canadians in Confederation* (Edmonton, AB: Lone Pine Publishers, 1988).

44 With a total of 46 of its 52 seats in the 1993 elections in Alberta (22) and British Columbia (24), Reform was essentially a two-province party. The 1997 and 2000 elections reinforced this regional judgment. Despite winning 24 per cent of the popular vote in Ontario in the 2000 elections, the Canadian Alliance could not take seats away from the dominant Liberal Party. In the West, however, the Canadian Alliance won 59 per cent of the popular vote in Alberta, 50 per cent in British Columbia, and 48 per cent in Saskatchewan.

45 Don Braid and Sydney Sharpe, *Breakup: Why the West Feels Left Out of Canada* (Toronto: Key Porter, 1990).

46 Not surprisingly, the two Conservative Party governments of Alberta and Ontario look a lot more alike on issues than either does vis-à-vis British Columbia. For example, quite a number of respondents in 1995 and 1996 (11 to 25 per cent) said provincial governments had gone too far in deficit reduction. In British Columbia, with fewer cuts, the response was in the 4 per cent range on the same question. 'Canada in 2005 Poll,' *Maclean's* (December 30, 1996/January 6, 1997), 20.

47 For all of its lightheartedness, the book written by a *Washington Post* reporter with the provocative title does acknowledge this difference between coastal British Columbia (Ecotopia) and the territory east of the Rocky Mountains (The Empty Quarter). Joel Garreau, *The Nine Nations of North America* (New York: Avon Books, 1981).

48 Westerners, disproportionately represented in the Reform Party, also resist

concessions to Quebec more than the rest of the country. Some 83 per cent of British Columbians, for example, oppose giving Quebec a constitutional veto over changes. 'Maclean's 12th Annual Year-end Poll,' Maclean's (December 25, 1996/January 1, 1997), 17.

49 Jeffrey Simpson, 'Losing the "Quebec Problem" would Create an "Ontario Problem,"' The Globe and Mail, 21 September 1996, editorial page.

50 Charles Kindleberger, World Economic Primacy: 1500–1990 (Oxford: Oxford University Press, 1996), 37–53.

51 Philip Resnick, Thinking English Canada (Toronto: Stoddart, 1994).

52 'Accommodation' involves for the realist the 'mitigation and minimization of political conflicts' but not the yielding of power. Hans Morgenthau, Politics Among Nations (New York: Alfred Knopf, 1948), 419.

53 Eric Kierans and Walter Stewart, Wrong End of the Rainbow: The Collapse of Free Enterprise in Canada (Toronto: Harper and Collins, 1989), 172–4.

54 'The net mix of gains and losses in policy capacity inherent in the FTA will probably result in a transfer of power to influence the course of the nation from government to the market, and the national or commonly shared character of the Canadian political experience will be diminished as a result.' G. Bruce Doern and Brian W. Tomlin, Faith and Fear (Toronto: Stoddart, 1991), 294.

55 Michael J. Trebilcock and Daniel Schwanen, Getting There: An Assessment of the Agreement on Internal Trade, Policy Study No. 26 (Toronto: C.D. Howe Institute, 1995).

56 Robert A. Young, 'The Breakup of Czechoslovakia,' in The Secession of Quebec and the Future of Canada (Montreal: McGill-Queens University Press, 1995), 145–68.

57 In a twenty-nation poll, over half of the foreign respondents and 88 per cent of the Canadian respondents viewed Canada as well-known for its tolerance and diversity. Angus Reid Group, Canada and the World (Toronto: Angus Reid Group, 1997).

5: Is Separatism Home-Grown or the Result of Contagion?

1 Jean-Marie Guehenno, The End of the Nation-State, trans. Victoria Elliott (Minneapolis: University of Minnesota Press, 1995); Kenichi Ohmae, The End of the Nation-State: The Rise of Regional Economies (New York: The Free Press, 1995). These writings follow a long exposition of this viewpoint in the international relations literature. Richard Rosecrance, The Rise of the Virtual State (New York: Basic Books, 2000); Martin van Creveld, The Rise and Decline of the State (Cambridge: Cambridge University Press, 1999); Stanley

Hoffmann, 'Obstinate or Obsolete? The Fate of the Nation-State and the Case of Western Europe,' *Daedalus* 95, no. 3 (Summer 1976); William H. McNeill, *Polyethnicity and National Unity in World History* (Toronto: University of Toronto Press, 1986), 82.

2 The classic discussion here is J. David Singer, 'The Level-of-Analysis Problem in International Relations,' in Klaus Knorr and Sidney Verba, eds., *The International System* (Princeton: Princeton University Press, 1961), 77–92.

3 'Whether a secessionist movement will achieve its aims,' observes Donald Horowitz, 'is determined largely by international politics.' *Ethnic Groups in Conflict* (Berkeley: University of California Press, 1985), 258.

4 Contrast, for example, the assumptions of Kenneth Waltz that the bipolar system determines the magnitude and probability of instability between states and to a great extent within the state, with the assumptions of Richard Rosecrance who places much more emphasis on the impact of historical process on instability within and between states. Kenneth W. Waltz, 'The Stability of a Bipolar World,' *Daedalus, Journal of the American Academy of Arts and Sciences* (Summer 1964), 881–909; Richard N. Rosecrance, 'Bipolarity, Multipolarity, and the Future,' *Journal of Conflict Resolution* 10, no. 3 (September 1966), 314–27.

5 Richard S. Dunn, 'Toward a New Balance of Power,' *The Age of Religious Wars, 1559–1715*, 2nd ed. (New York: W.W. Norton, 1979), 259–302.

6 Karl Deutsch, *Nationalism and Social Communication*, 2nd ed. (Cambridge: Harvard University Press, 1966), 105.

7 Liah Greenfeld, *Nationalism: Five Roads to Modernity* (Cambridge: Harvard University Press, 1992), 15.

8 Deutsch, *Nationalism and Social Communication*, 96–105.

9 J.L. Brierly, *The Law of Nations*, 6th ed. (Oxford: Oxford University Press, 1963), 165.

10 Since 1945, however, a nascent decline in warfare seems evident. Brian M. Pollins, 'Cannons and Capital: The Use of Coercive Diplomacy by Major Powers in the Twentieth Century,' in Frank W. Wayman and Paul F. Diehl, eds., *Reconstructing Realpolitik* (Ann Arbor: University of Michigan Press, 1994), 50. For an excellent summary of empirical findings on how non-rationality interacts with war decisions, see J. David Singer and Daniel S. Geller, *Nations at War: A Scientific Study of War* (Cambridge: Cambridge University Press, 1998).

11 J.R. Hale, *War and Society in Renaissance Europe, 1450–1620* (Baltimore: Johns Hopkins University Press, 1985), 13–45.

12 Regarding the diplomatic learning that has taken place, see Charles A.

Kupchan, *The Vulnerability of Empire* (Ithaca: Cornell University Press, 1994), 486–509.

13 Arthur M. Okun, *Equality and Efficiency: The Big Tradeoff* (Washington, DC: The Brookings Institution, 1975).

14 Robert Keohane, *International Institutions and State Power* (Boulder: Westview Press, 1989), 78.

15 Michael W. Doyle, *Empires* (Ithaca: Cornell University Press, 1986), 123–40; Jack Snyder, *Myths of Empire: Domestic Politics and International Ambition* (Ithaca: Cornell University Press, 1991), 21–65.

16 Charles F. Doran, *Politics of Assimilation: Hegemony and Its Aftermath* (Baltimore: Johns Hopkins University Press, 1971), 191–203.

17 Charles F. Doran, *Systems in Crisis: New Imperatives of High Politics at Century's End* (Cambridge: Cambridge University Press, 1991), 11–125.

18 Doran, *Systems in Crisis*, 237–59.

19 Anthony D. Smith, 'Nations by Design?' *National Identity* (London: Penguin, 1991), 99–122; Benedict Anderson, *Imagined Communities* (London: Verso, 1991), 36–46.

20 This analysis draws upon a private discussion with then Czech Cabinet Minister Vaclav Klaus.

21 For a discussion of diffusion processes in politics see Randolph M. Siverson and Harvey Starr, *The Diffusion of War: A Study of Opportunity and Willingness* (Ann Arbor: University of Michigan Press, 1991).

22 Michael Hechter and Margaret Levi, 'The Comparative Analysis of Ethnoregional Movements,' *Ethnic and Regional Studies* no. 2/3 (July 1979), 262–72.

23 Philip Schlesinger, 'Europeanness: A New Cultural Battlefield?' *Innovation in Social Science Research* 5, no. 2 (1992), 12–22.

24 On January 9, 1997, for example, the United States warned Turkey not to 'threaten the use of force against Cyprus.' But is the American public prepared to use force against Turkey, on the latter's doorstep, to halt a further division of Cyprus, having already intervened in the relations of Somalia, Haiti, Iraq, and China-Taiwan in the recent period? *Washington Post*, 10 January 1997. Divisive nationalism that is benign is likely to slip past even a vigilant hegemon, given its concern about more volatile situations.

25 Antarctica, the High Seas, and space remain the frontiers not yet conquered by the nation-state, yet even here inroads have been made. Some seven countries have staked claims on the frozen ice-cap at the South Pole; in some cases, the territorial seas beyond 200 miles (321 km) of coastlines are being colonized; space orbital slots and locations for communications satellites are among the hottest of national properties. Just as the domestic mar-

ketplace is owned by the individual firm, public places are owned by the nation-state.

26 The most radical step taken in these agreements are the binational trade dispute resolutions found in the FTA and NAFTA. For an imaginative extension see Wendy Dobson and Hideo Sato, *Are There Better Ways: Managing U.S.–Japanese Trade Disputes* (Ottawa: Carleton University, Centre for Trade Policy and Law, 1996).

27 Doran, *Politics of Assimilation*, 1–11.

28 'When this crisis is over, America needs to ask itself an even deeper question: How far does it wish to push the principle of self-determination? Bosnia is now too divided to design a government under which the three ethnic groups can live in harmony. But if pressed on a global basis, will the concept of ethnic self-determination not splinter the world into unmanageable confusion? And, at the extremes, what might it do to the cohesion of our own society?' Henry Kissinger, 'Bosnia: Only Just Beginning ...,' *The Washington Post*, 11 September 1997; David Cameron, *Nationalism, Self-Determination, and the Quebec Question* (Toronto: Macmillan of Canada, 1974), 143–57.

29 Jeffrey Sachs, 'Economics: Unlocking the Mysteries of Globalization,' *Foreign Policy*, no. 10 (Spring 1998), 109; Robert Gilpin, *The Challenge of Global Capitalism: The World Economy in the Twenty-First Century* (Princeton: Princeton University Press, 2000), 293–324.

30 Geuhenno, *The End of the Nation-State*, 45.

31 Ohmae, *The End of the Nation-State: The Rise of Regional Economics*.

32 Michael E. Porter, *The Competitive Advantage of Nations* (New York: The Free Press, 1990), 179–238.

33 Mildred A. Schwartz, 'NAFTA and the Fragmentation of Canada,' *The American Review of Canadian Studies* 28, nos. 1 and 2 (Spring and Summer 1998), 11–28.

34 Vamik D. Volkan, 'Turks and Greeks of Cyprus: Psychopolitical Considerations,' in Vangelos Calotychos, ed., *Cyprus and Its People: Nation, Identity, and Experience in an Unimaginable Community, 1955–1997* (Boulder, CO: Westview Press, 1998); Necati Munir Ertekun, *The Cyprus Dispute and the Birth of the Turkish Republic of Northern Cyprus* (Oxford: Oxford University Press, 1984).

35 Chris Delphin, 'The European Union and Conflict Resolution on Cyprus: The Effect of Cypriot Accession on the "Cyprus Problem,"' (Senior Thesis, Johns Hopkins University, Department of Political Science, April 2000).

36 Stephen D. Krasner, *Sovereignty: Organized Hypocrisy* (Princeton: Princeton University Press, 1999), 226.

6: Is Small Size a Stimulus or Obstacle to Separatism?

1 A first draft of this chapter was written in the spring of 1998, and in the next two years was presented in seminars and conferences in Washington, DC; Chicago, Illinois; Bologna, Italy; Bochum, Germany; and Oslo, Sweden.

2 Lester C. Thurow, 'Rise in Global Economy, Fall of Communism Shift Borders; Remapping the World,' *The Boston Globe*, 7 October 1997.

3 Robert J. Barro, *Getting It Right: Markets and Choices in a Free Society* (Cambridge, MA: MIT Press, 1996), 28.

4 Absence of a relationship between population size and level of per capita income was also found in an empirical study by Jack Sawyer, 'Dimensions of Nations: Size, Wealth, and Politics,' *American Journal of Sociology* 73, no. 3 (September 1967), 145–72.

5 Alberto Alesina and Enrico Spolaore, 'On the Number and Size of Nations,' *The Quarterly Journal of Economics* (November 1997), 1027–56.

6 This is exactly the opposite conclusion that James Madison came to in the *Federalist Papers* No. 10. He argued that factionalism is more probable in the small state because political parties and interest groups are not as likely to be cross-cutting or offsetting as in the larger polity where there is more room for diversity and choice. Put in economics language, the probability of local monopolies is less and balanced competition is greater in the larger polity. See also Robert Dahl and Edward R. Tufte, *Size and Democracy* (Stanford: Stanford University Press, 1973); Maurice East, 'Size and Foreign Policy Behavior: A Test of Two Models,' *World Politics* 25, no. 4 (July 1973), 560–5; Eric A. Nordlinger, *Conflict Regulation in Divided Societies*, Occasional Papers in International Affairs, No. 29 (Cambridge, MA: Center for International Affairs, Harvard University, 1972).

7 Jacob Viner, *The Customs Union Issue* (New York: Carnegie Endowment for World Peace, 1953).

8 R.G. Lipsey, 'The Theory of Customs Unions – A General Survey,' *Economic Journal* 70, no. 279 (September 1960), 496–513.

9 James R. Markusen, James R. Melvin, William H. Kaempfer, and Keith E. Maskus, *International Trade: Theory and Evidence* (New York: McGraw-Hill, 1995), 320.

10 M.C. Kemp and H.Y. Wan, 'An Elementary Proposition Concerning the Formation of Customs Unions,' *Journal of International Economics* 6, no. 1 (February 1976), 95–7.

11 Used here is a minimal definition of cycle as 'a period of time during which something becomes established, reaches a peak, and declines.' That 'something' is the per capita income growth rate. And the 'cycle' is the period of

time during which it completes a non-linear curvilinear pattern of change, rising to a peak and then turning into decline. There is no notion of repetition here (as would be the case in other definitions of cycle). Hence some readers may prefer the label 'curve' instead of 'cycle.' This same definition applies to the 'power cycle' concept treated later in this chapter.

12 Epitomizing this older literature on growth is the discussion by Richard Easterlin: 'The gap in the percentage of labor force in nonagricultural activity has continued to widen. With regard to GNP per capita, it can also be inferred, despite the limited data, that relative levels have continued to diverge.' 'Economic Growth: Overview,' in *International Encyclopedia of the Social Sciences* (New York: Crowell, Collier, and McMillan Inc., 1977), 404.

13 Perhaps the best expostulation of the catch-up thesis is Moses Abramovitz, 'Catch-up, Forging Ahead, and Falling Behind,' *Thinking about Growth* (Cambridge: Cambridge University Press, 1989), ch. 7, 220–42.

14 P.T. Bauer, for example, rightly calls into question the notion of the 'widening gap' as an overall description of the economic growth situation without going the next step which is a combining of the rich/poor gap and the catch-up thesis into a single more compelling explanation of relative per capita income change. 'The Vicious Circle of Poverty and the Widening Gap,' *Dissent on Development* (Cambridge, MA: Harvard University Press, 1971), chs. 1 and 2, 31–49, 49–68.

15 Joel Mokyr, 'Technological Change, 1700–1830,' in Roderick Floud and Donald McCloskey, eds., *The Economic History of Britain Since 1700*, Vol. 1, *1700–1860*, 2nd ed. (Cambridge: Cambridge University Press, 1994), 12–43; Daniel R. Headrick, *Tools of Empire: Technology and European Imperialism in the Nineteenth Century* (Oxford: Oxford University Press, 1981), Part One, 15–79.

16 Mancur Olson, *The Rise and Decline of Nations* (New Haven: Yale University Press, 1982). For a critique, see David R. Cameron, 'Distributional Coalitions and Other Sources of Economic Stagnation: On Olson's Rise and Decline of Nations,' *International Organization* 42, no. 4 (Autumn 1988), 561–604.

17 The logical progression here in terms of the building of a model of economic growth is E.D. Domar, 'Capital Expansion, Rate of Growth,' *Econometrica* 14 (April 1946), 137–47; Robert M. Solow, 'Technical Change and the Aggregate Production Function,' *Review of Economics and Statistics* 39 (August 1957), 312–20; Paul Romer, 'Increasing Returns and Long-Run Growth,' *Journal of Political Economy* 94, no. 5 (October 1986), 1002–37.

18 Charles F. Doran, 'Yardsticks,' and 'Operationalizing National Capability,' *Systems in Crisis: New Imperatives of High Politics at Century's End* (Cambridge: Cambridge University Press, 1991), 49–51, 51–3.

19   Charles F. Doran, Kim Q. Hill, and Kenneth R. Mladenka, 'Threat, Status Disequilibrium, and National Power,' *International Journal of Group Tensions* 4, no. 4 (December 1974), 431–54.

20   Doran, *Systems in Crisis*, 68–9, 261–7.

21   Charles F. Doran, 'Confronting the Principles of the Power Cycle: Changing Systems Structure, Expectations, and War,' in Manus Midlarsky, ed., *Handbook of War Studies II* (Ann Arbor: University of Michigan Press, 2000).

22   Charles F. Doran, 'Why Forecasts Fail: The Limits and Potential of Forecasting in International Relations and Economics,' Special Millennium Volume, *International Studies Review*, Davis B. Bobrow, ed., *Prospects for International Relations* (Oxford: Blackwell Publishers, Ltd., 1999), 11–41.

23   Doran, 'Confronting the Principles of the Power Cycle.'

24   Doran, *Systems in Crisis*, 93–116.

25   Doran, 'Confronting the Principles of the Power Cycle.'

26   William J. Baumol, 'Multivariate Growth Patterns: Contagion and Common Forces as Possible Sources of Convergence,' in William J. Baumol, Richard R. Nelson, and Edward N. Wolff, eds., *Convergence of Productivity: Cross-National Studies and Historical Evidence* (Oxford: Oxford University Press, 1994), 62–85.

27   Paul Krugman, 'Voodoo Revisited: Sorry Boys, Over the Long-Run a Maximum of 2.5 Per Cent U.S. Growth Rate Is the Limit,' *Foreign Affairs* (November/December 1995), 14–19.

28   More formally expressed, the theory of the secessionist state as expressed in terms of size and in terms of degree of integration is as follows:
     Size: If A is the state, B is the fragment that separates from A, and C is a regional trade grouping of which B eventually becomes a member, then when size alone is taken into consideration B will benefit insofar as $C + B > A$.
     Degree of Integration: When the degree of integration is also considered, and X is the degree of integration of the state, Y is the degree of integration of a regional trade area, and Z is the degree of integration of the larger trade system, then the secessionist entity will benefit when $Y \geq Z \geq X$.

29   Patrick Bolton and Gerard Roland, 'The Breakup of Nations: A Political Economy Analysis,' *The Quarterly Journal of Economics* (November 1997), 1057.

30   I am grateful to Gustav Schmidt, University of the Ruhr, Bochum, Germany, for this insight.

31   See 'Trade-Restricting Regulations,' in James R. Markusen, James R. Melvin, William Kaempfer, and Keith E. Maskus, *International Trade Theory and Evidence* (New York: McGraw-Hill, 1995), 280–1; Joseph Kalt, 'The Impact of Domestic Regulatory Policies on U.S. International Competitiveness,' in A. Michael Spence and Heather A. Hazard, eds., *International Competitiveness* (Cambridge: Ballinger, 1988), 221–62.

32 This function has three important characteristics: Among the small states
(those with small GDP), a state with larger GDP has a significantly higher
per capita income growth rate; this advantage in growth rate levels out
abruptly for a GDP of about that of the UK; the threshold growth rate that
results is about 3 per cent per year. Fit in terms of ordinary least squares to
these data, the function is of the type $5.96x/(1 + 1.97x)$ with a variance
accounted for of 54 per cent.

33 W.M. Corden, 'Economies of Scale and Customs Union Theory,' *Journal of
Political Economy* (March 1972), 465–75.

34 There is good empirical evidence that this supposition may have validity
here since increasing trade diversion seems to be a problem for the European countries associated with the European Union. See Gary Clyde Huf-
bauer, *Europe 1992: An American Perspective* (Washington, DC: Brookings
Institution Press, 1990), 23.

35 Maurice Obstfeld and Kenneth Rogoff, 'The Six Major Puzzles in International Macroeconomics: Is There a Common Cause?' Working Paper 777,
National Bureau of Economic Research, Cambridge, MA, July 2000.

36 'Saturated Solution,' *The Economist* (July 29, 2000), 76.

37 J. McCallum, 'National Borders Matter: Canada–U.S. Regional Trade Pat-
terns,' *American Economic Review* 85 (June 1995), 615–23; John F. Helliwell,
'Borders and Growth,' *How Much Do National Borders Matter?* (Washington,
DC: Brookings Institution Press, 1998), 92–112.

38 Gene Koretz, 'Bright Lights, Midsize City: What Towns Are Best for Business?' *Business Week* (November 2, 1998), 22.

39 Trading volume divided by GDP is likely to be 17 per cent higher for countries that speak English, according to a study by Shang-Jin Wei, 'Natural
Openness and Good Government,' Working paper, National Bureau of Economic Research, Cambridge, MA, June 2000; 'Closed Borders and Open
Palms,' *The Economist* (9 September 2000), 98.

7: What Kind of Canada in the Twenty-First Century?

1 Arend Lijphart, *Democracy in Plural Societies: A Comparative Exploration*
(New Haven: Yale University Press, 1977), 129. See also Kenneth D.
McRae, 'Consociationalism and the Canadian Political System,' Kenneth
D. McRae, ed., *Consociational Democracy: Political Accommodation in Seg-
mented Societies* (Toronto: McClelland and Stewart, 1974); Robert Presthus,
Elite Accommodation in Canadian Politics (Cambridge: Cambridge University
Press, 1973).

2 Thomas S. Axworthy and Pierre Elliott Trudeau, *Towards a Just Society: The
Trudeau Years* (Markham, ON: Viking, 1990), 16.

3 Guy Laforest, ed., *Reconciling the Solitudes: Essays on Canadian Federalism and Nationalism, Charles Taylor* (Montreal: McGill-Queen's University Press, 1993), xi.

4 A good start was Prime Minister Chrétien's three-point proposal: (1) to recognize Quebec as a distinct society; (2) to make no constitutional changes without Quebec's consent; and (3) to assist Quebec with workforce training and other services. Judith Webster, 'Government of Canada Introduces Unity Measures,' *Canada Quarterly* 4, no. 1 (January 1996).

5 Francois Aubin, *René Lévesque tel quel* (Montréal: Boréal Express, 1973), 169–73.

6 The foreign equivalent of the impact of careless behaviour on Canadian attitudes, as opposed to just Quebec attitudes, is the famous statement Champ Clark made in the U.S. Senate about 'annexation' to which is attributed the derailing of Laurier's 1911 Free Trade Agreement with the United States and his reelection chances. As always, history is far more complex than such anecdotes imply and richer in a variety of causal explanations.

7 Clarification of issues, however, can be helpful. Charles F. Doran, 'The Issue of Quebec's Sovereignty and Its Potential Impact on the United States,' testimony presented at the *Hearing Before the Subcommittee on the Western Hemisphere of the Committee on International Relations*, 104 Cong., 2nd session, 25 September 1996, 34–6.

8 For a discussion of Quebec's attitudes towards English Canada and the United States, see Alfred Olivier Hero, Jr., and Louis Balthazar, *Contemporary Quebec and the United States: 1960–1985* (Cambridge, MA: Center for International Affairs and the University Press of America, 1988), 199–231.

9 A.D.P. Heeney and Livingston T. Merchant, 'Canada and the United States: Principles for Partnership' (June 28, 1965). Mimeograph of original typed copy of the 'Merchant-Heeney Report,' from the personal library of Rufus Smith, in author's possession.

10 Howard Adelman, 'Quebec: The Morality of Secession,' in Joseph H. Carens, ed., *Is Quebec Nationalism Just? Perspectives from Anglophone Canada* (Montreal: McGill-Queen's University Press, 1995), 185–8.

11 John Saywell, *The Rise of the Parti Québécois: 1967–1976* (Toronto: University of Toronto Press, 1977), 89–90.

12 R. Kent Weaver, ed., *The Collapse of Canada?* (Washington, DC: Brookings Institution Press, 1992), 9.

13 John Breuilly points out that consent to the creation of a sovereign power in Europe resulted from the need of a national entity to defend its borders, a situation that is not relevant for Quebec. *Nationalism and the State*, 2nd ed. (Chicago: University of Chicago Press, 1993), 373–4.

14 Patrick J. Monahan and Michael J. Bryant, with Nancy C. Cote, 'Coming to Terms with Plan B: Ten Principles Governing Secession,' in David R. Cameron, ed., *The Referendum Papers: Essays on Secession and National Unity* (Toronto: University of Toronto Press, 1999), 283.

15 Alan C. Cairns, 'Looking into the Abyss: The Need for a Plan C,' in Cameron, ed., *The Referendum Papers*, 199–243.

16 Alain Cairns expresses well the philosophic dilemma in which the law must operate. He stresses three equalities: citizens, provinces, peoples. 'Constitutional Change and the Three Equalities,' in Ronald L. Watts and Douglas M. Brown, eds., *Options for a New Canada* (Toronto: University of Toronto Press, 1991), 77–100.

17 Earl H. Fry, 'Quebec, Canada, and the United States: The Economic Dimension,' *The American Review of Canadian Studies* (Winter 1995), 508–12.

18 Murray G. Smith, 'Canada and Economic Sovereignty,' in Joyce Hoebing, Sidney Weintraub, and M. Delal Baer, eds., *NAFTA and Sovereignty: Trade-Offs for Canada, Mexico, and the United States* (Washington, DC: The Center for Strategic and International Studies, 1996), 65. Consider also the interesting essay by Wendy Dobson, 'The Canadian–U.S. Relationship as a Benchmark,' in Wendy Dobson and Hideo Sato, eds., *Are There Better Ways: Managing U.S.–Japanese Trade Disputes* (Ottawa: Carleton University, The Centre for Trade Policy and Law, 1996), 35–76.

19 Jonathan Doh finds that Newt Gingrich's conclusion for the United States based on the 1995 referendum as an 'odd development.' Gingrich concluded that the vote was a 'warning signal' for the United States that bilingualism leads to divisiveness and that Congress ought to enshrine English as the only official language. Gingrich's concerns are not far-fetched. The problem is that language use by immigrants is not as much a legal matter as it is an educational one, and the latter costs money. Spanish ought to be offered in the schools for English-speakers, as well, in locales where Spanish is the preponderant language. 'Le Plus Ça Change – The Quebec Referendum and U.S.–Canada Relations: A U.S. Perspective,' in *North American Outlook*, Washington, DC, National Planning Association, 6, no. 2 (July 1996), 50.

20 Gordon Gibson, *Plan B: The Future of the Rest of Canada* (Vancouver: Fraser Institute, 1994).

21 Seymour Martin Lipset, 'The Importance of Political Culture,' in Larry Diamond and Mark F. Plattner, eds., *The Global Resurgence of Democracy* (Baltimore: Johns Hopkins University Press, 1993). For an insightful discussion of the role of cultural confidence in Quebec separationist thought, see Stephane Dion, 'Explaining Quebec Nationalism,' in Weaver, ed., *Collapse of Canada?* 97–110.

22 Fanny S. Demers and Michel Demers, *European Union: A Viable Model for Quebec-Canada?* 2nd ed. (Ottawa: Carleton University, The Center for Trade Policy and Law, 1995).

23 Jeffrey M. Ayres, 'National No More: Defining English Canada,' *The American Review of Canadian Studies* (Summer and Autumn, 1995), 186–9.

24 C. Fred Bergsten, *America in the World Economy: A Strategy for the 1990s* (Washington, DC: Institute for International Economics, 1988), 65–7.

25 Hon. Lloyd Axworthy, Foreign Minister of Canada, letter to the editor, response to 'Will Canada Unravel?' *Foreign Affairs* (January / February 1997), 168–9. This is an important point of agreement.

26 Harold J. Barnett and Chandler Morse, 'Mitigations of Scarcity in Complex Economies,' *Scarcity and Growth: The Economics of Natural Resource Availability* (Baltimore: Johns Hopkins Press for Resources for the Future, 1963), 126–47.

27 Special Committee of the Senate on National Defence, 'Linkages and Early Decisions About Space,' *Canada's Territorial Air Defence* (Ottawa, 1985), 37–40.

28 Mel Watkins, 'Ideology,' in 'A Canada–United States Free Trade Agreement: For and Against,' *British Journal of Canadian Studies* 1, nos. 1 and 2 (December 1986 / January 1997), 199.

29 According to polls in 1996 and 1997, between 30 and 40 per cent of Canadians regard it as likely that one or more provinces will decide to join the United States by the year 2005. 'Canada in the Year 2005 Poll,' *Maclean's* (December 30, 1996–January 6, 1997).

30 See the discussion by Robert Lewis, 'From the Editor,' *Maclean's* (February 15, 1999), 2.

31 Should Quebec leave, 47 per cent of all Canadians say 'Canada should just let Quebec go.' This includes 55 per cent who say so in British Columbia and 58 per cent who say so in Quebec. 'Canada in the Year 2005 Poll,' *Maclean's*, 41.

32 According to Statistics Canada, Ottawa spent $956 more per capita in Quebec than it received in taxes. According to Infometrica, *La Presse*, November 15, 1994, Quebec received per capita about $250 more than it paid to the federal government in taxes. Kimon Valaskakis and Angeline Fournier, *The Delusion of Sovereignty* (Toronto: Robert Davies Publishing, 1995), 68–9.

33 Howard Cody, for example, suggests a movement away from 'central government dominance' until the dual federalism era of 1883–1910 and then a movement towards such dominance until 1960 and then a movement away again to the present. 'The Evolution of Federal–Provincial Relations in Canada,' *American Review of Canadian Studies* 7, no. 1 (1977), 55–83.

34 Richard Simeon, *Federal-Provincial Diplomacy: The Making of Recent Policy in Canada* (Toronto: University of Toronto Press, 1972), 299–300; Robert Jackson, Doreen Jackson, Nicolas Baxter-Moore, *Politics in Canada: Culture, Institutions, Behaviour and Public Policy* (Scarborough: Prentice-Hall, 1986), 237–49.

35 Allen Smith, *Canada an American Nation? Essays on Continentalism, Identity, and the Canadian Frame of Mind* (Montreal: McGill-Queen's University Press, 1994), 321.

36 Alan C. Cairns, 'The Electoral System and the Party System in Canada, 1921–1965,' *Canadian Journal of Political Science* (March 1968), 55–80; Peter Russell, 'Can the Canadians Be a Sovereign People?' *Canadian Journal of Political Science* 24 (December 1991); Donald V. Smiley and Ronald L. Watts, *Interstate Federalism in Canada* (Toronto: University of Toronto Press, 1985), ch. 7.

37 G. Remillard, *Le fédéralisme canadien* (Montreal: Québec/Amérique, 1980); G-A. Beaudoin, *Le partage des pouvoirs* (Ottawa: Editions de l'Université d'Ottawa, 1982); Valaskakis and Fournier, *The Delusion of Sovereignty*, 61–4; Marsha A. Chandler and William M. Chandler, *Public Policy and Provincial Politics* (Toronto: McGraw-Hill, 1979), 10.

38 'If province differs with province, or region with region, a foreign negotiating party may exploit the differences among Canadians so as to weaken Canada's negotiating position.' Donald S. MacDonald, 'Three Perspectives on Canada's Future,' *Daedalus* 117, no. 4, (Fall 1988), 375.

39 Thomas G. Barnes, 'There'll Always Be a Canada and a Canadian Constitutional Crisis,' Special Issue, Charles F. Doran and Ellen Babby, eds., *Annals: Being and Becoming Canada* 538 (March 1995), 27–39.

40 David B. Dewitt and John J. Kirton, *Canada as a Principle Power* (Toronto: John Wiley and Sons, 1983), 5.

41 Respondents in a sample of twenty countries ranked Canada among the top two countries in the world as a preferred place to live. Canada ranks first in terms of quality of life. Angus Reid Group, *Canada and the World: An International Perspective on Canada and Canadians* (March 23, 1997).

8: Self-Determination and Democratic Pluralism

1 During the height of Ancient Athens' power, various elements of society did live in harmony with each other, including a population of metics (resident aliens) we estimate at about 8 per cent, although this harmony did not persist. Walter R. Agard, *What Democracy Meant to the Greeks* (Chapel Hill, NC: University of North Carolina Press, 1942).

2 Empirical political science provides support for rejection of the hypothesis that political instability and nationalist effort occur randomly across separatist movements. Political violence is by far more common in separatism associated with countries of low GNP; escalation to actual 'ethnonational crisis' is more common in countries of high GNP. Philip G. Roeder, 'The Robustness of Institutions in Ethnically Plural Societies' (paper presented at the American Political Science Association, Washington, DC, August 31–September 3, 2000); Val R. Lorwin, 'Belgium: Religion, Class, and Language in National Politics,' in Robert Dahl, ed., *Political Oppositions in Western Democracies* (New Haven: Yale University Press, 1966), 147–87.

3 Jacques Bertrand, 'Ethnic Conflict, Secession, and Democratic Transitions: The Case of Indonesia' (paper presented at the American Political Science Association, Washington, DC, August 31–September 3, 2000); James Manor, 'The Political Sustainability of Economic Liberalization in India,' in Vijoy Joshi and Robert Cassen, eds., *Future of Economic Reform in India* (Delhi: Oxford University Press, 1995); Gabriella Montinola, Qian Yingyi, and Barry Weingast, 'Federalism, Chinese Style: The Political Basis for Economic Success in China,' *World Politics* 48 (October 1995), 50–81.

4 Democracy in Ancient Greece was not different. 'Athenian policy was really determined by mass meetings of the citizens on the advice of anyone who could win the people's ear.' Arnold H.M. Jones, *Athenian Democracy* (Oxford: Basil Blackwell, 1969), 132. For the possibilities of freedom inside the democratic state, see Richard E. Flathman, *The Philosophy and Politics of Freedom* (Chicago: University of Chicago Press, 1987).

5 Alan Siaroff, 'Democratic Breakdown and Democratic Stability: A Comparison of Interwar Estonia and Finland,' *Canadian Journal of Political Science* 32, no. 1 (March 1999), 103–24.

6 Robin W. Winks, *The Relevance of Canadian History* (Lanham, MD: University Press of America, 1988), xiii–xiv.

7 Francis Fukuyama, *The End of History and the Last Man* (New York: Free Press, 1992); Samuel Huntington, *The Clash of Civilizations and the Remaking of World Order* (New York: Simon and Schuster, 1996); Shlomo Avineri, 'The Return to History: The Breakup of the Soviet Union,' *Brookings Review* 10 (Spring 1992), 30–3.

8 Ghia Nodia, 'Nationalism and Democracy,' in Larry Diamond and Marc F. Plattner, eds., *Nationalism, Ethnic Conflict, and Democracy* (Baltimore: Johns Hopkins University Press, 1994), 4–5.

9 Robert Putnam, Susan Pharr, and Russell Dalton, *What Is Troubling the Trilateral Democracies?* (Princeton: Princeton University Press, 2000).

10 Charles F. Doran, Cal Clark, and George Modelski, eds., *North-South Relations: Studies of Dependency Reversal* (New York: Praeger, 1983).

11 Ministerio de Cultura, *Encuesta de Equipamiento, Practicas y Consumos Culturales* (Madrid: Ministerio de Cultura of Spain, 1990); D. Convesi, *The Basques, the Catalans and Spain: Alternate Routes to Nationalist Mobilization* (Reno: University of Nevada Press, 1997); Richard Wyn Jones and Dafydd Trystan, 'A "Quiet Earthquake": The First Elections to the National Assembly for Wales' (paper presented at the American Political Science Association, Washington, DC, August 31–September 3, 2000).

12 P. Heywood, *The Government and Politics of Spain* (New York: St. Martin's Press, 1995).

13 Christopher J. Anderson and Christine A. Guillory, 'Political Institutions and Satisfaction with Democracy: A Cross-National Analysis of Consensus and Majoritarian Systems,' *American Political Science Review* 91, no. 1 (March 1997), 66–81.

14 Surely these were the assumptions in most of the republics that once composed Yugoslavia, even though many of the resulting states were quite multi-ethnic. James S. Fishkin, *Democracy and Deliberation: New Directions for Democratic Reform* (New Haven: Yale University Press, 1991), 78; William E. Connolly, *The Ethos of Pluralization* (Minnesota: University of Minnesota Press, 1995).

15 Richard Eichenberg and R. J. Dalton, 'Europeans and the European Community: The Dynamics of Public Support for European Integration,' *International Organization* 47 (Summer 1993), 506–10; David McKay, *Rush to Union: Understanding the European Federal Bargain* (Oxford: Clarenden Press, 1996).

16 The European Union, partly to regulate or 'regularize' contacts with regional entities while placating the state governments, has established an Assembly of European Regions. Regional governments, much like the states and provinces in North America, are establishing offices in Brussels to lobby the European Community. M. Keating and L. Hooghe, 'By-passing the Nation-State? Regions and the EU Policy Process,' J. Richardson, ed., *European Union: Power and Policy-Making* (London: Routledge, 1996).

17 Peter Lynch, 'New Labour and the English Regional Development Agencies: Devolution as Evolution,' *Regional Studies* 33, no. 1 (February 1999), 73–8; Peter Hall, 'Social Capital in Britain,' *British Journal of Political Science* 29, no. 3 (July 1999), 417–61.

18 *The Republic of Plato*, trans. Francis MacDonald Cornford (New York: Oxford University Press, 1963), 139.

19 Thomas D. Hall explores the strange origin of the notion of the homogeneous state. 'The Effects of Incorporation into World Systems on Ethnic Processes: Lessons from the Ancient World for the Contemporary World,' *International Political Science Review* 19, no. 3 (September 1998), 259–60.

20 See Frank Harvey's excellent analysis of the issue in 'Primordialism, Evolu-

tionary Theory and Ethnic Violence in the Balkans: Opportunities and Constraints for Theory and Policy,' *Canadian Journal of Political Science* 33, no. 1 (March 2000), 37–65. The reference quoted is Umberto Melotti, 'In-Group/Out-Group Relations and the Issue of Group Selection,' in V. Reynolds, V.S.S. Folger, and I. Vine, eds., *The Sociobiology of Ethnocentrism* (Athens: University of Georgia Press, 1986).

21 Ernst Mayr, *This Is Biology: The Science of the Living World* (Cambridge: Harvard University Press, 1997), 227–70; Colin Patterson, *Evolution*, 2nd ed. (Ithaca: Cornell University Press, 1999).

22 David Owen, *Balkan Odyssey* (London: Harvest Books, 1995); Susan Woodward, *Balkan Tragedy* (Washington, DC: Brookings Institution Press, 1995).

23 Warren Zimmerman, *Origins of Catastrophe: Yugoslavia and Its Destroyers* (New York: Random House, 1997).

24 Harvey, 'Primordialism, Evolutionary Theory and Ethnic Violence in the Balkans.'

25 Michael J. Sandel, *Democracy's Discontent: America in Search of a Public Philosophy* (Cambridge: Harvard University Press, 1996), 17.

26 Jon Elster, Claus Offe, and Ulrich K. Preuss, *Institutional Design in Post-Communist Societies: Rebuilding the Ship at Sea* (Cambridge: Cambridge University Press, 1998); Jack Snyder, *From Voting to Violence: Democratization and National Conflict* (New York: Norton, 2000).

27 For instance, suppose the three patients were ushered into three separate waiting rooms in which no information was available about who would be examined first and where each was told that there was a long line of patients ahead of him or her and no further information about his or her place in line was given.

28 Religious toleration emerged very slowly from the seventeenth century and onwards. Philosophers and social theorists like Hume and Bacon were not passionate about affinity between religious groups and about religious toleration. J. G. A. Pocock, *Barbarism and Religion*, Vol. 2, *Narratives of Civil Government* (Cambridge: Cambridge University Press, 1999); John Kekes, *The Morality of Pluralism* (Princeton: Princeton University Press, 1993).

29 As Plato foresaw, moral learning can be cumulative. *The Republic of Plato*, 114–15.

30 Michael Ignatieff, 'Nationalism and the Narcissism of Minor Difference,' *Queen's Quarterly* 102 (Spring 1995), 21.

31 Ian Angus, *A Border Within: National Identity, Cultural Plurality, and Wilderness* (Montreal: McGill-Queen's University Press, 1997), 162.

32 Carlos Fuentes, 'Introduction,' in Edward James Olmos and Lea Yberra, eds., *Americanos: Latino Life in the United States* (Boston: Little Brown and Co., 1999).

33 See Daniel Patrick Moynihan, *Pandaemonium: Ethnicity in International Politics* (Oxford: Oxford University Press, 1993), 84–5.

34 Alvin Rabushka and Kenneth A. Shepsle, *Politics in Plural Societies: A Theory of Democratic Instability* (Columbus, OH: Charles E. Merrill, 1972), 217.

35 Robert A. Dahl, *On Democracy* (New Haven: Yale University Press, 1998).

36 Hurst Hannum, 'The Specter of Secession: Responding to Claims for Ethnic Self-Determination,' *Foreign Affairs* (March/April 1998), 14.

37 By cooperation, we here apply Crick's definition of politics. Politics is 'the activity by which different interests within a given unit of rule are conciliated by giving them a share in power in proportion to their importance to the welfare and the survival of the whole community.' Bernard Crick, *In Defence of Politics*, 2nd ed. (Chicago: University of Chicago Press, 1972), 22.

38 Germany, for example, struggles to formulate a politically acceptable, fair, and tolerant legal regime concerning immigration. Lutz Hoffmann, *Die unvollendete Republik: Zwischen Einwanderungsland und deutschem Nationstaat*, 2nd ed. (Cologne: Papy Rossa, 1992); Charles A. Kupchan, 'Introduction: Nationalism Resurgent,' in Charles A. Kupchan, ed., *Nationalism and Nationalities in the New Europe* (Ithaca: Cornell University Press, 1995).

39 According to Inglehart, post-modernist values towards 'well-being' have shifted away from earlier values of 'survival.' The forty-three nation study includes both Canada and Ireland. Ronald Inglehart, *Modernization and Postmodernism: Cultural, Economic and Political Change* (Princeton: Princeton University Press, 1997), 333. Is it possible that as this shift in values occurs in Quebec and the rest of Canada, the greater political and cultural confidence that may result will coax out greater harmony in francophone and anglophone societal visions as well?

Index